ONE strategy

Organization, Planning, and Decision Making

Steven Sinofsky

Marco Iansiti

WILEY

John Wiley & Sons, Inc.

Published by John Wiley & Sons, Inc., Hoboken, New Jersey.
Published simultaneously in Canada.

The views expressed herein are the personal views of the authors and do not necessarily represent the views of their employers.

For general information on our other products and services, or technical support, please contact our Customer Care Department within the United States at 800-762-2974, outside the United States at 317-572-3993 or fax 317-572-4002.

Wiley also publishes its books in a variety of electronic formats. Some content that appears in print may not be available in electronic books. For more information about Wiley products, visit our Web site at http://www.wiley.com.

Library of Congress Cataloging-in-Publication Data

Sinofsky, Steven, 1965–
    One strategy : organization, planning, and decision making/Steven Sinofsky, Marco Iansiti.
      p. cm. –
    Includes index.
    ISBN 978-0-470-56045-7 (cloth)
      1. Strategic planning.   2. Business enterprises—Technological innovations. I. Iansiti, Marco, 1961-   II. Title.
    HD30.28.S476 2010
    658.4'012–dc22
                                              2009035915

Printed in the United States of America
10 9 8 7 6 5 4 3 2

To Melanie and Malena

Contents

List of Blog Posts

Acknowledgments

Author's note from Steven Sinofsky: Writing this book has offered me a chance to reflect on the work of the Windows and Windows Live team over three years of building a team and releasing some wonderful software: Windows Live (several "waves"), Internet Explorer 7 and Internet Explorer 8, and Windows 7. While this book represents my point of view, without the collaboration, communication, and even debate that took place over this time, these blog posts would not be possible. The thoughts, input, and points of view of so many members of the team are reflected in these posts that I think of this work as the work of the team much more than the work of any one person. At the same time, I'm most certainly responsible for the mistakes or misinterpretations that might have wound up in posts.

A coworker once suggested that "writing is thinking" and this blog offered a great chance to think through the answers to tough management questions—there's no better way to be prepared to answer a concern of a member of the team than to spend the time to write it down, and no better way to amplify the answer than to post it for all to see, comment on, and share. I'm deeply indebted to many amazing individuals who have been so supportive, not just over the past few years but throughout my professional life. Microsoft is a remarkable collection of people, each of whom has taught me a great deal, tolerated my shortcomings, and shown incredible patience while I continued to learn. At each step in my career, I have been blessed with wonderful coworkers and great managers, and have been part of awesome teams all coming together in an effort to build excellent software. I would like to offer my deepest and sincerest thanks to the Microsoft community, of which I am so fortunate to be a part.

I offer this book with the utmost humility. One must admit that in the uncertain worlds of product development and management, ideas that are perfect in one context are decidedly wrong in other contexts. The things that seemed absolutely right at one time might be absolutely wrong at other times. My hope is that in sharing these ideas and experiences I continue to grow and learn and that the teams I happen to be part of can experience the same. I also recognize that all of this work is a journey and that most of all what matters is that journey.

The dialog this book represents took place in a learning and growing organization. The reader is asked to fully consider this context and to recognize the value of the whole over small elements taken out of context.

Tren Griffin provided valued insights, guidance, and editing assistance for which I am grateful. I also wish to thank each of the reviewers at Microsoft who provided detailed and constructive feedback.

I wish to express my deepest appreciation to the Windows and Windows Live team, to the Office team, and to the Microsoft engineering community. Thank you.

For more than a decade, I've had the opportunity to work with Marco Iansiti, who saw the opportunity for us to work together to bring our complementary experiences to this book, and I thank him for that partnership.

Author's note from Marco Iansiti: This book project provided me with a unique opportunity to perform management research by examining an organization from within. When I started, I frankly did not have any idea what the book would ultimately be about. I was just fascinated by the idea of studying an organization as complex and important as the Windows team. I started by reading through blogs, talking with Steven, spending time with his team, and involving myself in the project itself. As I spent more and more time on this, it gradually dawned on me that something really interesting was happening. This was an organization that believed what it said, accomplished what it promised, and embedded its strategy in its way of doing everything. The strategy actually had integrity. There were no fractures, no broken promises, and no "heroes" that made everything happen behind the scenes. This organization did not promise things. It just delivered.

After years of being involved in senseless debates as to whether strategy drove operations or the other way around, here was an organization in which the two were one and the same thing. It simply made no sense to separate strategy development from execution in an environment that moved this fast. Strategy and execution had to remain 100 percent aligned, as the organization reacted to events like the world's worst financial downturn in recent memory, the architectural transition to cloud computing, or the rise of Google's competitive power. In this kind of an environment, there is no time to separate strategy. Strategy lives within each team member, who jointly develops it and executes it. Directed and emergent strategy are one and the same. There is only one strategy.

This book never would have happened without the help of countless people. First in line is my wife, Malena, with my children, Alexander and Julia, who had to put up with countless long nights and discussions about chapter headings, book titles, or cover designs. I am also grateful to Greg Richards, whose truly relentless pursuit of insight is a constant inspiration to me. Jeff Schneble, Jeff Marowits, Ross Sullivan, Karim Lakhani, Alan Mac Cormack, Roberto Verganti, Srikant Datar, and many other friends at Keystone Strategy and the Harvard Business School were also instrumental in making this book happen. I am also indebted to many generations of GMP faculty and students at the Harvard Business School, where innumerable discussions provided the foundations for this book. Finally, I am indebted to a long line of executives who helped shape the book's ideas and provided valuable feedback, including Sami Issa, Manpreet Khaira, Mehmood Khan, and Qi Lu.

Finally, Steven obviously deserves a special mention. Having known him for more than ten years, I have come to recognize his unique qualities as an inspiring and thoughtful leader, manager, and friend. I thank him for his patience, and most of all for his insights.

Preface

One Strategy describes a general approach for organizations to achieve a single, shared strategic perspective and translate that perspective into impact.

In doing so, this book investigates the interaction between strategy and execution by providing a unique blend of theory and practice. Marco Iansiti combines his research in strategy and innovation with Steven Sinofsky's experience managing the Windows team at Microsoft in order to describe what it takes to align a complex organization around one strategy. Marco's research provides the context for Steven's blogs and together they describe a real journey, with strategic integrity as the final destination, and with important managerial lessons encountered along the way. In doing so, the book examines the concepts, capabilities, processes, and behaviors that aligned around one strategy that helped to build a new release of Microsoft Windows—Windows 7.

Rather than stipulating what a high-integrity organization should look like, the authors offer readers the communications and experiences documenting the managerial journey of the Windows organization as it seeks to optimize the match between strategy and execution in developing the product. The book includes the series of dialogs between Steven and his organization, captured by Steven's blogs. These blogs, posted internally on the Microsoft Office SharePoint site to all Microsoft employees (http://my/site/stevesi/blog on Microsoft's network), tell the story of the Windows team as it progresses through the development of both the organization and the product. Given the large size of the organization, Steven found blogging to be a powerful communication tool to provide his perspective and to discuss a broad set of issues in depth, from organization to motivation, and from culture to budgets, especially when used in conjunction with traditional tools such as one-on-ones (1:1s), team meetings, office hours, and so on.

The blogs present a real view into the Windows organization and the issues it confronted as it searched for strategic integrity and strived to translate potential into impact in its organization and in its business. While these blogs are presented as though they were a series of memos, in practice blogging is a two-way form of communication and for that reason Steven is literally having a dialog with the Windows team. The blogs chosen are a subset of the more than 200 postings on the site. In addition, some of the blogs have been chosen from a public blog maintained by Steven prior to his joining the Windows organization (http://blogs.msdn.com/techtalk), as these were often referenced.

Perhaps most interesting is how the blogs reflect Steven's own experience and learning throughout his tenure at Microsoft. Steven is the first to point out that the dialogs with the team represent his opportunity to pass along the insights, experiences, and lessons learned from some of Microsoft's great managers—especially Jeff Harbers, Bill Gates, Pete Higgins, Chris Peters, and Mike Maples, who so greatly influenced, in fact defined, his approach and thinking early in his career. Steve Ballmer and Jeff Raikes were there to support Steven as he applied these lessons to the management of the Microsoft Office organization. During the course of building the new Windows organization, having the wisdom and support of both Bill Gates and Steve Ballmer afforded Steven unparalleled support, advice, and guidance on the topics of technology, business, and leadership. Building on the strengths of Microsoft gave Steven a unique foundation on which to further refine the concepts articulated in the blogs. While *One Strategy* documents the changes in the Windows organization, one must not lose sight of the foundation on which these concepts have been added—an incredibly talented engineering team rooted in the development of one of the largest and most successful software products ever created.

The blogs are integrated into the body of each chapter, providing a unique view into a real journey to strategic integrity. Except for fixing spelling errors and typographical conventions, or editing small amounts of Microsoft internal content, the blogs are presented "as posted." In cases where words were omitted or even garbled we have enclosed clarifications in [square brackets]. The blogs describe what went on in the Windows organization and are linked to commentary, frameworks, and examples drawn from other companies that have struggled with the same challenges, as well as original research.

By providing these blog posts "as posted" and unedited, the reader is brought into the reality of an evolving organization and project. Many of the blogs were written while reacting to events as they unfolded or were written within the context of the moment. In all cases, the posts reflect Steven's personal view of the situation and in no way reflect a corporate policy. Even on matters of policy, these posts merely represent a conversation—in the hallway, at the break room, or in a casual team get-together—and not a policy statement or definitive guide to how things are or should be at Microsoft in general. While many corporate communications are vetted, edited, or go through a feedback process, Steven's posts went straight from Windows Live Writer to SharePoint, and as such reflect the realities of that sort of conversation.

Chapter 1

Strategic Integrity

S trategic integrity is established by aligning strategy and execution at all levels of the organization.

Every firm has two strategies. The first is explicit, defined by official strategy white papers, memos, and presentations to turn executive vision into a series of competitive moves.[1] The second is implicit and defined by execution, and arises from the pattern of decisions and actions undertaken by the firm.[2] The first notion of strategy is "directed" since it stems from the top-down directions of senior management. The second notion of strategy is "emergent" because it materializes from bottom-up performance and originates from the aggregate behavior of the firm's middle managers and line employees. As organizations grow in size, and as uncertainty in the business environment increases, creating alignment between these two notions becomes increasingly difficult. A lack of alignment will fuel an unproductive duality that destroys strategic integrity and leads to catastrophic business failure.

Directed and emergent strategies diverge because strategy and execution are usually disconnected, defined at disparate points in time, placed in separate organizations, and driven by different people. But rapid change in the business environment requires constant adaptation and reassessment, which in turn necessitate an increasingly tight and responsive connection between top-down strategic priorities and the actual patterns of operational execution. Rethinking the strategy development processes, organizational capabilities, and decision-making systems to provide a better connection between top-down priorities and bottom-up actions has become one of the most important priorities on the agenda of today's executives.

Drawing from specific examples and detailed descriptions, this book describes a general approach for organizations to achieve a single, shared strategic perspective. Strategic integrity is driven by specific approaches to organization, planning, and decision making. Beyond the establishment of measurement systems that track performance to strategic objectives, matching strategy to execution incorporates many concepts and approaches that are traditionally separated from the strategy creation process. Not only should strategy match organizational capabilities, but the specific configuration of organizational capabilities should be part of the strategy development process. Also, successful strategy benefits from a much deeper and more participatory planning process than previously recognized. Participation drives alignment and promotes teamwork, while planning connects strategic vision to execution tactics. Together, these factors mold emergent and directed strategies into one.

The Enterprise and Its Unrealized Potential

Despite the devoted efforts of managers everywhere, the potential of an enterprise often remains unrealized. Companies today are confronted by unprecedented challenges caused by the unpredictability and complexity of their competitive environment. From automobiles to financial services, from consumer electronics to computers, many recent managerial missteps have created a common belief that established enterprises can no longer compete effectively. Large companies are often slow, driven by the wrong incentives, trapped in the wrong value systems, or simply too rigid and entrenched to adapt to turbulence. In the extreme case, these problems have caused spectacular failures, as seen in the telecom industry during the dot-com era or in financial institutions leading up to the financial crisis that resulted in the recession of 2008 and 2009. It may appear to some people that once a business achieves the very success it strives for, the next step must inevitably be failure. But there must be more opportunity for success as part of an enterprise; otherwise many waste a great deal of effort.

Bridging the gaps between conflicting strategies in large organizations is essential. Enterprises drive our economy and are essential to innovation. From the phones that we use to the media that carry their signals, products and services are increasingly complex and their businesses require constant innovation. Any notion that small ventures or volunteer communities can produce all of the innovations that society requires is untenable. Countless innovations require, by their very nature, significant resources, capabilities, and investments. While start-ups and spin-outs can and do create important new technologies, new businesses, or even new markets, they simply cannot solve the class of problems that is addressed by larger and more established firms. One cannot develop a spacecraft to explore Mars, revolutionize transportation to address environmental challenges, drive innovations in biotech and pharmaceutical research to deliver cures, or engineer an operating system that serves one billion customers without mastering the management of complex, multibillion-dollar organizations. There is a pervasive need to find new ways to align and manage large enterprises, especially given the nature of the problems that society must solve.

The challenges and opportunities in managing the enterprise are amplified by the fact that today's products are most often produced in partnership with many firms. Companies are embedded in business eco-systems, which are made up of large networks of partners, suppliers, and competitors that influence the value of products and services by produc-ing complementary or competitive offerings.[3] Having impact in such a setting requires an organization that not only reaches internal integrity, but also has the strategy and capability to align external communities. MS-DOS and then Windows were both successful because they created opportunities for millions of external software developers. Even Linux, originally developed by Linus Torvalds and a dispersed community of engineers, dramatically increased its impact when companies such as IBM, HP, Novell, and Red Hat aligned key parts of the community around a new strategy for success (focusing on the enterprise). Beyond software, automobile, appliance, and electronics companies must align suppliers and dealers, while pharmaceutical companies must connect with regulatory agencies and scientific communities. Ultimately, enter-prises have great strategic potential because they shape and influence vast assets and capabilities, both internal and external to the firm. If they manage to align these resources, in a way that remains coherent through times of change, their potential will translate into enormous impact on both business and social dimensions. But without alignment, the same potential is virtually certain to remain unfulfilled.

Strategy, Execution, and Inertia

Management research has examined the challenges enterprises face in translating potential into impact. The research spans a broad variety of studies that examine thousands of organizations across every industry, from cement kilns to digital photography, and from automobiles to financial services.[4,5] These research studies converge on the idea that organizations accumulate a kind of "inertia" over time, through the processes, incentive systems, routines, and relationships that shape operational execution. These routines and processes enable an organization to perform complex tasks, ranging from management of customer orders to interpretation of market research, and from choice of design features in product development to specific steps taken in driving to a particular operational improvement goal (e.g., "We always do it this way"). These same routines shape how the organization works, and are reinforced by the company's incentive systems, to make it efficient to do the same types of tasks over and over again. However, what makes it easy to perform repetitive tasks can make it nearly impossible for the organization to change.

Over time, routines established to optimize efficient execution converge into a pattern of behavior that defines the emergent strategy of the organization. Strategy therefore becomes the product of the firm's incentives, structures, and patterns of behavior, not the other way around. Over time, a very large gap can emerge between emergent strategy and any top-down, directed strategy, causing the firm's potential to stay unrealized. This may go unnoticed for some time, but will rapidly come to a head if the firm's environment begins to evolve.[6]

In times of change, attempts by management to alter the strategic direction of the company can easily expand the gaps between directed and emergent strategy. If the management of the enterprise recognizes the need for change and articulates new directions, subordinates will too often reject it and stay focused on established patterns of behavior. The organization will often tend to stay the old course either because it has not been given a new definition of success that applies to daily tasks and priorities, or because that new definition has not been fully embraced. Even if the need for change is recognized in certain operating units, more gaps may open as different units move in different directions. Gaps between strategy and execution will destroy alignment and make it difficult for the enterprise to respond effectively to competitive pressures.

Dell: Inertia, Failure, and Renewal[7]

Before 2006, Dell had often been hailed as the world's most successful personal computer company. For 20 years, Dell enjoyed tremendous success in the personal computer industry, driven by a powerful business model, which competitors repeatedly tried to imitate, and failed. The situation changed dramatically in recent years, with Hewlett Packard (HP) taking the lead and Dell falling behind. How did this come to happen?

Unlike most other computer manufacturers, Dell sold directly to its customers and established a unique information flow between customers and suppliers. This rapid and rich information exchange was matched by a high-velocity supply chain, and Dell was able to match customer orders with a lead time that was an order of magnitude shorter than competitors'. This had a direct impact on reducing inventory, returns, and even component costs, while dramatically improving cash flow and overall profitability. The speed of Dell's system enabled the company to respond to changes in customer needs and market requirements with unmatched velocity and efficiency. Dell was the darling of customers and Wall Street analysts alike, as its sales and stock price increased by orders of magnitude between 1984 and 2004.

Dell was perfectly optimized to fit its quick response model. The model influenced all aspects of the organization, from a ruthless cultural focus on efficient execution to a financial emphasis on rapid cycles, closing the books, and emphasizing "making the numbers" on a weekly basis, sometimes even on a daily basis. The people it recruited were focused on operational excellence and rewarded for the rapid and efficient completion of operational tasks. Dell did not always emphasize product innovation, since its computers were designed conservatively and exhibited a relatively small number of similar models, which could be stocked efficiently and shipped quickly to customers. As the organization grew rapidly during the 1990s and early 2000s, this model was continually reinforced, and its routines became second nature to the company's employees. The organization stayed efficient but, as it grew, lost its flexibility. Managers were doing "the right things" not because they were the right things to do but because it was the same way they had always been done. Their model became a driver of organizational inertia. As an insider stated, "The business model became cast in concrete, and business processes became increasingly ossified."[8]

In 2005, the personal computer industry continued to undergo incremental changes. Growth opportunities shifted increasingly to the consumer market, which favored notebook computers over desktops. This gradual shift increasingly challenged Dell's operating model, since consumers valued design innovation and liked shopping retail, particularly for notebooks. Dell evolved its strategies toward an increased focus on notebooks and on consumers, but unlike HP and Apple, which made significant investments in design and in retail presence,[9] Dell's operations simply did not follow suit. Dell continued to execute as it had in the past, focusing on supply chain management, channel efficiencies, and economies of scale, which provided an increasingly ephemeral advantage. Dell's relative lack of design innovation, R&D, sales channel diversity, and absence of focus on the consumer business led to increasingly poor financial performance.[10]

Dell's story is particularly surprising because the challenges it encountered were so gradual and incremental. The increase in notebook share is very incremental and predictable. This is not the Internet transforming the competitive landscape overnight, but a much more gradual transition, which takes place over essentially a ten year period. Could Dell's managers, immersed in their competitive environment, really fail to notice such incremental changes?

Most Dell executives were certainly aware of the changes way before 2004, but their knowledge did not translate into significant actions. Inertia had set in and it had become impossible for individual managers to change the company's course and react in a coherent fashion, until it was much too late. Despite a top-down strategy calling for change, the company was only able to form pockets of activity that argued for a new operational direction, increasing a focus on design, investing in a retail presence, with many separate groups advocating different approaches. However, these groups did not reach critical mass and succeeded only in creating stress, without real impact. This caused major fractures in the organization, especially when Dell began to miss its financial targets, and then "things really hit the fan . . . "[11] The organization lost its coherence, with different executives arguing for different strategies, blaming each other, and creating a managerial panic that resulted into significant financial mismanagement.[12]

In early 2007, Michael Dell came back as Dell's CEO in order to turn things around and realign the organization around a new strategy. Dell urged every manager to rethink his or her individual job in light of the new strategy and reexamine every aspect of the Dell model. Dell showed significant promise by mid–2008, when its performance was further challenged by recession.

Michael Dell rolled out changes in many key areas. He reorganized the businesses, which had hollowed out and lost key talents and skill sets. He rebuilt management capability, flattened the organization, and invested deeply to bring in new, hand-picked employees at every level, from the top executives to entry-level engineers. He moved to reinvigorate R&D to catch up with competition, particularly in consumer designs.[13] Dell expanded the company's product line breadth and focused resources on designing PCs in new ways, predicting features ahead of demand, stocking more inventory, and implementing new approaches to product distribution. In its most observable move, Dell moved to the retail channel, and now has its products in more than 10,000 retail outlets around the world. The company also redesigned its manufacturing process for lower-margin laptops—with less configurability, focusing more on build to stock and less on build to order. Additionally, Dell improved its customer support function and increased its competency in dealing with a less-technical customer base.[14]

It took significant managerial energy to repair old fractures and execute the new strategy in a coherent fashion. Michael Dell motivated his organization to develop, evolve, and communicate a new detailed plan and present progress on a weekly basis, with many meetings personally attended by him. The system went both up and down: He emphasized close top-down supervision while encouraging (and requiring) bottom-up participation. Gradually, the results began to emerge, and Dell appears once again positioned to succeed, even in these very difficult economic times.[15]

Why was it so difficult for Dell to change course? Dell's organization had learned over time how to live by a certain business model, and it was very successful. Management had optimized everything in the company to emphasize quick supply chain responsiveness, minimum inventory, and ultimate manufacturing efficiency. However, the routines that evolved did not lend themselves to the different challenges of the last few years, which required regaining an emphasis on notebook computers, design innovation, and product differentiation. Dell managers faced a significant challenge in changing course, since they had tightly aligned the organization's processes and incentives around the old environment, and the massive organization suffered debilitating inertia. Until Michael Dell came back and broke the dominant patterns, replanned activities from scratch, and changed organization, processes, and incentives, managers had no space to make different decisions and they continued doing the same old things, measured in the same old way, and driven by the same old incentives and goals.

There are many factors explaining Dell's challenges. The company had a great tradition of success in a relatively predictable environment. The organization also rewarded project managers for execution excellence and for hitting their numbers, providing an urgent incentive to execute on immediate tasks, but no incentive to look ahead. As the environment changed, even though it did so gradually and incrementally, the organization did not have the flexibility to adapt. The pressure that built up in the organization was not being released by means of any real changes in overall direction, and instead gave rise to fractures between groups and between directed and emergent strategies. As a result, the company kept going through its traditional motions without responding to the changing desires of its customers.

Inertia can make matching new strategies to execution as difficult as steering an ocean liner. Making the problem set harder is the fact that organizations are more fragile than most people imagine. If one attempts to take an organization in a new direction, without the right foundation, much of that organization will remain pointed in the old direction, creating stress, fractures between groups, confusion, delays, and poor execution. These fractures fragment the business and prevent an efficient flow of information, making it impossible to gain the critical mass needed for change. The fractures cause people to make the wrong decisions and can lead to business "failure."[16]

Inertia, with the stress and organizational fractures that it can cause, destroy the match between strategy and execution in countless examples. Inertia that may exist in engineering, marketing, general management, and finance, or between business partners and customers, will prevent teams from sharing information and making informed decisions. This wrecks the alignment between strategy and execution. Inertia and stress can do damage at different levels, including detrimental behavior of CEOs and other executives all the way down to mistakes made by engineers.

Inertia is challenging but not insurmountable, as the Dell example illustrates. Laying the groundwork to fight inertia takes time and enormous attention to detail and consistency across the many factors that drive the coherence and responsiveness of an organization. Much like turning an ocean liner too quickly or without the right infrastructure, inertia can lead to the creation of fissures large enough to sink the whole ship. On the other hand, with appropriate strategy and framework of operational principles, the enterprise can successfully counteract inertia and develop the coherence and flexibility required to do extremely well in today's turbulent business environment.

A Participatory Approach to Strategic Integrity

Breaking inertia and matching execution to new and evolving strategies hinges on the idea of strategic integrity. More than just ensuring that a strategy has traction, a close match between strategy and execution is crucial to be sure that we have the right strategy in the first place. Strategic integrity is not about crafting brilliant strategy or about having the perfect organization: *It is about getting the right strategies done by an organization that is aligned and knows how to get them done.* It is about matching top-down-directed perspectives with bottom-up tasks.

Creating a match between strategy and execution is rare. Historical research in strategy, innovation, and operations has shown that companies often isolate strategy development, marketing, and planning processes from the very groups that are responsible for execution, such as engineering, product, or operations. Additionally, these functions further fracture into increasingly small departments, teams, and subgroups without creating any processes or systems to reintegrate the disparate subgroups. Human nature tells us that few are likely to accept at face value a strategy handed "down" and even fewer are likely to execute it according to an inevitably poor plan, lacking the necessary detail. This fragmentation not only prevents strategy from being absorbed and implemented by the operational functions, it also prevents the right operational information to migrate up to inform and redirect strategy. Beyond financial information, this includes information about more difficult issues such as project schedules, customer needs and trends, technical feasibility, and partner viability. Above all, this separation avoids organizational accountability at every level—those responsible for the strategy can point to failed execution and those responsible for execution can point to a strategy doomed to failure. The effects of separation, fragmentation, and lack of accountability are exacerbated by increasingly static incentives and measurement systems. This pattern creates and amplifies misalignments and can contribute to stress and major fractures in the organization. This pattern also destroys the organizational coherence required for strategic integrity.

There are better ways to run an enterprise. Achieving strategic integrity depends on maintaining coherence in the organization and achieving a high degree of fit with evolving customer needs and environmental trends. Imagine an organization in which the articulation of strategy is not contained within the purview of a small number of senior managers or executives but is instead shared broadly across the organization. Engaged in a participatory planning activity that examines the creativity and feasibility of the strategy, the organization feeds back comments, arguments, challenges, and new opportunities. In this world, the organization not only improves the strategy, but also connects strategy to execution with integrity. Once execution kicks off, the organization is behind it. And when execution runs into challenges, the problems are visible across the organization and the strategy changes to overcome the obstacles that come into its path. Emergent and directed strategies are one and the same thing.

This book will show how the search for strategic integrity focuses on three drivers: planning, organization, and decision making. These drivers can create the kind of transparency, coherence, and fit that indicates a high-integrity organization and keeps strategy matched to execution during times of change.

Planning

Planning is the first driver. Planning is the main way the bulk of the organization participates in strategy development. In contrast with traditional top-down, basic financial planning, this planning process involves pervasive participation and combines top-down, bottom-up—and "middle-out"— inputs to examine high-level vision, tactical details, and everything in between. This kind of planning emphasizes carefully structured flexibility and transparency and drives alignment between disparate groups. In fact, the more participatory the planning process, the stronger the alignment of separate parts of the organization. And with more teams used to operating in concert, enterprises can avoid the fissures that so often plague strategic changes. In contrast with many management stereotypes, this kind of planning process increases the flexibility and responsiveness of an organization, not the other way around. It provides a clear framework for decision making and outlines a path for the framework to evolve and adapt as necessary without losing internal consistency.

Organization

Organization is the second driver. Integrity depends on building an organization with a reservoir of deep capabilities and on fostering the integration necessary to translate the potential created by these capabilities into impact. This implies building a deep foundation of traditional "disciplinary" excellence. By "disciplinary excellence" we refer to both generic knowledge of, say, engineering, sales, and marketing disciplines, and also to deep knowledge of the specific subdisciplines required. Additionally, integrity requires an organization to be structured for coordination and integration, with processes and behaviors that maximize the translation of knowledge into action.

Decision Making

Decision making is the third driver. Decision-making foundations start with the definition of transparent roles and responsibilities for members of the organization and continue with the establishment of clear levels of empowerment and accountability. Furthermore, the foundations extend to a system of shared values. These values are built on ethical behavior, but go way beyond it to include transparency, customer and partner focus, technical excellence, openness, and directness.

In essence, operating with strategic integrity implies teaching an enterprise an internally consistent set of principles for planning, organizing, and making decisions. Furthermore, it means using these principles to drive execution, guide choices, and make strategies come alive.

Windows Strategy and Execution

In March 2006, Steven Sinofsky was asked to manage the newly formed Windows and Windows Live R&D organization.[17] Leaving his current assignment as the Senior Vice President of Microsoft Office, Steven started working with the Windows and Windows Live (WWL) teams as the latest product generation, Windows Vista, approached shipment. Steven would focus on the next product release, which would become known as Windows 7 and also on realizing the vision of a suite of software and services to complement Microsoft Windows, known as Windows Live.

Windows is built on a tradition of achievement, with extensive revenues drawn from a sequence of successful products, starting with Windows 3.0 in 1990. With Windows 3.1 in 1992, Windows greatly improved its user interface and its internal design, which enhanced its ability to multitask, edging out competitors such as IBM's OS/2. Windows 95 was possibly the most successful introduction. With enthusiastic customers lined up the morning before the product's launch, Windows 95 included important innovations in the product's graphic user interface, access to the then-nascent Internet, support for powerful plug-and-play standards, and 32-bit microprocessor architecture. Other successful releases followed, such as Windows NT (for workstations and servers), Windows 98, and Windows XP, introduced in 2003.

Although the success of Windows is undisputed, by 2006 the business had come under pressure. The Internet, hailed by many as a "disruptive" force, was transforming the software industry and powering new generations of services and applications. These created new risks for Windows. New companies were gaining rapidly in influence, such as Google, which might come to dominate a new world of Web-only software. Additionally, older companies such as Apple had found a new life, introducing an impressive array of competitive products that were gaining share and threatening the core business. Some of Microsoft's responses to these challenges had not gone as anticipated. Analysts and the press had been quick to point out that Windows Vista was not achieving its promised targets of schedule, features, or quality.[18]

The Search for Strategic Integrity

This book describes a journey, with strategic integrity as its final destination. It is organized in two parts. Chapters 2 through 4 frame the main concepts and describe the setting of the book, providing its context and foundations. Chapters 5 through 9 focus on implementation and articulate the search for strategic integrity in detail, examining real, practical implications for planning, organization, and decision making. Chapter 10 concludes by summarizing and framing the book's ideas and connecting these experiences to other companies and industries.

Chapter 2, "Strategy: A Participatory Approach," exposes the core framework of the book by providing an overview of the strategy development and execution transformation driven through the Windows organization. It begins with the original expectations by the leadership team and continues with a summary of key changes made. The chapter describes a framework for strategic integrity, driven by planning, organization, and decision making. The chapter introduces the framework to discuss the management of the Windows and Windows Live business as well as the external approach used in reaching out to the ecosystem.

Chapter 3, "The Foundations of Strategic Integrity," hones in on the concept of strategic integrity, motivates it, and explains why it is the key to keeping the enterprise aligned, innovative, and adaptable in types of change. The chapter provides the grounding for the framework discussed in Chapter 2 and relates the idea of strategic integrity to concepts of integrity from other fields, motivating the importance of organizational coherence, and fit, and adaptability. The chapter relates the concept of integrity to the drive for innovation, and the translation of potential into impact. The chapter then focuses on strategic integrity in action in the Windows organization and examines its responsiveness, organizational coherence, and fit with customer needs.

In a changing environment, the match between strategy and execution cannot be static and survive. This implies that achieving and sustaining strategic integrity is founded on flexibility, adaptation, and, especially, innovation. Chapter 4, "Integrity and Innovation," focuses on the role of innovation in matching strategy to execution. Matching strategy to execution must build on innovation and leverage the complex capabilities of the enterprise while avoiding the classic pitfalls of inertia and disruption. The chapter articulates some key ideas for meeting these challenges and for crafting and executing innovative strategies at Microsoft, specifically, and in the enterprise more broadly.

Chapter 4 concludes the four foundation chapters of the book that define strategic integrity, link it to planning, organization, and decision making, and discuss its general implications. The planning, organization, and decision-making framework is discussed in great detail in the following five implementation chapters, which examine in depth each of the strategic integrity drivers.

Chapter 5, "Planning: Innovation, Risk, and Agility," homes in on planning as the first driver of the strategic integrity framework. The chapter starts by arguing that strategic vision is matched to execution by instituting planning at all levels in the organization. The planning approach described is iterative and integrative, top down, bottom up, and middle out. The chapter describes the planning process in detail and draws from the actual planning methods that are used in the Windows group.

Chapters 6 and 7 focus on the second strategic integrity driver, organization. Chapter 6, "Organization: Matching Capabilities to Strategy," focuses on how to achieve the deep foundation of disciplinary excellence and the strong cross-functional integration that is necessary to achieve high-integrity execution. A high-integrity organization will focus on the people that really do the work—there is no substitute for real deep capability and understanding. At the same time, it is also crucial that the right skill sets are combined and integrated to achieve a coherent result. The chapter describes Microsoft's approach to creating functional excellence and cross-functional integration, including an approach for organizing product development. Chapter 7, "Organization: What Managers Do," narrows in on management. It examines how managers can build the capability, effectiveness, and trust that coaches, empowers, and inspires an organization. The chapter is full of detail on the pragmatic approach taken and on the resulting impact on the organization.

Chapters 8 and 9 examine the third strategic integrity driver. Chapter 8, "Decision Making and Value Systems," describes core decision-making values, such as accountability, delegation, and empowerment. Additionally, it describes values employed behind specific types of decisions, such as those influencing quality and customer and partner needs. Furthermore, it discusses learning, as it impacts both value systems and specific processes. The chapter relates how a strong value system, and more traditional integrity notions, complement an effective planning process and an efficient organization to strive for strategic integrity. Chapter 9, "Personal and Organizational Growth," takes the perspective of the growing manager. It articulates a value system and specific approach toward personal growth and career development.

Chapter 10, "Lessons from Aligning Strategy and Execution," concludes the book, summarizes its ideas in a comprehensive framework and expands the discussion to companies in other industries.

Notes

1. See H. Mintzberg, J. B. Quinn, and J. Voyer, *The Strategy Process* (Upper Saddle River, N. J.: Prentice Hall, 2003), p. 4; and K. Andrews, *The Concept of Corporate Strategy* (New York: McGraw-Hill: 1987).
2. Ibid. See also R. Burgelman and A. S. Grove, *Strategy Is Destiny* (New York: The Free Press, 2002); R. H. Hayes, G. P. Pisano, D. M. Upton, and S.C. Whelwright, *Operations, Strategy, and Technology* (Hoboken, N. J.: John Wiley & Sons, 2005); and G. Gavetti and J. W. Rivkin, "Seek Strategy the Right Way at the Right Time," *Harvard Business Review* 86, no 1 (January 2008): 22–23.
3. M. Iansiti and R. Levien, *The Keystone Advantage* (Boston: Harvard Business School Press, 2004).
4. There are many papers and books on this topic, including P. Anderson and M. L. Tushman, "Technological Discontinuities and Dominant Designs: A Cyclical Model of Technological Change," *Administrative Sciences Quarterly* 35 (1990): 587–605; R. Henderson and K. Clark, "Architectural Innovation: the Reconfiguration of Existing Product Technologies and the Failure of Established Firms," *Administrative Science Quarterly* 35 (1990): 9–30; and C. Christenson, *The Innovator's Dilemma* (Boston: Harvard Business School Press, 1997).
5. M. Iansiti, *Technology Integration* (Boston: Harvard Business School Press, 1997).
6. The classic example here is probably Intel's exit from the DRAM business, chronicled by Burgelman and Grove, *Strategy Is Destiny* (Free Press: 2001).
7. Marco Iansiti's research has focused on a large number of enterprises struggling with organizational inertia, including this study of Dell Corporation.
8. Interview with a senior member of the Dell turnaround team, August 20, 2008.
9. See, for example, P. Kunkel, *AppleDesign: The Work of the Apple Industrial Design Group*, with photographs by Rick English (New York: Graphis, 1997).
10. From 2005 through 2007, Dell's consumer sales as a percentage of its revenue, fell from 15.5 percent to 12 percent.
11. Interview with a senior member of Dell's turnaround team, August 21, 2008.
12. Ibid.
13. Michael Dell acknowledges importance of fashion in the consumer technology market: "We are kind of in the fashion business. We have been putting quite a bit more energy into this. It will be reflected in future products."

14. Interviews with members of the Dell turnaround team.

15. Ibid.

16. See, for example, Henderson and Clark, "Architectural Innovation: the Reconfiguration of Existing Product Technologies and the Failure of Established Firms"; Tushman and Anderson, "Technological Discontinuities and Dominant Designs: A Cyclical Model of Technological Change"; Iansiti, *Technology Integration*; and Gavetti and Rivkin, "Seek Strategy the Right Way at the Right Time."

17. As announced ("Microsoft Realigns Platforms & Services Division for Greater Growth and Agility: Steven Sinofsky joins PSD to lead Windows and Windows Live development, *Microsoft PressPass,* March 23, 2006, http://www .microsoft.com/presspass/press/2006/mar06/03-23PSDReorgPR.mspx), Steven's responsibilities included managing the development of the Windows client operating system and the Windows Live suite of services (internally known as Windows and Windows Live or abbreviated as WWL throughout this book). He would later be joined by Bill Veghte, the senior vice president for the Windows Business, and Jon DeVaan the senior vice president for the core operating system development. The three worked as peers in partnership with Steven to "assume[ing] responsibility for process and planning of future versions of Windows."

18. See Robert A. Guth, "Microsoft Delays Windows Vista Again," *Wall Street Journal*, March 22, 2006.

Chapter 2

Strategy

A Participatory Approach

Despite countless books on strategy and countless books on execution, strategy and execution often diverge.

The following scenario is all too common: During a senior briefing meeting at a Fortune 1000 appliance firm, the CIO (chief information officer) presented a comprehensive strategy and project portfolio that started with the needs of the company's customers and worked its way down systematically to define clear priorities for the dozens of major innovative information technology (IT) efforts (e.g., succession planning, currency hedging) that he claimed were already underway. But in other 1:1 meetings, lower-level engineers presented a dramatically different picture. A top-down strategy was nowhere to be found, and priorities were completely different. Front of mind for these employees was the task of integrating the mass of disparate IT applications that were running the different operating units so that the data could be aggregated at the corporate level for basic reporting purposes.

As this typical scenario demonstrates, managers are all too often caught in the gap between top-down and bottom-up perspectives, between directed and emergent strategies, or in the cracks between different parts of the organization that are following different perspectives. The senior management of a corporation may be trying to implement a deliberate strategy of fostering "innovation," while the operating managers are dealing with technical feasibility or cost efficiency as a real day-to-day priority. "How can we get senior management to stop dreaming?" is often the question asked by those with "line of business" responsibility. "How can those with line responsibility get with the program and execute on the strategy?" is often the question asked by senior management. The answer to both of these questions lies in creating broad participation in both strategy development and execution. Achieving strategic integrity requires a process that brings alignment to the entire organization, top down, bottom up, and middle out.

During the second half of 2006, the Windows[1] team began to implement a participatory approach to strategy development, delineating how each component of the organization needed to adapt to confront its challenges. As the task of developing the new strategy began, the team embraced a powerful framework to create alignment and translate potential into impact. This framework, with foundations in organization, planning, and decision-making systems, provided the guideposts to create an organization capable of translating strategy into actions. The plan extended to cover not only the firm's internal operations but also those of its business ecosystem.

The Windows Business

Windows is a successful business with an exceptional customer base around the world. Windows is complemented by Windows Live, a suite of Windows software plus online services that comprises Hotmail, Messenger, SkyDrive, Groups, and Photos, among others. Both Windows and Windows Live represent platforms in which customers and partners of many types build unique software that build on the value delivered to provide unique software applications and services.

When Steven Sinofsky began to manage the newly formed Windows team, the Windows business was faced with new forms of pressure and was also under a variety of competitive challenges. Pressure both internally and externally on the team created by the delay and initial challenges of Windows Vista was present in many parts of the organization (and the industry) and formed the undercurrent of strategic debates. Competitively, Apple, with its focus on design innovation and marketing prowess, its media service offerings, and its compelling personal devices, was making significant inroads in the operating system market. Google, with its dominant search franchise and its significant investment in software R&D and infrastructure, was becoming a force in software technologies, platforms, and applications. Other challenges came from myriad other start-ups and enterprises, each offering a different computing alternative.

Several technological trends made these challenges harder by creating potentially disruptive forces, such as cloud computing and mobility. With cloud computing, software programs were run on remote computers (large networks of servers) and delivered as a service to a computer via the Internet and through the browser. With mobility, not only were PCs becoming increasingly portable, but traditionally portable devices such as cellular phones were becoming de facto portable computers. Cloud computing and mobility could be either a threat or an opportunity for the personal computer, depending on whether the PC operating system continued to deliver improved value to its customers and partners.

These challenges gave rise to innumerable debates and discussions throughout the Windows organization as well as outside the group. These debates represented many different points of view. Some people wanted to emphasize rapid iterations on Windows Vista, introducing new features and bug fixes on a monthly or even weekly basis with a primary focus on addressing the in-market opportunity of Vista. Others suggested cutting the Windows team in half in an effort to address one perceived cause of the challenges faced in the development of Vista. A few people even advocated abandoning the traditional Windows code base, to start developing a new Windows from scratch, perhaps even with a different team. Despite the variety of initial opinions, the debate soon converged on the central, fundamental need to add real, concrete value for the Windows consumer. Despite pressure to introduce a new product in the very short term (whether that was possible or not), the Windows team decided to take the time to make sure that the next version had a major impact and incorporated real innovation. This decision, in turn, created a need to reinforce the organization and align execution capabilities with a new, developing Windows strategy.

A Vision for the Windows and Windows Live Organization

The continued competitive challenges and technological change faced by Windows made the pressure on the teams to deliver stronger than ever. The teams needed to reconnect strategy with execution and make sure that the Vista experience, in the words of Steve Ballmer, would "never happen again."[2] Steven Sinofsky wrote the following blog after the first meeting of the Windows Senior Management Team, in which the group's managers discussed how to approach these challenges. The blog captures the original vision of the senior team, which led to the concepts and approaches described in this book. The title of the blog comes from a question asked to Steven at that meeting and represents the start of a two-way dialog.

Q: When You Look Down the Road, What Do You Think the Organization Will Be Like?

Today we had a chance to get together as a "senior management team." The format was Q&A and I want to thank everyone for their open and frank questions. I definitely want this dialog to continue. I ended the meeting with my open request to show up at any team meetings or group meetings—just invite me.

I wanted to share one question that came up, which I really liked and I thought the answer is something I should try to write down. I will elaborate a bit since I've had a little more time to think about it.

Question: We definitely hear you on trying to understand the larger organization and that we need to develop some shared view of what we are doing. When you look down the road, what do you think the organization will be like?

I took this question to be one of "[W]hat are the qualities of the organization I aspire to be part of?" I think there are a couple of things that really come to mind:

- An organization with a rhythm
- An organization where we're all on the same page even if we're working on different products or releases
- An organization that manages itself by consensus
- An organization that values engineering at the core and is structured around our core engineering disciplines
- A team that builds products that people *want* to have and create a *buzz* in the broadest possible way

Rhythm is a super important thing to a team. When everyone knows where we are and what to expect it makes it very easy to work together and it makes it very easy for our products to reflect goals of being great for customers. We don't all have to be at the same spot at the same time, or have product cycles that are the same length, but we do need to have some sort of rhythm so we can talk about where we are or where we need to be. What I think this is not is sometimes easier to talk about. If we don't have a rhythm, then some of us are in crisis mode or some of us are trying to wait on a decision from another group, or worse a decision from me, but if we know what to expect when then things can flow smoothly. It also means that we don't have to have "special" meetings and people do not have to drop what they are doing to prepare or "review" things, but rather features are designed, code is written, [and] services get deployed at some interval that the whole organization understands and works with. We know when to work across the team and when the right time to make commitments should be.

Being on the **same page** is a big part of what you should expect from me and what I will work with my direct reports on ensuring. We need to be working from a "framework" that allows people to spin as fast as they need to in their area, but to also know the "bounds" of the work they do. We don't want to create a set of overlapping or conflicting teams that need to resolve everything by a tricky cross-group process. Of course we will have connection points across the organization, but to the best of our ability we will define these connection points upfront and be clear about the team responsible for arriving at customer-friendly and business-savvy decisions, without thinking that "escalating" is right. The ideal goal is that when a new person joins our team they can read one document and have a sense for the breadth of products we work on and the organization that supports those products is clear and follows from it. When another group in the company wants to work with our team then who you work with is not a multiple choice test or a multi-group process, but one that is clear and easy to understand.

Consensus is an incredibly important tool for deciding how to move forward. It is also very powerful in terms of being on the same page and working as a team. I know a lot of people **groan** when they hear this because it sounds like endless meetings and people who don't agree just circling endlessly. In the end, two peers will know way more about a problem and proposed solution than some common manager, so it is important for the maturity and depth of our team that peers be able to reconcile things. Obviously having a good framework and a clear organization are critical to this. At the same time people need to compromise. We don't want to compromise in lame ways that customers see—sort of "splitting the baby." Rather we want to have real compromise where sometimes you "give in" and sometimes the other person "gives in." The reason is simple—this is social science and developing new products doesn't have a definitive right answer. What works is the cleanest experience for customers and if we have two very nice and clean approaches then we should be able to just go with one without a huge battle. I know this sounds much harder than it looks and I know this is a bit utopian. All I can say for sure is that I know that (a) if something makes it to me to decide, then I have failed somehow and (b) that if two people can't agree on picking one great path and settle on one mediocre "compromise," then those folks probably failed our customers.

Engineering is what we're all about. I want people whether they are in development, testing, program management, design, usability, planning or other disciplines to know that our organization cares deeply about being the very best in those disciplines. I want people to know that you can strive to be a manager or strive to be the best non-manager you can be and either way you can move up the career ladder, get recognized, contribute significantly, and be a senior member of the team while working as a core technical contributor. Some people will aspire to be general managers, but that is not the only career path and certainly not the only way to get promoted. If you look at the Office organization we have VPs (and TFs [Technical Fellows]) in dev [software development], test [testing], program management, and we're always working to make sure we have the most seniority and most depth in the core technical disciplines. Closely related to this is making sure that when you join our team from college or elsewhere, you can look up the management chain and see a lot of depth in your job function. If you are a new tester, you see a couple of layers of increasing test experience and seniority and you see role models and people to aspire to be like. We have been hearing a lot how Google is an "engineering company" and Microsoft does not feel like that. I know we used to be perceived as an engineering company and I know we are in our heart—we need to make sure people feel that way whether they are new employees or current employees. Two posts from my old blog related to this are http://blogs.msdn.com/techtalk/archive/2005/09/18/471121.aspx (about general management) and http://blogs.msdn.com/techtalk/archive/2005/09/24/473599.aspx (about team size). I want to caveat both of these with what I said at the meeting, which is that what we've done in Office might not make sense in our new team and part of the "transition" is learning and reaching a consensus on how to move forward.

And of course the reason we're here is because we want to **build great products.** We want to have the most page views. We want to have the most revenue. I think all of this follows from building products people will line up to buy, from having services that people will beg to get accounts on, and from having a genuine buzz around them. If we can do those things, then people will buy more or advertise more.

Obviously these represent a set of aspirations. Some might be *corny* or you might think they are too high level to be actionable. But I know when I think about the place I want to come to work [to] every day, these are things that can contribute to making work fun, challenging, and can also make our lofty goals achievable.

Feel free to send mail, challenge these views, or just use this as a basis of discussion at a team meeting we can have together.

What do you think?

—Steven

This blog represents the vision, the aspirations, of the Windows management team. The blog's main themes focus on building organizational integrity and reconstructing a "whole" organization, mending the fractures and fissures left by past experiences. This organization is focused on deep, disciplinary skills, and values engineering and technical recognition.

The team's vision is to be on the same page, working with the same rhythm, and making decisions from a common framework. The framework functions as a great plan to define objectives and narrow in on the right approaches, distributing tasks to allow local independence while establishing clear boundaries.

Furthermore, the vision argues for a participatory, "consensus" decision-making culture, one that drives to better and more robust solutions by emphasizing diversity, maturity, and depth in the resolution of different views, and by relying on a sound planning framework and a clear organization. Additionally, the vision emphasizes the importance of deep, disciplinary expertise in all critical areas, from development to planning. As shown in the next section, these aspirations really capture the essence of the approach that was actually implemented.

The team has a clear and rich vision: to have rhythm, be on the same page, value engineering, and build great products that people want. The organization needs deep capability and needs to reward both engineering and management skills, creating significant recognition for seniority and, especially, contribution. Moreover, the organization needs to develop a clear working framework, one that allows people to react quickly within their area, knowing the bounds of the work that they do. Interestingly, escalation signals a problem, as it implies that frameworks for planning and decision making have failed.

This blog is particularly important because of the context of the meeting and the challenges faced by Steven in coming to Windows from Office. At the time of the senior management meeting and of the blog, Steven had just started his new job. Any time a manager moves from one job to another, especially moving from a "rival" group, a number of concerns are sure to arise. Some were worried about not having big dreams for Windows going forward, as they viewed Office less than positively along that dimension. Others were concerned that their fiefdoms would be subsumed in the more uniform Office culture that Steven came from. Some were skeptical of the advice and coaching of people with Office experience, since they felt Windows was inherently more difficult and certainly had its own unique culture developed due to the product's engineering requirements. Others were concerned about the nature of the technical and managerial ladders or career paths under Steven. Others felt strongly that Steven's responsibility was to create a vision and top-down direction, and were already expecting answers at the meeting. People were already asking for Steven's schedule to set up review meetings, to validate their directions and keep doing what they were already doing. Steven clearly used the forum of the meeting, followed by the blog, to gain closure and ensure communication, and to set a different direction for the team. Clearly, things were going to be different going forward—the new approach had started to emerge.

Living the Windows Vision

The following blog was written exactly one year after the previous one. It guides the reader through similar themes and shows the impact of the changes made during the first year. As this next blog shows, the aspirations are turning into reality as it describes the changes made to the Windows group over a period of 12 months. The changes aimed at consolidating the organization, creating a whole entity with the aspirations outlined in the previous goals blog, including a common planning framework, clear, a functionally deep organization, and strong, participatory decision-making foundations. The blog organizes these themes under the headings of organizational efficiency, planning, and decision making. As we shall see in great detail in the following chapters, these three headings represent important drivers with which to search for strategic integrity. The title also provides an indication of the scope of the blogging conversation, stretching to more than 200 pages at this point with posts averaging about 4 or 5 pages twice a week.

12 Months and about 120,000 Words Later . . .

Friday marks the first 12 months of our new Windows and Windows Live organization (and also the 100th post to this blog) so it seems like a good idea to take a step back and look at the progress we have made together and think about the work left to be done.

Before getting started, I wanted to thank everyone on the team and all of those that have been supportive of the team and the work we have been doing for the past year. Together we have embarked on a great deal of change and put in place many new operational methods, and none of that would have been possible without the open minds and cooperative efforts of those involved. Thank you!

I also want to use this as a chance to reinforce the "open inbox" that I (and all the leaders on the team) maintain. Some of the best input and best conversations I've had have been with people who just send mail or stop me in the halls. It is one thing to see averages and deltas from the mean on an employee survey, but the real improvements in our team come from written comments or conversations. This substance is what really has helped to make a big difference in how our team is evolving.

We have had a year that at times has seemed rather focused on process and operations, which is in a sense by definition, but also at times a bit less than ideal. Last spring we were still months from finishing Vista and our first wave of Live services would start to slip months beyond their originally planned dates. Yet we came through that and through the midst of significant changes in organization and structure we released Vista, a plethora of Live services, a major release of Live Search, and Internet Explorer (IE) 7. To a person, everyone contributed to delivering an amazing amount of software. At the same time there was a consistently expressed desire to do things better, and so that has been the motivation for the focus on the "how" we get things done. As I said in our announcement in March we will aspire to have the best engineering organization in the company—one that is focused, with modesty, on discipline, expertise, agility, and creativity, and above all is a learning organization. Across every dimension we have been working hard to instill a sense of clear accountability with the resources and framework to be successful. I also committed to help us achieve these goals with transparency of process and this blog has been part of this work. And of course we want to move forward with a renewed emphasis on planning our work, and working those plans.

With all of these changes it is important to point out that it takes time to see the results. Some would have hoped for faster results, and others would have hoped for less change. We are a work in progress for sure. Nothing says that more than the fact that we are just getting started with big releases of software—a new wave of Live services, a new release of Internet Explorer, a new release of Search, and of course a new release of Windows (and [its service pack] SP1). In the hallways, folks ask me every day, "[H]ow's it going?" and I generally think it is more than rhetorical— I think people really want to know how things are progressing. Things are progressing well. I am very optimistic. Things are upbeat. I do indeed have the benefit of a broader perspective and some "altitude," which helps. I know that some of the challenges many individuals face on a daily basis—the challenges that seem to get in the way of getting work done—are still there and did not disappear overnight. I know that some new challenges have appeared. But I don't have to look far to hear feedback about things moving forward and heading in the right direction.

It is worth looking at three of the main areas of feedback that correspond to three of the biggest changes we have made as an organization and provide a "state of the organization" view of **organization efficiency, planning,** and **decision making.** It is hard to separate these changes because they are interrelated. We can make changes in our organization structure because we are more focused on executing on a plan. We can create a plan that reflects the whole team because we put in place more empowered decision makers. But I also recognize that for each of these areas we have much work to do, few concrete results, and for some the jury is still out. That's why I think it is good to take a step back and make sure to communicate and acknowledge that the management team does understand where we are today and also to share the sense of optimism that we each have.

> If you want the short version of this post . . . we have created an organization that is flatter, has fewer managers, and is much more focused on core engineering values. With this organization in place, we have embarked on a product planning process that is about bringing the best ideas to our products in a timely and thoughtful manner. And because of our structure and because we are operating with a plan we are in a much better position to make and stick to decisions. Yet this is a work in progress and I recognize that for many the changes have not been enough or fast enough, or that the changes have not yet erased the challenges in daily work. It takes time for these changes to pay off and time for them to move through the whole organization. With the evidence of early results, such as the Live and Search plans and the progress we have made as a team on Windows and IE I believe we all have reasons to be optimistic and that we will see results of our efforts as we enter execution mode on our work. Our software will be used by over a billion people by the time we finish this next wave of products—that is an awesome responsibility and an amazing opportunity for us all in our careers.

Organization Efficiency and Engineering Focus

In many posts to this blog and in many of our team meetings we have talked a great deal about the organization's statistics, such as how many people at what level, how many direct reports managers have, how big teams should be, and how many managers and management layers there should be. This is an area where it is easy to be concrete and so was the first one we acted on as an organization. Across Windows and Windows Live (and COSD [Core Operating System Division]) we have worked hard to put in place a team that values the engineering disciplines and streamlines our engineering organization and I think we have made progress.

Last year on average an individual contributor had 7 managers between him/her and me. On average we have reduced this to 3 or 4. I think that is probably the most dramatic change. It is also one that has come in handy as we recruit from colleges this year. It is amazing how sensitive college candidates are to this detail and how often I was asked on campuses and in email exchanges with candidates—being compared to Google (an organization that has 4000 engineers these days) favorably definitely helps. We are also asking more of our managers, but not as much as some folks might have thought—we do have more reports for most managers now, but on average this is only 1 or 2 more reports (because previously many managers had only 2 reports). I want to give a lot of credit to all of our managers—they have been leading a big change even in the face of some uncertainty. And many people on the team have new managers, which is a two-way street of newness, and everyone has done a great job working through those transitions. I've had some conversations with folks where they ask if we are moving to a model where if you are a manager then you are a "pure" manager and only manage people—nothing could be further from the truth and what we have tried to emphasize is the desire to have managers contributing at a much deeper technical level than in the past, and this is possible because of a combination of more managers working within an engineering discipline and a much more focused planning process that frees managers from the burden of "keeping things under control" to focus more on execution of the plan.

The biggest part of our organization's change has been the focus away from silos of product units to a focus on disciplines working together. It goes without saying that this was controversial and also a change that for many amounted to a feeling of resetting career goals. We have in place about 30 engineering triads of development, testing, and program management representing our 1000 or so developers. Some are still adjusting—wondering who will ultimately decide (they will) or what happens when dev/test/pm don't agree (they will work it out, based on consensus), and so on. Until we go through the whole ship cycle, or at least the full planning cycle, it will be the case that some are still waiting for a VP to swoop in and take away the empowerment of the triad—it won't happen :-). It is super clear that most people understand the increased level of responsibility that they feel. I've had incredible discussions with GPMs [group program managers] who own planning themes or big bets and they are definitely seeing the reality that the buck stops with them—without their plans we simply won't have features in that area. I've had conversations with SDETs [software design engineering in test] who talk about what it is like to be part of the planning process for the very first time. And in talking to developers who for the first time are taking a step back and looking at the code assets during MQ [Milestone for Quality][3] and thinking about what we should do. All of this is part of taking a discipline-specific view of the work that needs to happen. We are focused on mastering the crafts of dev, test, and pm rather than everyone gravitating to more generalist roles.

I've also talked to some members of the team who think we replaced one type of inefficiency with another—that is, we replaced silos of product units with cross-team meetings. On the one hand, there is some truth to this, but that comes from the fact that there is no org structure where we develop our products unencumbered by the relationships to other products. On the other hand, we are adjusting to operating in a way that optimizes for executing within a planned framework. We are still building trust across the teams and still learning how to work together. We were used to a manager clearing the way, usually by isolating the team or forging arm's-length relationships with other teams, rather than a focus on collaboration and consensus. Some folks have said it feels like we went from 1 boss to 3. My view is that we are now much more accurately reflecting the specializations and skills necessary to create world-class software, but I recognize that this puts a high burden on managers staying in sync with their discipline peers and communicating. This is no different than the expectation in a tiny team of one dev [development manager], one pm [product manager], one test [test manager] except we are trying to scale this to a larger group. It might seem harder now, especially because we only see the work and not the end result. I've personally experienced this transition before so perhaps that is why I have confidence that once we go through the product cycle it will be much clearer and we will all be surprised at how much more natural collaboration happens.

We are still adjusting to having to incorporate many different perspectives and inputs from our engineering team at each step in the product cycle. We are seeing test involved early on for the first time. We are seeing program management working to get out front while also accountable to development for detailed specifications. It is clear that every discipline is reaching new levels of discipline involvement and if you think about it in terms of the CSPs [career stage profiles][4] we are seeing more people touch more of those areas than we have had previously. I think this is a good sign for the growth of individuals on our team and our longer-term health as an organization.

We start the second year of our organization with a streamlined organization that is much more focused on engineering and collaboration.

I know it will take time for every member of the team to experience the positives of these changes and it is easy to focus on the change and see the less-than-positive elements. It might even be the case that over time some will find this new level of accountability and empowerment to be too challenging. Of all the changes to the team this is the one that will have the biggest long-term benefits for the careers of engineers. If I could pick one thing that we still need to improve it is the communication through-out the team and across the disciplines. We are still not sending around (locally) enough meeting notes and not sharing information more freely. And part of that is asking people to be more receptive to "raw data" and less demanding of "tell me what is important" because with empowerment comes the need to process more data and manage the flow of information. For our process to work smoothly we do need more communication.

Planning

About six weeks after I moved into this new role I remember reading that when asked about the next release of Windows Steve Ballmer said "that will never happen again . . . it'll never happen again." If I wasn't awake and alert, I definitely was after reading that.

Of course I know that my commitments (as published) were very much focused on planning. The option open to me was to simply put in place the best process we could and hope we could all follow it, without trying to make it seem like it was a "playbook." That was a big challenge for me. I know many folks thought that I pulled the planning process out of my back pocket, and certainly I had my fair share of stories about Office, but the truth is that the process we embarked on tried to take into account the unique situations of each of our teams. The Live teams wanted to remain as agile as they had been. The Windows team needed to finish Vista. The Search team had monthly improvements and a well-known set of features to work on. Yet it was clear that the team at large was hoping for more of a definitive sense of "[W]hat will we accomplish?" and "[W]hat does success look like?"

A big turning point and in a sense our first real team event was when Marco Iansiti from Harvard came and taught us about the benefits of planning from the perspective of two case studies.[5] While we did not walk away from this day with the magic answers or the specific plans, we did develop a shared sense of the importance of planning and the value that thoughtful planning can bring to product development. Even though that was back in October, people still comment about "not in the direction of goodness" and "we need to be building more keels" in reference to the *Challenger* case and the Team New Zealand case. I learned a good lesson about team building in how having those shared experiences, even if not entirely applicable to day-to-day work, is very valuable.

These discussions led to the "WWL Planning Process" slide that we have used dozens of times in offsites and meetings. In a sense this slide made the planning process seem more rote and mechanical than it is in real life. Early on many worried (in email to me) that the process would not yield any creativity and that it squeezes the creativity out of product development. Many worried about the trust we were putting in the teams to develop the plan and had expectations of executives swooping in. And of course the biggest worry people expressed was that it all was going to take too long. We're behind and need to get ahead so how can we afford the downtime to plan, was a common refrain.

The first team to move from planning to plan was the Live Experience team. We made a deliberate choice to focus on getting the plan in place as the highest team priority (perhaps in contrast to the Windows team where we have been focusing more on developing the operational aspects of the larger team and COSD). In a few short weeks it became clear that we did indeed unleash a lot of creativity. Our first lesson as a team was that the hardest part of the "WWL Planning Process" is figuring out what ideas to decide to do. It was really great to see the prototypes and the detailed feature lists. This creativity culminated in the Vision rollout (jointly presented by the WLP [Windows Live Platform] and WLX [Windows Live Experience] teams) that showed clear commitments to specific scenarios. We have tons of work to do and like any product cycle we will go through milestone checkpoints, recalibration, and so on. But we did learn together [that] putting the process in place did not constrain our creativity.

The core of the planning process is the idea that good ideas can come from anywhere and that the role of those leading the planning themes is to make sure they go out there and ferret out those ideas, and those with ideas need to seek out those working on the plans. The idea of "middles-out" planning is definitely new. JulieLar and ChrisJo and I have talked many times about how those on the team and others all think we have "the plan" in our Drafts folder waiting to be sent out, and sometimes there are those on the team that are waiting for us to hit send regardless of what others think up. We are deep in the process on the Windows product now and it is definitely the case that people are feeling the sense of accountability for the plans. One GPM [Group Program Manager] who used to be a PUM [Product Unit Manager] told me that they feel way more responsible for the plan of their team than they ever have before. They know that the plan will fit within the vision and that they alone are responsible for that, and previously they felt that the "worklist" would just sort of get created and before they knew it their primary job was to avoid having too much work put on them, making it impossible to get done the few things they thought should get done. This is just one case, but it is a general theme. Of course I still have to earn the trust of the team and so do all of my direct reports. I was once asked if I plan on redesigning the Start button 80% through the project and I took an oath not to do that in front of the WEX [Windows Experience] team, but I still have to follow through on that. Our team is learning how to consider all points of view and bring those together into a plan. It might look a bit chaotic right now and we will iterate and get better. More than most changes, the "what goes into the plan" is likely to be the one that is the most opaque while it is transpiring. If you have any questions and are not sure about what is going on, please ask rather than assume nothing or something worse is going on.

We are also seeing the benefits of "downtime," despite the misnomer. The time is not idle at all—all the teams have done (or are in the progress of doing) some excellent MQ work. Each of the leaders of development has worked hard at documenting development practices that will be used for quality, security, performance, etc. Our test discipline has done some great work on automation and frameworks. On the Windows team we continue to dive into postmortem feedback around test tools and bug tracking and using the MQ time to be concrete about our goals and exit criteria. Yet it is fair to say that some are still frustrated by our lack of "coding" right now—some believe that "we know what features we want to do so we are wasting time not coding." Of course it could very well be that we might end up doing precisely some of those features, but we also know that developing these features with upfront thinking in terms of specifications and test plans will at the very least make delivering those features more reliable, if not make those features better. I know I have to ask for patience for some.

The most challenging area for me in terms of planning has been the expectations of the end result, the plan. By talking so much about the plan,

I believe I have inadvertently raised the stakes of the plan (the vision document) too high. I think many are expecting the plan to be the most amazing document with detailed killer features that describe how we deliver a knock-out blow to the competition. The plan will not have that (sorry). I expect the plan to be detailed and to be clear in the value to customers. But the real details of what are home runs or merely solid hits are up to the team. If you could really mastermind a product plan to know you would have a hit, then there would be many more successful companies (or maybe many fewer, just the ones with hit products). Perhaps this is the most counterintuitive part of the plan. The plan is about removing risk (the schedule, the ability to get the work done, the resources, etc.) but it cannot remove the uncertainty ([D]id we pick good features to do[?], [W]ill people like the features we pick[?], [W]ill we have expressed the features well[?], etc.) In the past few weeks I have definitely heard from people that they expect the plan/vision to be more "exciting" or more "killer." I've never seen a plan that looks like a winner before you start that also looked achievable. The Office 2007 UI [user interface] was just one pillar of the product and if you would have asked me in 2004 if the UI would be as paradigm shifting as it has been perceived, I definitely would not have said that. We will all learn together the value of the plan and also how to recognize good plans and feel pumped to begin development even if we know that what we have accomplished is outlining the goals, if not the actual results.

The other area of planning yet to be tested, and the source of concern, has been flexibility. The reality is that when working with a plan our team will be more agile than if there was no plan in place, as counterintuitive as that sounds. We will have a clear sense of our priorities and the costs of making changes and new decisions. We will be able to adapt to changes in the marketplace or in our progress because we will know what remains to be done. Some are still skeptical of this and so together we will learn and adapt going forward.

There is work to be done. We have to write the vision for Windows and Internet Explorer. We have to develop prototypes and make sure our release meets the business goals we have. In Windows we have had two planning checkpoints and we are zeroing in on the product vision and we can feel excitement building. Perhaps the biggest challenge ahead of us is in doing a detailed development schedule that we require and one that has very high scheduling integrity. This is going to be critical to our success and will ask the most of our disciplines—pm needs to have specifications (that can never be detailed enough), dev needs to have schedules (that can never be granular enough), and test will need to be forgiving that pm and dev are both not 100% certain. I am sure this will stretch the team and our triads in new ways, but we are all in this together.

Decision Making

No topic caused more angst in the postmortem than decision making. Often this is a code word for "random executive" or "deadlocked managers." It also described the feeling that almost everyone has when you feel like you know the right answer but can't get something done. Improving decision making cannot be done by putting in a decision-making process (in fact, many groups put those processes in place only to see those processes get overridden). Improving decision making takes organizational trust. It takes a common framework. It takes clear roles and responsibilities.

I would say we have the start of all of these in place. But this is also an area where it is easy to find many examples where things are not friction-free. We make big products. We have many competing needs. We will always have challenges in having an environment where one person has 100% control over everything they might do. I know that either frustrates or surprises people. I have been asked by many what it is like to be a "business leader" and I remind people that even at my job I have no say in tons of things that matter a lot to whether our work is successful (when thought of from the 4 Ps of marketing [mix]: product, price, promotion, placement, I only have say in 25% of the business, at best). But we have built our team, both in terms of feature teams and in terms of engineering structure so that we can have a balance if we all operate from a shared plan. Decision making has the key ingredients of a plan and an engineering structure that reinforces roles and responsibilities. I know the jury is still out.

The first order of business for our team was putting in place the engineering-focused organization so it is super clear that decisions about engineering get made by engineers, and that those decisions can stick because they are grounded in the technical realities of our products. When it comes to the schedule, the test plans, and the architecture I know for sure that we will not be second-guessing these down the road.

The second priority is to establish a common framework for making decisions or a common set of priorities. The product vision that outlines business goals, tenets, and clear scenarios makes it a built-in prioritization tool for the product. The key here is that we agree on the priorities and on what it takes to get them done. We agree at the outset that these goals, while aggressive, are achievable and that everyone has a deep understanding to begin the project and the resources necessary to complete the project in a timely manner.

Taken together we have moved from a model of "butts on the line" or the "hero" model of working. We won't look to a single person to go above and beyond to accomplish our work. In terms of decision making this is very important because those modes of working have a way of tearing down any orderly decision-making processes and replacing them with "out of my way this needs to get done" work styles that upend even the most robust plans.

And finally we are going to be clear about work that crosses the whole product we make. We are seeing this as we create the vision where we are going to prioritize the 2 or 3 "big bets" (as we have done with Live Wave 2) and making sure we share these bets and staff them accordingly. We have moved from a model where groups believe they decide their own set of features only to see that burdened by endless inbound reprioritization.

Without a doubt the biggest part of decision making that we are looking to change, and one that still is somewhat "foreign" to people, is *escalation*. It is still the case that we have too many things where people think they need VP approval. If you want to spend $1M then that is probably VP approval, but if you want to decide on the features for your area, you have the authority to do so. We also still have many decisions where people do not agree with the decision and escalate to reverse a decision—I hope folks understand that escalating a decision is not a way to reverse things. The hope is, again, that those making decisions have done the work necessary to understand points of view and take into account the full context of a decision. If you learn something new or have new data, then change your mind rather than force members of the team to drive an escalation process. The way to avoid escalation is in communicating and making sure you are taking into account all the stakeholders—freedom to make decisions is not freedom to ignore the landscape.

With our engineering-focused organization we are also expecting more from our group managers[6] with respect to decision making. They are on the hook to drive the processes of engineering and do so without pushing the process down the organization. We have minimized the "staff" functions for running our team. We can do so because we are working to make the process of following the plan less challenging by being more consistent and less confrontational. We are still early in this regard, but watching the visions come together gives me reason to believe these changes will come naturally from the work we have done to date.

This next year will be a year of execution. We are about to roll out the plan for the next wave of Search investments. We are approaching M1 [Milestone 1] completion for Live Wave 2. We will soon have a vision for Internet Explorer. And we are entering MQ for the next release of Windows. The best organizational learning happens while doing actual work and we are doing that now. So we have clearly left the realm of theoretical and meta-discussions and are turning the crank. It is exciting.

A big part of execution mode, so to speak, is that it is now up to the team to succeed. Management, process, and memos can only take us so far. Taking the development foundation we have built together and delivering products is up to every member of the team giving 100%.

This has been a challenging year for just about everyone on the team. It has also been a rewarding year. We are a team ready to execute. We are a team ready for the challenges of execution. And above all, ready to take those on together as a team.

—Steven

This "12 Months" blog captures how the aspirations of the "Vision" blog turned into reality. The blog captures the key changes made by the Windows team to restructure the organization and build the foundations for strategic integrity. The changes focused on three important drivers, which make up the strategic integrity framework shown in Exhibit 2.1. These are integrity in organization, in planning, and in decision making. The diagram starts at the bottom by describing the foundations, the essential ingredients on which all else is built. It goes on to summarize the structure that make the foundations work in practice. Finally, it describes the most important resulting qualities, the objectives for each driver.

The framework begins by focusing on organizational integrity. A high-integrity organization is founded on technical depth and on the capacity to execute. The idea is to build very deep functions that accumulate extensive technical competence and cover a diverse skill set, including program management, development, test, and others, as described in detail in Chapter 6. The capabilities built in such a fashion

	Organization	Planning	Decision Making
Drive the Pervasive Qualities	• Efficiency • Transparency • Integration	• Participation • Realistic • Commitment	• Empowerment • Well grounded • Consensus
Design the Structure	• Connected • Flat or flatter • Clear boundaries and clear connections	• Multidisciplinary • Top-down, bottom-up, middle-out • Pervasive	• Clear roles, responsibilities, and dependencies • Framework (plan)-based • Shared load
Create the Right Foundations	• Demonstrated capability for execution • Functionally deep, knowledge, no shallow areas • Technically passionate and skills-driven culture	• Market-driven and scenario-based planning capabilities • Adaptive, flexible processes • Analytical methods	• Accountability • "System focus" • Quality consciousness • Measurement- and learning-driven value systems

Exhibit 2.1   The Strategic Integrity Framework

are shared across the organization by means of a structure that facilitates integration. By combining clear organizational boundaries with clear horizontal connections between subteams and a flatter hierarchy (see Chapter 7 for how flat) the organization avoids silos and works to create a coherent force to tackle challenges and opportunities.

The organization is characterized by three pervasive qualities. The organization is efficient and avoids redundant resources and administrative bureaucracy that reduce the effectiveness of execution and erects barriers between managers and engineers. The organization is accountable, since organizational boundaries and connections are clearly defined to focus the capabilities required to solve individual problems, which over time will build organizational trust. Finally, the organization is transparent, since the lack of administrative bureaucracy, the flatter structure, the organizational clarity all work to create an environment that avoids politics and evokes openness, directness, and accuracy.

Beyond describing the organizational qualities, structure, and foundations, the blog also describes the specific steps taken by the Windows team. These started with rebuilding a foundation of expertise through critical hires, investing in each of the functions, and defining clear horizontal connections for coordination and integration. The functions were reorganized into fewer levels, reducing the average number of layers of management between Windows leadership and an individual contributor from seven down to three or four. The flatter organization reduced the overall number of managers needed and streamlined the transfer of information. It created a much more efficient structure, improving both information flow and transparency. The more efficient structure reduced the amount of daily managerial "control" needed, releasing the time for more creative, "real" work. Ultimately the organization is more balanced, collaborative, and innovative.

The framework continues with planning integrity. The foundations of high-integrity planning are deeply analytical, covering the breadth of technical challenges involved in strategy execution. As such, they provide a way to validate the feasibility of any proposed strategy and feedback specific changes and improvements, based on deep, specialized knowledge, empirical evidence, and scenario-based analysis. The planning process is not a single top-down exercise, but is instead connected by iterations involving a broad set of people. The structure of these iterations defines waves of effort across the organization, thereby linking the different organizational subunits in a top-down, bottom-up, and middle-out fashion. The scope of planning is broad, all the way from business goals to specific technical details defined in customer scenarios, as discussed in Chapter 5. The process is pervasive and involves all team members. Everyone has a chance to participate in examining the strategic frameworks and comment on their accuracy, as they work on their specific technical areas. Finally, the rhythm of the planning process is crucial to achieving both innovation and convergence—there is a time for expanding options and there is a time for narrowing in on actions, to make sure that impact is maximized.

The planning process is participatory, realistic, and commitment based. Planning is participatory because it involves the whole organization and builds alignment by drawing on the entire team to shape the strategic effort. Planning is realistic because it is built on deep, technical foundations, with a process that establishes the feasibility of a strategy as it defines it and as it builds alignment and support for its execution. Finally, planning is based on clear, real commitments, since it provides an initial set of guidelines for what to do, but also establishes a precise framework with which to evaluate and drive changes, clearly establishing a committed structure for decision making. In essence, planning represents the organization's joint commitments in transforming strategy into action.

The Windows team defined a planning process that pulled the organization together and shared the development and execution of strategy ties in a systematic way. The process was detailed and technical, and it required a substantial investment in time and resources. It is worth noting that after 12 months, Windows and Internet Explorer, the most significant efforts in Windows *were still in planning and early execution* (more on this later in Chapter 5)—the team was not buying time, but as we will see, spending considerable time up front across the entire organization would become the norm. Rather than rushing into a project (as many had believed to be necessary), the team engaged in a deep and detailed process to develop a clear framework that described the connection between strategy and execution and that included clear objectives, priorities, schedules, and a detailed set of customer scenarios. Rather than just reducing resources in order to reduce complexity, the team redeployed resources to get more done. One might imagine the challenge in keeping the organization focused on *merely* planning while the demands for quick-fixes only grew.

The Windows planning process relied on everyone (literally) to both contribute ideas and check on their feasibility. The process was all encompassing and iterative, going top-down, bottom-up, and middle-out, thereby developing both vertical and horizontal connections in the organization. The result was a participatory process that was both creative and realistic. Moreover, the process fostered adaptability since the detailed plan was not cast in stone, but instead created a framework for rapid iteration and responsiveness as the external environment evolved (see Chapter 5). In essence, the approach fused directed and emergent strategy into a single, coherent, adaptable entity.

The framework is completed with decision making. The organization accumulates the required capabilities, planning establishes how these capabilities translate into high-impact execution, but it is decision making that ensures the plan is executed with the consistency and quality required for a high-integrity outcome. As described in detail in Chapters 4, 8, and 9, high-integrity decision making is founded on some crucial common values, which shape the decisions of all team members. Establishing clear accountability is an important foundation, since it defines who ultimately owns the decisions and drives their execution. "System focus" establishes a holistic approach to decision making, shining light on the performance of the whole and on the repercussions of decisions in one specific domain on the rest of the system. The focus on quality and completeness reinforces these notions, driving the integrity of the final outcome by emphasizing the value of the whole. Finally, an emphasis on measurement and learning continually reinforce the establishment of deep functional knowledge and technically focused planning, keeping capabilities current.

The approach taken by the Windows team delineated clear roles and responsibilities for strategy development and execution, which cut across the entire organization. This completed the connection between the organization, the plan, and the details of individual decisions. Reflecting a situation all too familiar in the software industry, Windows in the past was accustomed to a "hero" culture of getting things done, with a small number of people bearing a much larger fraction of authority and responsibility than others. In the past, despite the consumer view of Windows as a single product, the organizational reality faced by the leadership was one where most of the work was done by isolated and disconnected teams—each heroes of their own silo. The online services efforts in the past were even more disconnected, having defined themselves as "innovative and agile" and expressly not connected in any way (more on this in Chapter 3).

The new framework reshaped past practices by driving home clear roles and responsibilities, a participatory planning framework, and clear organizational connections. This supplanted the traditional hero culture by empowering a much larger group of Windows team members to make decisions within a clear definition of shared boundaries and objectives. Clearer definitions in turn created trust between individuals and individual departments and improved transparency. Ultimately, this translated into good decisions, decisions that stuck and that did not suffer from second guessing because they were grounded in real technical understanding, knowledge, and support, and driven by the consensus of a diverse and talented organization.

Naturally, describing these pillars did not make them happen. As we shall see in the remainder of the book, the Strategic Integrity Framework was sustained through many additional communications by Windows management, dozens of blogs, and thousands of e-mails, meetings, and individual conversations (we will describe Steven's typical schedule in Chapter 7). Additionally, the ideas were constantly reinforced by real decisions and actual behavior throughout the project.

As described, the organization, planning, and decision-making drivers capture the changes made in the internal workings of the Windows and Windows live Team and set the stage for much of the remainder of the book and the success of Windows 7. However, the internal perspective is only half the puzzle. A successful Windows strategy also influences resources that are external to the Windows team, scattered across the vast ecosystem of partners that drives much of the innovation that differentiates Windows from its competitors. The internal approach should be reflected in the way the team deals with its external partners. Internal integrity should drive external integrity.

Strategy, Execution, and the Ecosystem

Strategic integrity should extend beyond a firm's borders, enveloping business partners, customers, and firms providing complementary products and services. To be complete, the vision that guides internal operations must be intimately connected to the activities and dependencies of key parties outside the firm and must create real value for them. In the case of Windows, this requires taking into account the vast network of firms and customers that have grown around its flagship operating system and associated software.

The PC ecosystem, of which Windows is a part, spans tens of thousands of organizations large and small across hardware, software, and services. There are component makers such as Intel, nVidia, and Seagate that form the components of the PC. PC manufacturers such as HP, Dell, Sony, and Acer develop unique combinations of hardware, together with software and services, bringing PCs to the many different types of customers. Hardware manufacturers such as Canon, Brother, and Logitech develop cameras, printers, input devices, and an amazing array of peripherals that also include Windows software to complement the hardware. In addition, around the globe there are firms that sell, support, and customize the hardware and software used in businesses, schools, and organizations of all types. The ecosystem is vast. There are a hundred times as many people that build Windows-compatible software and hardware outside of Microsoft than inside the company. This means that any Windows product release has a huge ecosystem-related impact, and that the execution of Windows strategy extends way beyond Microsoft resources.

To maintain its integrity, any Microsoft Windows strategy needs to deliver productivity and innovation in the PC ecosystem. The ecosystem was "smarting" from the previous product cycle as the product delay, feature changes, and market execution all made for a difficult environment where trust would need to be rebuilt. The following blog describes the approach Windows followed in providing ecosystem opportunities, and complements the previous two internally focused blogs.

Perspectives on Partnering and the PC Ecosystem

Microsoft's history is intertwined with the history of thousands of partners.* The role of partners has been a hallmark of how Microsoft approached the technical and business challenges of the software industry. In the past decade or so this symbiotic relationship has become known as the *PC Ecosystem*. It, if one could refer to it as a single entity, comprises one of the most far-reaching, most interdependent, most innovative, and even most lucrative assemblages of people, investment, and effort in the history of business. Consumers benefit from the cooperation, competition, and partnerships that are the hallmark of the PC experience. Unlike the history of mainframe and mini-computers, no single corporation can make all that is necessary for the experience of using a PC for home, school, or business. When you crack open a case of a new PC and think just about the hardware there are dozens of entities represented by what is inside. And if you could peek inside the disk drive you would see an amazing number of partners providing the software that resides

---

*A *partner* is any person, company, or team that builds for or contributes to PCs running Windows. That includes companies that make hardware, OEMs that make PCs, independent software vendors, consultants, trainers, and also all the teams in Microsoft that do similar or related activities.

on that platter. And of course with the internet, the PC experience now extends to an essentially unlimited number of people collaborating, competing, and delivering innovation to your desktop (or your laptop . . .). Developing Windows, Internet Explorer, and Windows Live means we have an important role to play in this ecosystem. We provide a broad horizontal layer, a platform, upon which many partners depend both "above" and "below" us. That dependency is 100% mutual and in order to keep the experience healthy we must work in a way that helps partners to do more than build on Windows. We want partners to love Windows!

As we have been planning Windows 7 and as we have gotten feedback about the Vista product, it is clear that we can do much better for partners. That is not to say we have done poorly at all—Vista is a marvel of partner opportunities and partner efforts that really shine. Rather we need to look at what we do in how we build Windows and ask ourselves if we have the right framework for making decisions and ask ourselves if we are doing everything we can to make partners successful. I know we can do more, so that partners of all kinds love Windows!

One way to think about partners is that we are making a big investment in them. We are depending on them to deliver, to create [and] enable new scenarios, and create new opportunities for how software is great and PCs are amazing. We depend on partners to build hardware components, PCs, and peripherals. We depend on partners to help customers to set up systems, secure them, and maintain them. We depend on partners to build vertical systems that turn a PC into a cash register or a design workstation or a CT scan. We depend on partners to deploy Windows on 100,000 PCs for a global enterprise or to connect a single PC to the internet in a home.

We make these investments by writing code. We develop APIs [application programming interfaces], services, and extensibility that allow partners to accomplish [these] myriad activities. We make these investments in partners by our efforts at documentation and technical "education" so developers and designers can make the most of our software. We make these investments by our outreach and evangelism efforts through conferences like TechEd, MIX, and the PDC [Microsoft sponsored conferences for software developers and IT professionals] so partners can talk face to face with a broad set of Microsoft employees. We have significant parts of our entire company focused on partners in every office around the world. We bet big on R&D [that] enables partners and we double down with the effort to reach out and work with partners. Our entire business depends on these efforts—every line of code, every bug fix, and every touchpoint has a partnership angle.

Partnership is a two-way street, and my sense is that despite all of Microsoft's effort I think we in product development need to take a fresh look to see if we are doing everything we can to strengthen the ecosystem. We do not have a choice. Our partners have a choice. In fact our partners have lots of choices. Our partners are businesses. Businesses take capital and invest it, expecting a return. A PC maker takes capital and decides to build a PC—maybe a Windows PC, maybe a Linux PC, or maybe they build an "appliance" with embedded software. A graphics card manufacturer might choose to make cards for PC gamers by making really powerful cards, or they might choose to make graphics cards for consumer game machines, or they might make them for new mobile devices. A hard drive maker might choose to focus on reliable PC drives or maybe drives for a DVR running an embedded (competitive) OS. To us, sometimes these all look like more places to sell PC components, but to a partner these are all choices in how to deploy limited capital. Just like we can't do all the features we would like, even though they are all just code, a hardware company can't supply every type of customer because each has unique needs and requires incremental investment. When there are trade-offs to be made we have to be doing everything we can to make sure a partner sees the "ROI" of investing in the PC ecosystem as the highest possible ROI.

One could look at these and say, "[T]he volume says the PC should win." While volume plays an important role, there are pressures on both sides of the price/volume equation. Mobile devices are becoming increasingly powerful and certainly more powerful than the MS-DOS computers I started out on (or even more powerful than the Windows 95 baseline machine). And mobile devices are shipping in incredible numbers. For graphics, networking, wireless, storage, and other hardware partners, there is a high-volume alternative. For software developers there is a new outlet to focus their efforts on. At the same time, the price side of investing in the PC ecosystem runs the risk of becoming too expensive. That is, the investment dollars required to be part of the PC ecosystem mean your return on that investment might not be a justifiable option. If the cost of getting a Windows logo, building a Windows driver, making a Windows application, or attaching a peripheral to Windows is high enough (whether in money or intellectual capital), then a smart business person will look for other alternatives.

Therein lies the challenge that we must face as we decide on how to build Windows 7. We must look at the costs it takes to be part of the PC ecosystem and make choices that both reduce the cost and increase the return on investment. We need to make sure Windows remains the incredibly smart investment it has proven to be over the past 20 years. Windows is a great platform to invest in. We can make it better. We need to consider how partners view their opportunities and costs associated with the PC ecosystem.

The value of the PC ecosystem rests in the variety of choice, the competitive marketplace, [and] the amazingly endless possibilities of PCs, hardware, and software. For a business there is an incredible "volume" to tap into by investing in the PC ecosystem. As developers we just get to assume that the business folks see the volume opportunities in the PC ecosystem marketplace. Similarly, as developers what we need to recognize is that we have a lot of control, and responsibility, in terms of how much it costs to be part of the PC ecosystem. The "profit" or "margin" (being loose in financial terminology) is the part of the equation where our efforts can have an impact. Technical work that partners do is part of the R&D costs and we need to be sensitive to that.

The three areas worth focusing on as they pertain to Windows 7 are **Compatibility, Requirements,** and **Innovation.** Every day from Sept. 4 onward we can impact the PC ecosystem with the choices we make. This is a call to action.

Compatibility

Several of our Windows 7 tenets are about compatibility—and we are defining compatibility in the broadest sense:

- **Design for interoperability.** We are committed to making Windows work well with products from other manufacturers, in accordance with the principles established by Microsoft leadership.
- **Win 7 will target the same client hardware configurations as Windows Vista.** We will deliver a good experience on Windows Vista logo'd hardware with a minimum of 1Gb of RAM, while also taking advantage of [the] latest hardware.
- **Win 7 will be compatible with applications and device drivers on Windows Vista.** There will be no adoption blockers relating to compatibility in migrating from Windows Vista to Windows 7. Deprecated

features and technologies will be identified and made public as part of Beta1 and mitigation plans to address compatibility impact.

The essence of these project tenets is that any partner that invested in Windows Vista should be confident in knowing that investment is secure with Windows 7. We won't go backwards in terms of compatibility.

Yet Windows Vista was a big release and we have certainly seen the feedback about compatibility (applications and devices). Some have said we did not invest enough or deliver enough compatibility with Windows XP—that is, Vista could represent a discontinuity in the ecosystem. We have introduced discontinuities before—we have changed file formats in Office, driver models in Windows, [and] development tools that are loved have changed significantly. Some have blogged very eloquently about, perhaps, the rose-colored glasses with which we collectively remember the Windows 95 transition (I have long forgotten the dozen network cards I went through as PnP [plug and play] kept frying them as the drivers were debugged). I think in short order, customers will see the value delivered in Vista as the whole ecosystem has had time to adjust—as one personal example, I just installed an nVidia 8500 GT card in my desktop machine. It installed flawlessly. The driver downloaded from Windows Update flawlessly. Everything was great. I have updated my graphics capabilities from a score of 1.0 to 4.2 :-). I'm pretty happy. My machine is zippy. I see lots of cool stuff. It was not as smooth a ride as we would like and I know that some might share stories that weren't as successful at this time.

BUT, the question for this essay is really whether in all the changes, not collectively but individually, we made the right trade-off in terms of how much it would cost a partner (IHV, ISV, VAR) to transition their assets (code, hardware designs, knowledge) to Vista. We need to walk in the shoes of the [thousands] of partners that make up the ecosystem and make sure that every single change we asked accomplished [three] things:

1. Improves the PC experience in significant and novel ways for customers
2. Delivers significant value, that is, a return on the investment customers make
3. Provides an opportunity for the partner to have a significant return on investment for dealing with the change

If we are not compatible, then we must answer these questions and answer them well. And if you are a partner, it turns out the tide might be turning and we need to pay the closest attention to [number 3] since partners are on the hook to their shareholders for that ROI. How does this manifest itself? If a partner's asset is not compatible with Vista, then they need to invest money to be compatible. Some examples might be to run their app in standard user, deal with a new driver model, update how they handle security certificates, rewrite some code due to an API change, train their IT staff in Vista deployment, and so on. None of those things deliver immediate value to their customers—in fact, just like the trade-offs we make, it might have a negative value because when doing this work they are not serving their customers' immediate needs. That is, there might even be a perception that doing this work is value subtracted from the partner's business. Yikes!

Let's walk through an example. Imagine we're an ISV [independent software vendor] that makes a popular consumer software package for Windows. We deliver new versions of that software every year in the fall for back to school. We listen carefully to customers and we know there is an insatiable demand for new features in our product. Because our schedule is very tight and the need for our software to be ultra reliable [is paramount] we always feel that we're never delivering all we could to our customers. Like every software project, we are perennially behind and schedule challenged, though we have a 10-year track record of fall releases. Supporting our software is hard for us because we have so many versions out there (we release yearly) and not every customer buys a new copy every year, but we actively support two versions at any given time with patches as needed, which is rarely. It turns out that some changes in Vista cause our current and previous versions to no longer run reliably on Vista. Because the Vista schedule moved around we were never really sure when we needed to have this work done—would we need to support just our latest one due out in the fall and the current one, or the current one and the one before that? So we just held out and really focused on all those feature requests from our customers. Then Vista releases and our software doesn't work. We look bad. And we have no choice but to just say that this is clearly Microsoft's fault. Microsoft says we did a beta for 2 years and 500,000 people so ISVs had plenty of time to "respond." Of course the customer is caught in the middle and thinks that both us and Microsoft stink. The reality is that from our ISV perspective we had no incentive to go back and patch two versions of our product just to keep it running—all that work did was take away our developers from meeting the customer needs.

There is no doubt Vista is more secure, has a great new user interface, integrated search, better networking, and so on. Yet some ISV software first needs to dig out of a hole to run, before we have written any code to take advantage of these new things. And both of those investments take time away from the competitors we (the ISV) face and the customers asking for the features we are being asked for by our customers.

You can see this dynamic playing out whether we are talking about an ISV who needs to fix their code to be compatible with Vista, a hardware maker who needs to make drivers for Vista, a person who trains people to use Windows who has to take time out from training people to go learn new technologies, or a corporate IT staff that needs to stop serving their internal customers to figure out a plan for integrating new technology.

There is absolutely no doubt that we deliver massive value with a new operating system release. No doubt at all. At the same time we have to respect the reality that customers weigh that value with the cost of taking advantage of or offering that value to their customers. Since breaking from the status quo is always a near-term cost, the medium to long term has to deliver incrementally more value—that is, the return on investment needs to be there.

As developers, we have a lot of control over how much of a compatibility cost we introduce to the ecosystem. We too often make decisions that feel like "this is a small change" yet our ability to add up all these changes, present them to customers, and then present a compelling story as to the total cost is limited. For Windows 7 we are going to begin to think about this more deliberately. The tenets are clear—we aren't breaking anything that works on Vista. So it isn't a negotiation or a decision—we already decided. That is something we are doing to make sure the cost/value equation tilts favorably to partners and we are doing that by taking on the cost ourselves.

Requirements

Readers of my blog know that I'm not a big fan of "requirements." Personally I find requirements a bit too assertive for me and I think requirements have a tendency to drive cooperating parties apart rather than bring them together. There is room for requirements of course—physics, mechanical issues, open specifications, and layering often impose requirements that are necessary for a system. On the other hand, requirements can be easily abused and turned into a way to "force" one party to do something that they might not be predisposed to do. Putting aside the mechanism of requirements, such as a specification, interop document, or logo program, and thinking instead about the partner investment model, requirements are just another element of the ROI equation. Work items that are requirements to be part of the PC ecosystem need to be added up and define some of the costs side of investing in the ecosystem. Once again, if the requirements are too high, then someone thinking about investing their assets in the PC ecosystem might take the opportunity to invest elsewhere. A recent study [has] shown that partners actually care far more about their own success and profitability than they do about the ecosystem's or Microsoft's success and profitability—ok, I made that up, but the point is that we have to walk in the shoes of a partner.

Just as with compatibility, it might be that the partner is not anxious to spend their resources on this baseline work. There could be many reasons. It could be that a partner works in a hyper-competitive area and is very efficient at manufacturing, but just doesn't have the dollars to invest in new software. It could be that the partner is very sophisticated in a specific market (like CAD or supply chain) but has limited bandwidth to become sophisticated in an area like PC networking or security. It could be that the R&D costs for the product are already high and the partner experiences margin pressure even before looking at the types of things they might need to do to be part of the ecosystem. These are all real-world business problems.

I believe that every potential "requirement" we have is developed with the utmost desire to make the PC ecosystem amazingly robust, secure, and excellent all around. However our ability to come up with requirements always has the potential to exceed the partner ability to absorb the required effort. So while we have the customer's interest at heart, if partners aren't able to afford to do the work, then customers never experience the benefit. That's bad. And compounding such a situation is that more often than it should be, the experience of the partner's product that doesn't follow these requirements is worse for the customer. In other words the partner loses because their product fails. We lose because we don't have a partner in the ecosystem. And customers lose because they once again are caught in the middle.

Let's talk about an example. I want to use a real-world example from this week but I want to make it clear that this is just an example and I am not trying to pick on a team or single anyone out, despite the fact that by definition it will seem that way. The team was super well-intentioned and very earnest in their efforts, so please take this as an instructive case study that is part of being a learning organization. We were talking about UFDs (USB Flash Drives) this week at the M1 checkpoints. For me a core question with our current UFD experience in XP and Vista is why when I plug one in does it take so long before I can get the files off of it—as we have all experienced, the whole point of a UFD is that you plug them into machines you haven't used before and so going through the "Installing Device . . . Device Ready . . . AutoPlay" thing is sort of irritating when you are in front of a customer trying to get your PowerPoint presentation onto a podium machine. Well it turns out we have a ton of amazing things that can happen if a UFD maker does all the right plug-n-play work in their firmware, so we have "requirements" and a logo program. But that logo program has a cost, and it turns out that there are probably a ton of drives out there without a logo (I don't know how many, but I learned over 100M UFDs were shipped in 2006). We do a better job in Windows for logo UFDs. But we don't really handle ones without a logo very well. Who loses? Well I don't think the UFD makers really lose—they seem to be doing pretty good volume. Windows probably doesn't lose because people aren't making buy/no buy/upgrade decisions over this since it is probably under the radar. But really customers lose—every day some number (we don't know because we don't have SQM data[7]) [of] people experience this hiccup. So we had customer interests deeply engrained in our efforts, but the manifestation of that created an experience that ultimately was poor for customers.

I know there are tons of technical reasons, testing matrices, and very complex engineering at work. I picked a simple example I am sure. It is easy to come up with examples where if we either tried to support all the variants it would be impossible or the combinatorics would be nutty. My point is that our requirements have a cost for partners and we do not have the focus on the cost that we should. We should think about how when we talk to customers about requirements we should have an "estimated cost" next to each. We should model the economics of this and make sure that for a given category of partner we are making sense. For example, if a partner sells 1M UFD drives at $5 and our "requirements" need one developer for six months, we just cost the partner $250K and it isn't likely the margins are such that they can support that 5% cost.

And we also need to think about the all-up costs of requirements. For a partner that touches numerous systems there are requirements across all of those. So a partner that makes scanners might stumble across a new driver model, a new image format, a new USB logo, new UI in the shell, new security infrastructure, new guidelines for the control panel, new accessibility models, and so on. Yes, this is what it takes to build software in a modern world, but the average maker of scanners probably doesn't have a 20-person feature team ready to write software for each model scanner they make.

One point I want to be really clear on is about "forcing functions." I don't use the term lightly and it is a term I just don't ever want to hear people using. It drives me nuts. If we think something is important, then we need to make a case for getting others to support us. It might be counterintuitive to partners; then if that is true we have to get better at how we talk about the "ask." We have changes we want to make because we feel we know things about the ecosystem; then we need to share that information and build the case for partners. Everyone behaves rationally when presented with customer problems, technical support, and opportunities to improve things for customers and their business.

What we need to do is reduce the costs or "requirements" and also consider how we design our systems so that the requirements are about making things incrementally better, but without following those requirements things are great anyway.

As part of Windows 7 we need to look up at [all] our logo programs and will do so from a product management perspective. We need to take a fresh look at the goals of the programs, from our perspective **and** the perspective of the logo recipients. We need to align our respective goals better and get a better understanding of the cost and benefits of logos, from a broad ecosystem perspective.

As a side note, the above refers to the engineering around partner programs. It turns out that from a partner perspective the sales and marketing elements of these programs are where they often perceive the big opportunity—the visibility, the referrals, the marketing "dollars," and so on. So the equation is more complex, and one way we can reduce the cost or increase the ROI is to have significant benefits for partners along these business avenues. This is where work between the development team and PMG becomes critical when defining partner activities.

Innovation

Reading these first two areas one might think that there is no way to push the envelope around innovation. Or one might think that the best thing to do is focus on just those partners that are willing to invest in the ecosystem and not worry about the others. We need to be careful. For Windows to be healthy we need a lot of partners. We need a lot of people involved. We need depth and breadth. We need it to be economically feasible for lots of participants doing lots of things. And we need partners willing to take a chance and we need to create environments where taking that chance can be done and folks can focus on where they see the work, not where we see the work.

Innovation is the heart and soul of Microsoft. We are [all] here to do new things and change the world with our work. So we are going to do things that are "bets" and we are not going to constrain ourselves to doing only things that fit within the challenges described above. We are going to do things that are just crazy nutty—like build new UI metaphors for Windows, make Windows work as a DVR, handwriting recognition, WWAN support, and so on. We will have breakthroughs and we will make mistakes.

To bring these innovations from idea to prototype to market will require partners. Sometimes we will think of these innovations as incubations and work with a single partner for a short time. Sometimes we will just do some work and sign up as many partners as we can who are willing to make the bet with us. Or we might start out with one partner, get some traction, and sign up more. Other times we might see the partner doing something cool and do what we can to encourage and nurture the external activity.

One of the lessons we have learned with many of our recent innovations is that we are doing an amazing job at innovating in the core technology—think of this as the "device driver" level or the "API." But are we are leaving too much work to partners, third parties, or just others to fill in the scenario? What happens is sort of a corollary to the customer in the middle, which is that we end up doing a lot of work that is innovative but customers don't see it because we don't complete the picture. We need to define our contribution to innovation more broadly so that it is possible for partners to do their part and customers to see the result in some finite amount of engineering time and effort. This is sort of a *batteries not included* challenge we sometimes face. It is why we have been so focused on scenarios as we plan Windows 7.

In addition there are two things we need to consider as we go down this path. First, partners still have all the economic issues we talked about above and we need to respect these. And second, we can't just label everything we do as innovation and that allows us to have relatively unbounded costs to the partner to be part of this new ecosystem. In other words, even with brand-new things that no one has ever heard of we should be much more deliberate about how we think of costs. We should shoulder more of the work, not less, so that we can accelerate bringing innovations to market.

I want to be super clear because it is easy to snap to an extreme perspective in reading this note. Innovation is key to the long-term health of the PC ecosystem. There is already a case study on how an ecosystem can gradually decline without a wide array of partners, a lot of risk-taking, and investment in innovation—that is the PowerPC-based Macintosh system. In that world, the cost of being part of the ecosystem was too high. It made more sense to be part of the vibrant PC ecosystem. We see how much that ecosystem is valued today.

So this does not mean we will cease to innovate, or only do things we know a priori will work. What it means is we will be deliberate and know the costs of the innovation and know who is willing to make the bet with us. It is super important to understand and internalize the difference between that and just saying that we will merely focus on safe bets.

5 Ways Everyone Can Help Strengthen the PC Ecosystem Building Windows 7

I wanted to conclude with a short list of 5 things each developer, tester, [and] program manager can do as we enter milestone 1 [M1] and start to build Windows 7 that would make the ecosystem stronger for partners (and remember the definition of partner includes everyone we touch as part of Windows development):

Everything that runs on Vista runs the same or better on Windows 7.
This one is pretty self-explanatory. We just don't break anything. We just follow the Windows 7 project tenets.

Build as much of the platform as we can, but don't stop there.
Windows is a platform. But we also have to make a product that does stuff. We have to use our own APIs and services. If we claim we are creating something reusable or something that enables a specific solution, then we need to reuse that service or create the solution *before* we ship.

Know the costs of using our platform to complete the customer experience. We should know, before we ship and before we evangelize something, how much it will take for a partner to live up to the expectations we're creating. We should be able to talk in terms of lines of code, developer hours, costs per device, etc. Keep in mind the cost not just of your area, but the total cost to a partner for the whole release of Windows. This covers the opportunity cost side of the equation. These costs are not about forcing partners to do something, but about enabling partners to do something cool that they benefit from.

Be super clear about the benefit of the ecosystem work required, both the target customer and the value they place. This means we should be able to say clearly why the customer will value the work we are asking of the ecosystem and who is going to benefit from the work. A big part of this is that this cannot be a picture painted independent of the costs in #3 but when you look at the costs and look at these benefits they should make sense together.

Have a clear plan for partners that don't buy into the platform work we are doing and what the customer experience is like. Sometimes partners won't be able to buy into a new offering. It might be a time delay and they eventually will. It might be impossible. But the end user might still use that printer, scanner, phone, WAN ExpressCard WAN, UFD, etc. We must deliver a reasonable experience to those customers. That might even mean doing a ton of work and letting the partner spend their energy on further differentiation, rather than the "make it work" effort. A good example of this is all the great work on class drivers in Windows—the more class drivers Windows has, the better off everyone from partners to OEMs to end-users ends up.

There are probably a lot more. If there is a common thread to all of this, it is [to] walk in the shoes of the partner—their perspective really matters and we need to understand it super well.

What else do you think we can be doing to help partners to love being part of the PC Ecosystem?

—Steven

The definition and execution of strategy in the PC ecosystem involve thousands of organizations outside Microsoft. Windows performs a crucial "keystone" role in its ecosystem of partners. Like keystone species in a biological ecosystem, a keystone in business is a highly connected entity whose behavior is central to a much broader community. Take the keystone away, and the whole community is disrupted.[8]

The blog shows how the Windows team, as a keystone in the PC ecosystem, competes and innovates as a network. The dynamics of competition between Microsoft and Apple, for example, are not only driven by innovation in the two companies, but also by the performance of the thousands of partners they work with. The blog argues that it is imperative for Windows to provide interoperability, opportunity for its partners, and choice for its customers. The blog ends by outlining five clear ways everyone in Windows can help strengthen the PC ecosystem.

The blog defines a perspective for extending the Windows search for strategic integrity to the partner network (see Exhibit 2.2). The focus is on attracting a partner network that is productive and innovative.

Note: The exhibit represents the thousands of software and service companies that have partnered with the Windows franchise to deliver

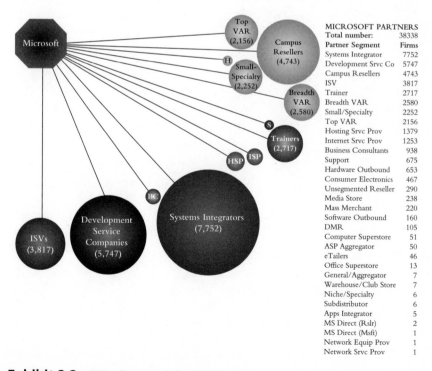

MICROSOFT PARTNERS	
Total number:	38338
Partner Segment	**Firms**
Systems Integrator	7752
Development Srvc Co	5747
Campus Resellers	4743
ISV	3817
Trainer	2717
Breadth VAR	2580
Small/Specialty	2252
Top VAR	2156
Hosting Srvc Prov	1379
Internet Srvc Prov	1253
Business Consultants	938
Support	675
Hardware Outbound	653
Consumer Electronics	467
Unsegmented Reseller	290
Media Store	238
Mass Merchant	220
Software Outbound	160
DMR	105
Computer Superstore	51
ASP Aggregator	50
eTailers	46
Office Superstore	13
General/Aggregator	7
Warehouse/Club Store	7
Niche/Specialty	6
Subdistributor	6
Apps Integrator	5
MS Direct (Rslr)	2
MS Direct (Msft)	1
Network Equip Prov	1
Network Srvc Prov	1

Exhibit 2.2 Windows and the PC Ecosystem

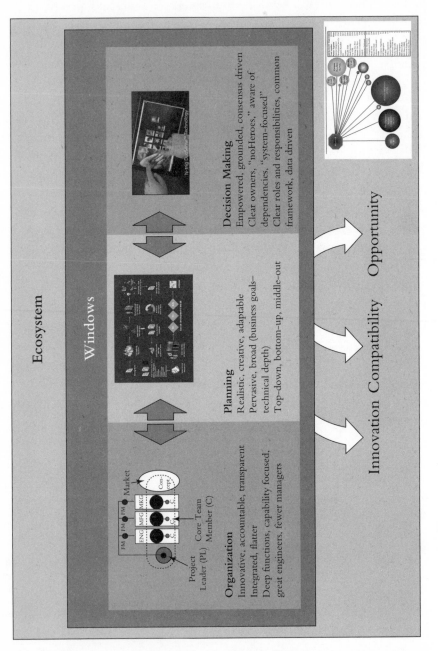

Exhibit 2.3 Windows, the PC Ecosystem, and Strategic Integrity

complementary products and services. It does not depict hardware and component providers. There are three main ecosystem drivers: compatibility, opportunity (through reasonable requirements), and innovation. Compatibility (interoperability) is a foundation of any ecosystem that is built on complementary products. Requirements definition is essential in creating a productive business model for partners and driving much of the cost involved in working with the Microsoft platform. Innovation drives the upside, and the blog describes how Windows 7 can be crucial in generating significant partner opportunities by enabling them to innovate in new and old directions. Ultimately, Windows' focus on compatibility, opportunity, and innovation must serve to create an attractive and sustainable business model for its partners to maintain the integrity of the ecosystem (see Exhibit 2.3).

A Participatory Approach to Strategy Development and Execution

Chapter 2 begins the journey to strategic integrity by examining the basic steps taken in rebuilding the Windows and Windows Live team and its relationship with its massive ecosystem of partners. After 12 months and an enormous amount of work, the Windows team had embraced a participatory approach to strategy development and execution. Windows restructured its organization, created a deeper base of technical expertise, and a flatter, clearer, and more transparent structure. The group rolled out a new set of goals and an all-encompassing planning process, which generated, communicated, tested, and evolved each new strategic direction. Windows defined clear roles and responsibilities and created a strong foundation for decision making. Finally, the Windows team defined clear processes and guidelines for extending its strategy to the ecosystem. The search for strategic integrity was gaining real traction.

Notes

1. Steven Sinofsky's responsibilities included management of the client or "front end" of Windows and Windows Live, working in partnership with Jon DeVaan and other senior executives then reporting to Kevin Johnson. He was also responsible for bringing the engineering resources across the broader organization together

to create the product and execution plan for Windows 7 and Windows Live. The blog posts refer to the overall planning of Windows across the organizations, while some specific references to "Windows and Windows Live" refer to the scope of Steven's direct management responsibilities. For the first year of this assignment, Steven also managed Microsoft's Web Search engineering before Satya Nadella assumed the responsibility.

2. Barbara Darrow and Paula Rooney, "CRN Interview: Microsoft CEO Steve Ballmer," InformationWeek, June 4, 2006, http://www.informationweek. com/story/showArticle.jhtml?articleID=188703406. Ballmer's full quote follows: "Look, we have one product—it just happens to be our most famous product—that has a bigger gap than it will ever, ever, ever have again in its release cycle. That will never happen again. I know how we got there. I'm not going to go through all that. I know what we're going to do differently. I'm not going to go through that. It'll never happen again."

3. MQ is preproject work aimed at "cleaning up" and "housekeeping."

4. CSPs represent the descriptions of job skills and expectations at each stage and level of career development.

5. Through a chance meeting in 1997, Steven Sinofsky and Marco Iansiti met at Harvard Business School and have maintained a working relationship since then. In the fall of 1998, Marco arranged for Steven to spend his Microsoft sabbatical as a visiting scholar helping to teach a class with Stefan Thomke. Steven has taught in many of Marco's HBS classes, with Marco occasionally returning the favor back in Redmond.

6. A group manager in the organization is the senior discipline leader of a major part of the product. Group managers manage on average 45 engineers and report to Steven's direct reports.

7. SQM data is the internal name for Customer Experience Improvement data.

8. See M. Iansiti and R. Levien, *The Keystone Advantage* (Boston: Harvard Business School Press, 2004).

Chapter 3

The Foundations of Strategic Integrity

I ntegrity is central to the effectiveness of strategy.

   Personal integrity invokes connotations of honesty, wholeness, and transparency, and embodies the notions of consistency (coherence), responsiveness, and fit. Similarly, to achieve *strategic* integrity, an organization needs to reach coherence around its strategic potential, sense competitive fit, communicate inconsistencies with honesty and transparency, and build the capacity to respond as the environment changes.

   The concept of integrity has many facets. In addition to integrity of strategy, one can think of many other notions, including integrity of character, integrity of organization, integrity of product, and integrity of management. This chapter goes into different notions of integrity and why they are particularly important to the effectiveness of strategy. Moreover, the chapter links these notions to the strategic integrity framework discussed in the previous chapter and provides its motivation and foundations.

Perspectives on Integrity

The idea of integrity has a long history, tracking across many fields, which provide many useful points of view. The integrity of a human being starts with his or her body. Each of us is truly remarkable in that we are whole beings, in which a large number of constantly evolving elements work together in almost perfect coherence as we continually adapt to our surroundings—at least for a few years of our lives. Take our immune system, which, as described by John Holland, "must change or *adapt* (from Latin, to fit) its antibodies to new invaders as they appear, never settling to a fixed configuration. Despite its protean nature, the immune system maintains an impressive *coherence*."[1] The human body, and its immune system, maintain their coherence and adapt to fit ever-changing conditions, keeping individuals unique and whole, maintaining their integrity in almost any setting. The objective in strategic integrity is for enterprises to do the same thing, maintain their coherence and adapt to fit an ever-changing strategic context.

Physical integrity is only the beginning. For most of us, the word "integrity" evokes a powerful association with our behavior, personal truthfulness, morality, and ethical conduct—a person of "character," if you will. No lies and no broken promises. Personal integrity teaches us that to be and remain whole, a person must have a foundation of character that drives each of his or her actions. This foundation provides a critical, internally and externally consistent framework that helps us evaluate the many disparate challenges that we encounter. This foundation enables us to achieve a coherence of purpose, adapt, and continue to fit with our evolving environment. Again, the analogy can fit the enterprise. Integrity requires an organization to develop an internally and externally consistent framework, what we discuss in detail in Chapter 5 as the plan.

The field of design provides another point of view. The concept of design integrity similarly refers to a product being internally coherent (where each component is perfectly matched to the others) and fitting with its customer context. The Porsche 911 has been perfected over decades of design improvements and reflects a point in which every detail and every knob, suspension coil, piston, and leather seam works to convey a coherent image of "911ness," which drivers have grown to love. The car is honest—it does not lie in the information it conveys to the driver; it is transparent in describing the slippery nature of road conditions through the feel of the steering wheel or the pressure of the seat on the driver's thighs. The car's holistic experience for its customer is coherent and there are *no broken promises.*

The Isuzu Impulse of the late 1980s reflects the opposite extreme. It was designed by Giuggiaro and his team to have the image of a powerful, aerodynamic sports car, with a lovely external design and a beautiful, dark, interior. As the driver entered the automobile, she would be surrounded by the sporty feel of the beautiful dashboard. As she turned the key, she heard the rumble of the sporty engine. But alas, as the car sped up, the sporty experience was completely shattered. The car was built on a truck chassis and, not surprisingly, drove like a truck.[2]

In a business setting, the notion of strategic integrity implies achieving coherence across the organization as it translates the potential of a given strategy into actual impact, as strategy and organization evolve to fit a changing business environment. A high level of strategic integrity will achieve the same level of capability, consistency, transparency, and responsiveness as the Porsche. A business with strategic integrity is fundamentally aligned, transparent, and provides an honest assessment of strengths and weaknesses, of successes and failures. When the road is slippery, it will convey that information to the driver. When integrity is lacking, the organization will lose the capability to master the tasks at hand, limit the flow of information, isolate the knowledge of critical people and departments, fracture, systematically misinterpret the results of tests and market research, and even engage in financial misconduct. When integrity is lacking, lies and broken promises will be daily common occurrences. When integrity is lacking, the business will look like a sports car and drive like a truck.

On Lies and Broken Promises

The following blog articulates important values that have impact well beyond the classroom. It does so by sharing an experience from Steven's college years, thus showing the personal nature of the dialog created by blogging.

An Allegory of Van Gogh and Batteries

In college I enrolled in a class, *History of Modern Art*. I enjoyed the class immensely and without a doubt it proved that those pass/fail classes you are *forced* to take outside your major can also be a super important part of your college experience. The class was a survey of art from 1851–1951. What was most memorable for me was not just the knowledge gained, but the experience of learning from someone who poured their heart into teaching.

The professor started the class on the first day opening herself up to ridicule in front of a bunch of folks no doubt enrolled in the class to satisfy a requirement. She talked about the power of art, the way art shaped history, and how much art meant to her personally. The class format was intense. About fifty of us met in a very old lecture hall with a steep rake to a big desk at the bottom. It was dark. The professor would go through a hundred slides (in a carousel, if you can remember those). She did not rattle off facts or analyze brush strokes but the focus was on the passion, the feeling, and the commitment the artist had to the work (the impressionists had quite a tough time gaining street cred for their work, which is why the class started with the *Salon des Refusés*).

The professor was often emotional and always deeply involved in each work she clearly put great care into selecting for us to talk about. She felt that to get the most out of class you had to be there in person, absorb the environment, and give it your all. She promised to pour her heart and soul into the class and share with us her passion for the work. She only asked for one thing in exchange, which is that we come to class to share the passion, and not to tape record the lecture or try to take notes, but to experience the art. That seemed like a fair deal, since after all I had 5 other classes where I got writer's cramp from switching colors on my 4-color Bic.

About half way through the semester we were studying Van Gogh. It turns out that the professor, who had already demonstrated her passion in discussions of the Impressionists, was a big-time expert and fan of his, having just written a book for a really big 1980s exhibit in New York on post-Impressionists. To say she was really into him would be an understatement. Her passion was evident from the minute we walked into class—filling the lecture hall with anticipation.

We had journeyed through *Starry Night*. We were exhausted as she gave her all talking about the work, Saint-Rémy, and so on. Amazingly she had more to give. On the screen appeared Van Gogh's famous *Self Portrait* and then followed with talk about his ear, mental disease and so on. Tears flowed from the professor's eyes. Then all of a sudden . . .

Crash.

Bang.

Roll. Roll. Roll. Roll.

Clank.

The crash and bang were from a tape recorder (analog) falling from a desk and the rolling was four AA batteries making their way down the long rake of the auditorium, landing at the feet of the stunned professor.

Silence overwhelmed the room. Anxiety replaced anticipation.

Composing herself, the distraught professor lifted the batteries and held them in her clenched fist, clearly at a loss for words, looking up to the darkened class. After a pause that seemed like an eternity all she said was, "you broke a promise," as if to say that she was doing all she could to uphold her part.

Of course the class continued for the remainder of the semester. Things weren't quite the same. We all knew and felt how our class had let her down. But more importantly what happened was that a member of the class missed the point—the point was to give your passion and commit to the class, not to try to memorize some words, ascertain a few facts to be learned, or merely game some system for a grade.

I thought about that class a lot today as I read a new story that contained direct quotes from a post on this internal blog.

—Steven

My inbox is always open.

Strategic effectiveness hinges on organizational coherence. Coherence, in turn, has its roots in clear behavioral norms, like understanding what belongs inside a group and what can be shared with the outside world. Coherence builds on trust between team members, and trust is a fragile thing. Leaks, often the tool of the disenfranchised, can create major problems and destroy the larger whole. Leaked information can be dishonest and fracture the integrity of an organization.

The blog provides a specific example and highlights the challenge of building the kind of value systems that underlie a high-integrity organization. The hard-hitting blog takes a very focused approach. The next blog takes a broader cut at similar issues.

Integrity, Strategy, and Innovation

The following blog provides a more comprehensive view of integrity in engineering innovation. The view extends well outside engineering to other functional disciplines and to general management.

Engineering Integrity—7 Elements of a High-Integrity Engineering Organization

As we go through M3 checkpoints for Windows 7 and IE 8, it has been extremely positive to see the level of integrity in the engineering work we are doing. Commonly, integrity refers to moral principles, which of course would be a core Microsoft value. In the context of engineering projects, the definition of integrity takes on more specificity and refers to *the state of being whole, entire, or undiminished* and *a sound, unimpaired, or perfect condition*. Think of integrity as a *state of* robustness. From this structural integrity perspective, I think it is fair to say that to date as a team we are running a very high-integrity engineering project and that is fantastic to see. When we think about projects that have been difficult to control, that have lacked a sense of completeness, or have ultimately failed to meet expectations, it seems that what one could point to was a lack of engineering integrity.

In sticking with the magic number 7, below are 7 elements that we're seeing, which I also think of as *7 tips to make sure the engineering plan and management are high integrity*.

Integrity in how and what we measure.
Integrity in features as part of a larger whole.
Integrity in cross-group partnerships.
Integrity in working with external partners.
Integrity in work lists and schedules.
Integrity in accountability.
Integrity in knowing what we know (and don't know).

(Pay close attention to the seventh element, since that is where there is ample room to grow and learn and to make sure we don't take too literally the inclusion of *perfect* in the above definition.)

Integrity in how and what we measure. No item of an engineering project is more important than having integrity in the data we use to measure our progress, and no item is more open to "abuse" than the data. One of my favorite books on management[3] points to many examples in business where measuring something actually generates the wrong behavior or the side effects of measuring something yield the wrong results. One of the classics of course is measuring bug counts—measure the find rate and your drown developers or single reports are broken up into multiple bugs or duplicates, measure the fix rate and you encourage withholding bugs until the fix is assured, measure severity and the focus shifts away from attention to detail, and so on. Thus understanding that if we choose to measure something, we are also choosing both to exclude some data and realize the direct action of the measurement. Trying to correct this by adding yet another *counter-measure* only yields a Rube-Goldberg status report that few can understand and even fewer acknowledge or act on.

Really understanding the role of "scorecards" or "red, yellow, green" is incredibly important to a team. My unease with these types of aggregate, top-down measures (and with scorecards in general) comes from seeing more of the downside than the upside. So for me, the best integrity in measurement comes from real data (such as performance benchmarks based on scenarios) and from within the teams measuring their own progress against higher-level goals. So for example, reporting aggregate bugs counts across teams generally leads to weird behaviors more than it leads to a coherent understanding of a project. What we're seeing as we progress is that teams are clearly accountable for the overall quality of their area, and the importance of rolling up data beyond a feature team is being reduced (thankfully). We put a ton of emphasis on the roles of dev manager, test manager, and group program manager because that is the scope of measuring the progress of the team and the determination of what gets measured and acted upon. Of course their relationship to their management is where the discussions should happen about how well this accountability is working.

Third, the inappropriate use of metrics in cross-team work can rattle an entire project. Once metrics are used as a relative "ranking" of teams, teams start trying to just not be the worst or to finish second-to-last, rather than focusing on being the very best. Thus driving all the wrong actions across the team. With a high-integrity measurement system within a team, there is no big role for trying to compare teams or further complicate the situation with such "rivalry."

We've worked very hard on Windows 7 to improve the overall measurement of the project, but just as importantly we have focused much more ownership and accountability of measurement to the group managers, and reduced the amount of aggregate and top-down reporting. The focus is on execution and our commitment to excellence, not on the numbers to the exclusion of other elements.

Integrity in features as part of a larger whole. The project starts off with a definition of what we will set out to accomplish for customers.

The integrity of the whole project depends on each team delivering their part of the vision as we set out to deliver it—that is not just the letter of the vision, but the spirit as well. As we progress through the milestones and the pressures of completing and completing well and on time mount, the high-integrity project is one that does not lose sight of the overall goals. A high-integrity project is one where decisions are made as part of the broader context, not just what is locally optimal. During the checkpoints we saw some great prioritization where teams actively prioritized the vision scenarios over other work and actively worked to make sure the project scenarios overall remained the highest priorities. This is a substantial change from past projects for sure.

Integrity in cross-group partnerships. Working across groups is hard, as we have talked about many times. The seams between groups is where definitions change, processes change, and priorities change—that is going to happen no matter how near or far the least common ancestor node in management rests. But any engineering project of substance or scale will involve cross-group partnerships. Maintaining these partnerships as a high-integrity element of execution is critical to project success. There are a number of project tensions that drive potential failures of integrity between groups:

- Measuring different things, yet assuming measurements are the same scale. As an example, one group thinks another's bug counts are too high, yet aren't aware that the group chooses to keep legacy bugs active longer even if they don't plan on fixing them.
- Lacking clarity in the deliverable, yet assuming clarity. While often this is a communication challenge, this can also be the lack of understanding of the overall problem or solution. A great partnership needs to be more than an upfront agreement and needs to spell out the steps and end-result.
- Optimism. By far the biggest hit to a high-integrity partnership is optimism, on either side of the relationship. Whether the optimism is in finishing the code for delivery or integrating that code, failure to have a high-integrity schedule spells doom.

We have so many cross-group efforts in Windows 7 and our success rate is very high. Cross-group is hard and we are aggressive at trying to make these scenarios work because that is what distinguishes our software from the competition. We don't expect to bat 1.000 but by any measure we are doing extremely well. And where we are not where we'd like to be we have done a great job recognizing that and admitting we can't get the work done so we can recover gracefully and allocate our efforts to a higher payback area. That's a trait of a well-run project.

Integrity in working with external partners. As difficult as it is to maintain high-integrity internal partnerships, it is perhaps more challenging to develop and maintain high-integrity partnerships outside Microsoft. Of course Windows is only as good as the ecosystem it supports, as we all know. And also, as we all know, the work in partnership with the ecosystem for Vista was not what many had hoped (though we did make amazing progress in the ecosystem since RTM). The challenges in working high-integrity partnerships with third parties are immense as our interests, while aligned, are also likely to have conflicting elements or at least varying perspectives that need to come together.

One area of Windows 7 that I believe has made enormous progress at improving the integrity of the Windows 7 project has been the work we have done with the PC manufactures. In an effort led by our product planning team we have developed a deep, high-bandwidth, and high-integrity channel with the OEMs, which we call the *OEM Technical Forum*. We approached our relationship from a fundamentally new perspective, looking at their challenges and opportunities and understanding what they would like to see from Windows 7. And we listened. We documented what we have learned and made sure we were hearing the issues correctly. Then we acted on what we learned. We didn't do everything that everyone wanted (for any number of reasons) but our dialog had integrity so our results, and ultimately the partnership, has moved to be a high-integrity element of Windows 7.

Integrity in work lists and schedules. Whereas integrity in overall measurement and integrity of cross-group work are generally thought of as feature-team level actions, the role of schedules in a high-integrity system is one that gets to the heart of individual accountability. A schedule is only as good as the spec, the work items, and the test plan. And each of those are only as good as the schedule the individual working on them makes them. Without this aspect of the project having the highest integrity, it is extremely difficult for the rest of the project to progress effectively.

Previous projects have focused much less on the individual schedule and much less on the structure of milestones and so this has been a big change. M1 completed on time but was a new experience. M2 finished nearly perfectly relative to schedule with much, much more getting checked in, and yet was much smoother. We expect M3 to go very well. The primary driver of this has been the degree to which everyone has embraced accountability at the TFS [Team Foundation Server] feature level. Folks are doing a fantastic job identifying and costing work items (work items that map to the vision) and then tracking them throughout the milestone. This takes cooperation across dev, test, pm and that has gone super well.

Integrity in accountability. It is impossible to have a high-integrity system without accountability. The heart and soul of integrity in an engineering project requires every individual on the team to understand that the integrity of the whole project depends on the integrity of their work. A triad working on a feature is only strong if all three folks are operating effectively. A feature team is only as strong as all the triads pulling together can be. And the project as a whole requires all the teams to have integrity in their work. This "Russian Doll" approach to a high-integrity project is accountability, and that requires a solid foundation starting with the individual.

For sure no *cultural* element of how our team works has changed more than accountability. It is clearly no longer the case that when something goes wrong you can find others to "blame." First, blame isn't really part of what needs to happen at all and it is great to see folks recognize that (gone are the "risk areas" of a project that always, as if by magic, point to the other teams). For some, this was a challenging or even scary aspect of how we worked—the reality that projects actually depend on the success or failure of an individual's work can be quite a shock. Of course as we moved through the milestones it became clear that we all do our best work when we know what we need to get done and we know that we are on the hook to get it done. That is the real meaning to the concept of *commitment*.

It is early and we are still not yet at the highest level of *performing*.[4] I am certain that we are on the path to be the best performing engineering organization we can be. A big part of that is because we work on the most widely used software on earth and thus we are required to reach that high level, but that alone isn't enough (neither necessary nor sufficient). I can see it in the confidence in which we went through M3 Checkpoints. I can see it in the specificity with which questions about features are answered. I can see it in the deep understanding of the quality efforts. One example I just got in email while typing this was a summary of the performance work on one aspect of the Windows client. The clarity of understanding, the priorities in what was addressed, and the visibility and end-user benefit were all world class. It was a great example of building a high-integrity product.

Integrity in knowing what we know (and don't know). Too often at Microsoft when someone is asked a question the answer is binary—either yes or no. We love to be definitive and absolute and it comes from working on software. The essence of a high-integrity project is also knowing when to say "I don't know" and knowing that sometimes the best thing is to go and learn more. It takes a lot of guts to say "yes" to something. It takes a lot of stamina to say "no." But it takes a lot of integrity to say "I don't know." Taking the time to learn more, put together a plan of action, and then execute on the plan is what builds a high-integrity system.

Integrity in what we know and don't know is what gets to the core of *promise and deliver*. I admit it bothers me when people look at a well-planned (high-integrity) project and label it as "under-promise and over-deliver." We never used that and I view that sort of work as low-integrity (in the moral sense). It takes a high-integrity engineer, high integrity in all the definitions, to take the time to really understand what is not known and refine what is known and plan and execute so we ***promise and deliver***.

That is the essence of a high-integrity project.

While integrity can be a loaded word, for an engineer it has a very specific set of attributes that relate to the ability to define, execute, and deliver on a project. The work we are doing to build an empowered team and deliver innovative products that impact the world has integrity as the foundation. As we march through our milestones and see the effects of this work it is becoming clear that we are doing very well as a team. It is great to be part of this team.

—Steven

The integrity blog describes the foundations of the Windows organization. Laying this foundation and reinforcing it through consistent patterns of management behavior and decision making is probably the most important success factor in implementing the strategic integrity framework described in this book. The different elements are well described in the blog, and apply just as well outside of engineering, to other functional and managerial roles. They are integrity in measurement, in being aware of the broader context, in working with different groups, in working with external partners, in commitments (work lists and schedules), in accountability, and in knowing what we know and don't know.

The seven elements of the integrity foundation specifically address critical problems encountered in the execution of any strategy. Strategy can run into execution challenges because of poor or biased information (technical, market, financial), because of a lack of systemic thinking, or because of a lack of internal or external integration. Lack of clarity and accuracy in commitments and accountability are other common problems as is a lack of honesty in what is really known. As a result, strategies are dead on arrival, as managers even struggle to figure out what their organization is actually doing—what projects are being resourced, what objectives have been achieved, what surprises are just around the corner, or which decisions are being made, explicitly or implicitly.

Previously, Chapter 1 described the problem of inertia, which prevents organizations from reacting to different types of change in technology or the business environment. But if the organization is built on a foundation based on integrity there are fewer surprises, more honest and accurate measures of progress, a broader sense of how each component fits in the whole strategy, as well as more transparency and clearer connections between different groups, inside and outside the company. Ultimately, integrity results in better knowledge of where the organization really stands, in better unity, coherence between different subgroups, internal and external and fit with its environment. Inertia could not last in this context.

Integrity in Action

Obviously, laying out integrity elements in a blog is not enough to make them happen. It is important to reinforce them constantly, in each decision and in each action. Integrity works because it lives within the organization and its daily activities, not because it is mandated by top-down edict. There must be a culture of integrity. The next two blogs are not about integrity per se, don't talk about it directly, and don't even mention the word, but they do link to each of the seven integrity elements. They focus on subjects that are crucial to innovation and strategy execution, such as creating a good plan and transforming a vision into reality. What is perhaps most interesting about the blogs is *how* they approach these topics. They don't push the team—they contain no big words, no stretch goals, no competitive challenges, no ambitious visions. No rallying the troops about saving Windows. In essence, they tell it like it is—and build integrity in action. (*Note:* "Dilithium crystals" is from a blog in Chapter 5.)

Please, Just One More Ride . . . Staying Sane during Development

One of the hardest parts about working from a plan is, well, the plan. Every day our projects bump up "against" the plan. What's the scoop on dealing with this? It feels so rigid. It feels like most days we can be going backwards. It feels like we might miss shipping the right product. The answer lies in having patience, confidence, and also knowing that we have a future of many releases to come.

When I was about 10 years old we moved to Florida. Of course that meant we were near Disney World (not Disneyland!) and I immediately had my sights set on planning our visits. Back then you really had to plan a day at the park. Each of the rides took a different ticket ("A" tickets for silly busses down Main Street, "C" for Mr. Toad's Wild Ride, "D" tickets for the Mission to Mars, and of course the coveted "E" ticket for Space Mountain and the Haunted Mansion). The fact that tickets came in pre-set combination books and combined with the long lines, it really took some logistics. It was not uncommon to see families sitting at the benches on Main Street plotting out the day. As Florida residents we chose to attend more often than not in the off-season (like right now!) which shortened the line constraint, but added the constraint of reduced park hours.

So I would make a list of the rides to go on and planned how to maximize the cool rides throughout the day. (At this point you are thinking that between this and dilithium crystals I was clearly some sort of problem child. Not to worry!) Invariably throughout the day something would go wrong—a line would be too long, a ride would be closed for repair (Mr. Toad always seemed to be closed), we'd get excited about a ride we didn't plan on (sometimes you just gotta see the Hall of Presidents— Lincoln stands up!), or we just needed a break. Of course that meant we didn't go on all the rides we wanted to. At the end of each of these trips I remember always asking my parents, "[S]o next time can we go on Pirates of the Caribbean **first!??!**"

A little thing happened along the way to next year that put a wrinkle in these plans. Every winter Disney would be busy building new rides and because we were local we would see them on the news and everyone would be excited to ride those first next time. And it wasn't long before I forgot about the last trip and the rides I didn't get to go on.

It goes without saying that I had the time of my life each and every time I visited the Magic Kingdom. But still, the best laid plans . . .

Our projects have many of these same characteristics. That is we go through the plans of the release, things happen along the way, and as we finish up we start to think about what we will do first for the next release, only to have those ideas not seem as cool once we get started again. Hmmm . . .

It is worth expanding on each of those concepts briefly, but it is also important to reiterate one very important point. When we roll out a vision to the team—a vision that is the product of months of work across all the stakeholders—it represents our commitment to Microsoft, each other, and our customers. We need to be sure we deliver. However, as we have talked about before,[5] the idea of having a plan is a way of increasing agility and a way to make sure we are building a product that delivers on a set of scenarios we know customers will value.

Do we have enough good ideas in the plan? Our problem is not the lack of ideas. Our problem is not even the lack of good ideas. Our challenge is picking the set of ideas that "make the most sense." The challenge with that metric is that we have to think about a lot of different constituencies. That is what the planning process is designed to accomplish. We decide on business goals, customer feedback points, and strategic initiatives. We come up with a balance of those. We see what is achievable. We allocate resources. We move forward. Like picking the rides to go on, you make different choices depending on the group (if I had to take my sister on Small World one more time I was going to crazy—that song!) or on the weather (If You Had Wings is air conditioned), and so on—you can't go on every ride (not enough time, not enough tickets). Then the really big challenge is executing on the ideas we chose (or getting through all those lines). I don't think we can underestimate the difficulty in executing a plan. Software projects are notorious in their inability to execute effectively. With so much at stake we need to be the world's best at execution. And we need to be world class at choosing what to get done.

What if our plan doesn't include something we really want to do? The easy thing is to say we should re-prioritize things and add it. We can always do that. As long as we have a solid spec and enough development time, that is certainly a possibility. However, we should really be careful about doing this. The biggest challenge with "something we really want to do" is that there are **a lot** of things we really want to do. I mean there are an infinite number of things we could do. From the day we start planning we have more ideas than we have time or people to do the work. So by definition producing a plan is a process of narrowing the set of things we will do. Along the way we will always (100% guaranteed) decide not do to things we would really like to do. Some of these things will be super big and hard and so we might not feel so "bad." Some of these will be really easy to do and seem cool, and so a bunch of us might be bummed. But the bottom line is, and we all know this to be true, is that we can only do a finite set of things and we can't kid ourselves about how much we can get done on a schedule.

What if customers *really* want something that isn't in the plan? This is certainly a variant of the first challenge, though instead of the motivation for doing a feature coming internally it comes directly from customers. We hear from customers constantly in all sorts of different ways, so we can hear about a customer request (or demand) at any time during the product cycle. Hearing from customers is always great, because it means they care and they have a vested interest in what goes into our products. Some of these are big huge features, and quite often they are refinements that genuinely make things better. But just like my parents telling me how much they would like me to go on the Carousel of Progress (that song!), we just can't do all the requests. The limitations here are just the same as above. It is hard to overstate this challenge with respect to our products like Windows, HotMail, Messenger, Internet Explorer. These products are used by gazillions and we all know just about everyone we encounter has ideas on how to make these products better. If we include corporate feedback then we also get very detailed, often strategic, input that covers a huge number of customers. When you start to think about the numbers involved you realize that even one request that represents 0.01% of our customers is still enough customers to fill SAFECO field. It is difficult to say "no" to this many people. But given that just a few hundred requests likely exceeds our development resources (assuming these requests are discrete and achievable) we simply have to.

In both of these cases, we have a path to success that does not just involve hoping that everyone just forgets what they ask for. We have the ability to build new rides for people. The essence of the plan is one where some percentage of the plan is about direct customer feedback, but we also put a lot of energy into enabling our software to do new things for customers. Most customer requests are generally centered on refinements to existing scenarios, or *articulated needs*. Our job is to implement those, especially when our own work on a scenario in a release failed to complete a scenario. By far the scenarios with the most impact for customers are when we provide customers with solutions that are *outside the box* or address *unarticulated needs*. These are the features and scenarios that have the potential to be viewed as breakthroughs. It is incredibly difficult to entice customers to buy new PCs or sign up for new services if all we can offer is "fixed some issues you might have had." On the other hand, if you can crisply articulate how a product or service enables some whole new life-changing work then people will beat a path to your door, as we say.

If we have done our job and come up with a compelling plan, managed to make it through all the discussions of "shouldn't we add X" and get the product or service done and get it to customers, we've definitely reached that magic moment. The fun really begins as customers start using the software and the feedback loop begins. And that also brings us to a state of mind that should free us, knowing that we can indeed make these difficult decisions along the way—the moment when we realize that there is another release coming and we can plan it, execute it, and deliver it to customers. Even though we had all these difficult decisions along the way, the power that comes from knowing there is a future is what allows us to move forward. When we start to think that everything has to get done this release it means we have failed to recognize that no matter how hard we try we cannot get *everything* we want into a release. We just can't. So too much is never enough. This is almost always an extreme failure point for projects—the idea that just one more feature will make it work.

At Disney, it was that one last ride that also caused me to miss the monorail to the parking lot and then I had to take the silly boat, which took an hour, and then I was really cranky the next day.
—Steven

This is a blog is about innovation. It encourages the team to think "outside the box" and address "unarticulated needs." But it gets to innovation in an unusual, measured, and transparent way. There is no innovation black box. There is no innovation skunkworks. The usual air of secrecy and drama is replaced by transparency and clarity of objectives. The blog stresses the need to determine exactly what the team can do, in a careful and transparent fashion—does not try to push the team to do "more." No stretch goals or "big hairy audacious goals." Words like "balance," "achievable," "making sense," capture the character of the writing. The plan, which the team iterates on to generate improvements, provides the common organizing framework for the effort. It is a plan that evolves, that adapts to changing market conditions and technological realities, but also a plan that is developed in careful detail, capturing the reality of what the team can actually expect to accomplish in the given period of time. While adaptable, caution is expressed about making changes. The plan is designed in a conservative way because it represents a real commitment. No fibbing or broken promises.

This next blog continues the same theme, but it addresses later stages of an innovation project, as the team comes closer to shipping its results. This blog is noteworthy in setting a tone that management's role is to tell the team to do less as a project nears completion, not to do more. Not only is this counterintuitive in general, but it is especially challenging for a product like Windows where the demands for new features, changes, or fixes is essentially constant and infinite.

In Chapter 8, we will see the other side of this dialog as the discussion points out the nuances and risks to doing less when it comes to quality and the inevitable trade-offs all projects face. The limits of time, resources, and how much can get done are the defining characteristics of a project cycle. The emphasis on accountability and alignment in the strategic goals of the project are the key to successful decision making. Too often, we see the final "big decisions" made at the top of an organization, where there is likely neither the time nor information to make a proper decision. Instead, the leadership focuses on framing the subtlety and nuance that each member of the team must learn to acknowledge and manage.

"Cutting Is Shipping"

As we enter milestone 2 of Windows 7, and just having done the same for "IE 8"—oh, wait, it is official so no more quotes needed :-), it is worth taking a step back and looking at how the process evolves. The core problems we face are the same one face[d] by every project team:

- the things we aspired to do turn out to be harder than we thought or at least take more time than we thought
- we learned more about what we wanted to do with respect to the partnerships involved
- some of the features we thought would be cool, turned out not to be so cool
- some things we thought would be just ok, turned out to be really neat
- and so on . . .

Some folks think that when we go through the planning process and write everything down that we have created a recipe for the release—that any one ingredient is missing or wrong and the cake fails to rise or the soufflè falls. As we have talked about many times, the vision is not an aspirational document, but our commitments—that speaks to the level and amount of work and the timeline. It is also a directional document in terms of the specific features. That means we expect to deliver on the spirit of each and every vision area and each and every scenario, even if we do not deliver on the specifics as we envisioned them. Sometimes the release goes extremely well and the specifics of what we deliver match exactly the early prototypes. Most releases are not so picture perfect.

What separates a good team from a great team is how the process is managed in going from one reality (the vision) to the next reality (through each milestone). Good teams make the date and have high quality. Great teams focus on the spirit of the vision and work the schedule and work lists to make sure the vision remains intact, not *just* that we hit the date with high quality. The process of figuring out what work to do as we enter the middle milestone is the critical point and it is where great teams are made.

As each dev manager looks at the schedule for their team and each GPM looks at all the features yet to be done, we face the first challenge of "too much work, too few dev hours." The process that is then kicked off is the normal one of prioritization and "adds/cuts." There is a natural tendency to prioritize "locally" and to make sure all of "my" features are the ones that get done. This is the case for pm, dev, and test. That is PM wants their domain to show and get done. Devs want to continue on the depth work on the code they have been writing rather than move on. Test wants to make sure the details of the area they were working on get done. This is good, but it might not be great.

What we need each of the teams to do now is take another look at the vision. We need each team to say, "[T]he work we are doing is the best balance of depth in our area with meeting the overall goals of delivering on the vision." What this really means in practical terms is that each team needs to look not just at their own feature list, but the full list of features for the product. It means you have to get out there and talk to all the partner teams that can make a scenario come to life. It means that for us to be successful we will necessarily give up on some depth so we gain the integration across teams. For our customers to really see the release "pop" we need to focus on the seams between our features. We all know the first things to go are those features "far away" or those work items that seem like "[G]ee, I haven't heard from them in a while so I bet they don't need this anymore."

Where we fail is right here, right now when teams think and act locally. We know we have cuts to make. Making the right cuts is what matters.

The emotion we all share now though is one of pain or a sense of loss. How can we really be successful if we "cut" when we know there is more to do? It is tough.

There is always more to do. If not, that is when we are in real trouble. When we set out the project plan and the vision, we had every intention of completing the whole thing. In fact a key criteria of creating the vision was that we said it was the plan for the team—we would ship the product this way. But we did learn. We've added a lot of polish and depth to the scenarios—not a lot of different features in different areas, but a lot of connection points across features and a lot of polish. We need to get these done. At the same time it means we are going to do less in other areas. Some would say that means we are selling out or being too "date focused."

We are not. We are just doing what engineering have always done, which is work within the constraints of the project.

When we go to sell Windows 7 we will have a cool web page that says all of the features in the release (actually more like a big book of features since there will be hundreds of them). What we don't do is publish a list of all the features we thought about doing and "cut." That list is only for our collective memory. The good news is that if we have done a good job on disclosure and not gotten ahead of ourselves, then the big book of features exceeds expectations a lot and folks get pretty darn excited. We have seen that already with Windows Live Wave 2 and with Vista SP1. We are putting together the list of features that will be out there for IE 8's beta and we know already that the list is way more than people expect (yes, we had a bit of a disclosure challenge last week which we need to work through).

So for me it means that I get more and more comfortable with the release as we cut things. It means we are focused. We are heading towards our goal of having a great release. We are making progress.

We are at the high-velocity part of the project. Things are changing very fast. Work lists are adopting in real time. There is a lot of activity. It is all healthy. What makes it even better is to be sure to communicate and to be sure to focus on our overall project goals. If we ship the features in the vision with the spirit of the vision on time with great quality, then we will have a great release that exceeds expectations of customers.

Cutting is a healthy part of the cycle. When we get to M2 start, we will all feel more focused and have a very clear view of the end-game for Windows 7.

When we cut things we know we are getting close to shipping. And shipping is what it is all about.

—Steven

PS: Also, stick to our guidelines, which are not to let M3 fill up now. M3 will get filled up as we learn more about M2 exit. I promise that teams that are filling up now will not have healthy and cleansing adds/cuts at M3, but they will be way less fun than that.

The purpose of these blogs was not to preach about integrity—the blogs were written as a dialog to discuss a variety of questions asked in various forums. Without being explicit about it, these blogs do emphasize and reinforce each of the seven components covered in the integrity blog above. They emphasize integrity in measurement, by driving data driven decisions, relying heavily on test driven milestones, and clear, detailed customer behavior observations. They emphasize looking at the broader context in the way the planning process pervades the entire organization, and in the serious way the vision document is treated. The vision is not just communicated; it is embedded in the organization—vision and milestones are reality, not expectation, because they are based on facts.

What separates a good team from a great team is how the process is managed in going from one reality (the vision) to the next reality (through each milestone).

The blogs emphasize working across groups and encourage the team to develop awareness of important interactions both internal and external to Windows and Microsoft. The blogs articulate commitments to schedule and plans, and constantly reinforce the importance of accountability.

[T]he vision is not an aspirational document, but our commitments—that speaks to the level and amount of work and the timeline. It is also a directional document in terms of the specific features. That means we expect to deliver on the spirit of each and every vision area and each and every scenario, even if we do not deliver on the specifics a we envisioned them.

Finally, the blogs constantly emphasize a philosophy of decision making based on clarity, transparency, and honesty—knowing and admitting what we know and don't (or didn't) know.

The core problems we face are the same ones faced by every project team:

- The things we aspired to do turn out to be harder than we thought or at least take more time than we thought
- We learned more about what we wanted to do with respect to the partnerships involved
- Some of the features we thought would be cool, turned out not to be so cool
- Some things we thought would be just ok, turned out to be really neat
- And so on . . .

And here . . . Ultimately, integrity works to embed vision, plan, process, and values deep within the team. The team lives its strategy, as it drives toward innovation.

Preserving Integrity

Integrity can be a fragile thing. We have seen many examples in our history in which once successful organizations gradually began to fall apart.

Ranging from the *Challenger* disaster to the AIG debacle, once successful organizations can begin to lose their integrity. There are many reasons for this, but one common failure mode is associated with stress, which is one reason for the following blog.

Stress or Pressure?

One of the things that is really important to me is making sure working on Windows and Windows Live is a *low-stress* job. Stress is evil; in fact stress is defined as:

> **stress**: strain felt by somebody: mental, emotional, or physical strain caused, e.g., by anxiety or overwork. It may cause such symptoms as raised blood pressure or depression.

The thing about stress is that it is both physical and emotional. Stress is all about a loss of control (anxiety). Loss of control comes from not really knowing the goals, not understanding what success looks like, and in our vernacular about being random. Stress comes because the work required is incompatible with your capabilities or your view of success. Stress is about a mismatch between your reality and the reality of your manager or team.

Stress in the workplace is 100% incompatible with building great software.

On the other hand, pressure is all around us. We have pressure to succeed. Pressure to get the build right. Pressure to get the design right. Pressure to go live with content. Pressure is a motivator. Pressure is defined as:

> **pressure**: urgency, as of affairs or business

The thing about pressure is that it comes from within. Pressure is about the plan. Pressure is about your own goals (affairs). By operating with a plan and the details of that plan [that] were created by the team we transform what might be stress into pressure. Pressure comes because you want to be successful against the goals you have set out. Pressure comes because the peers you depend on are expecting you to deliver what was communicated. Pressure is about the constant force in our environment to deliver on the plan we developed together.

Pressure in the workplace is how we stay on our toes and put forth our best efforts. Performing under pressure, while challenging, is what helps us as engineers to make great choices and use the constraints to our (and our customers') advantage.

No one works well under stress—the physical toll is real and provable. Some folks don't work well under pressure. You don't have to put yourself under pressure, but we're a competitive company and like a great athletic team we do want that effort to go above 100%, but we can do so in a constructive way by using pressure to our advantage.

We've got some pressure going on now on our team. IE 8 in the final milestone. Integrating the M1 build of Windows Live. Windows 7 moving to M3. We're excited. The pressure is real. It is pressure like being in the World Cup because we know what got us here and we know what it takes to be successful.

—Steven

PS: Yes these words are similar. The beauty of words is the subtle differences that make them special.

PPS: I'm just excited to use the new build of LiveWriter—and the whole Wave 3 suite!

Stress undermines strategic integrity. Stress is problematic because it causes strain and strain causes organizational fractures. Pressure is about drive, motivation, and excitement. Pressure is inspiration and positive reinforcement.

Stress is often caused by unreasonable expectations—goals that are stretched to the breaking point, overly aggressive revenue growth or profitability targets, unreasonable schedules (often imposed unilaterally from the top of the organization). Avoiding unreasonable targets is one of the key reasons why planning is such an important driver of strategic integrity. The role of planning will be picked up in detail in the next chapter.

The blog argues that "stress is all about loss of control." It is easy to see why setting unreasonable targets would cause an organization to get "out of control" trying to achieve them. We saw this with Dell in Chapter 1, as the system broke down trying to adapt to a strategy that did not fit its organization and business model. This point of view is particularly interesting in light of the traditional meaning in a manufacturing system of being "in control." Being "in control" means being within the statistical control limits, essentially indicating that the system is delivering according to plan. In our innovation system, the control analogy implies that we want an organization to sense its performance, adjust its responses, and be measured in its reactions. We want to stay within the plan, or carefully change the plan. We don't want to go "out of control," risk low-quality decisions, and damage to the project.

The *Challenger* disaster provides an important example, and was also one the team studied in an early training session described in Chapter 2. The fateful decision to launch Space Shuttle *Challenger* was made in a set of meetings that turned highly adversarial, with serious arguments between the managers and engineers involved, who ended up actually screaming at each other. The intense stress of the situation destroyed the integrity of the team, with people taking sides and abandoning any appreciation of the whole. Available measurements were imperfect, and what observations they did have were interpreted with strong bias (either to launch or not to launch). Additionally, there was no honest admission of what knowledge was lacking or of what data might be needed to make the best decision. True, as many have pointed out, many of the root causes can be found in the development of the Shuttle Rocket Booster system—but without the stress of the moment, the Shuttle would probably never have been launched.

Pressure, on the other hand, positively reinforces the integrity of the team. Pressure is the drive to be successful and meet your goals. Part of turning stress into pressure is having a good plan, so that we know how far the system can go and "stay in control." Pressure is about doing your best—not trying to go beyond it and failing. Pressure is about competence, and figuring out what it takes to be successful.

> The pressure is real. It is pressure like being in the World Cup because we know what got us here and we know what it takes to be successful.

Making Strategic Integrity Dynamic

This chapter has described the foundations for strategic integrity. The chapter described different perspectives on integrity and described factors that connect great strategy with great execution and that preserve that connection over time. The connection between strategy and execution, however, cannot be static. Internal stress is not the only problem. As time passes, the business environment will change and an organization must learn to respond to external challenges without losing its internal coherence. Making and preserving this connection between strategy and execution in times of change deserves a special focus and is the topic of the next chapter.

Notes

1. J. Holland, *Hidden Order* (Reading, Mass.: Helix Books, 1995).
2. See K. Clark and T. Fujimoto, "The Power of Product Integrity," *Harvard Business Review* 68, no. 6 (November–December 1990): 107–118.
3. R. D. Austin, *Measuring and Managing Performance in Organizations* (New York: Dorset House, 1996).
4. See http://en.wikipedia.org/wiki/Forming-storming-norming-performing.
5. See the post "Agility in the context of planning" in Chapter 5.

Chapter 4

Integrity and Innovation

C hange will challenge the integrity of any strategy, and any match between strategy and execution.

Any match between strategy and execution must adapt in order to endure. Adaptation, in turn, requires innovation, as companies search for new ways to anticipate or respond to changes in their environments. Whether we look at operating systems or Internet search, executing great strategies requires innovation, as shown by Windows 7 or by the Bing "decision engine" service.

Innovation and Strategic Integrity

What is innovation? This blog provides some answers and starts to paint a picture of the challenges and opportunities created by innovation in the enterprise. This post, one of two, was written as a guest post on Microsoft's internal Human Resources blog hosted by the Senior Vice President of Human Resources, Lisa Brummel.

Follow-Up: Innovation and Organization

What is innovation? Well, dictionary definitions tell us that it is a new invention or a new way of doing something. That's a good start. I think for a business you also have to add the notion of "a new way of doing something that has impact" and that impact needs to create sales or at the very least substantially enhance the "glow" of the company. TiVo changed my life, but the company has been challenged in making the most of their invention. We probably will never get as much credit for the invention that is the Office 2007 user interface, but when you think of the positive impact it will have both on our business and on the customers around the world, that is pretty cool.

The interesting thing is how we often think of innovation as "ah ha" moments (Velcro, Post-it, Lucite). Those are great. Chasing those singular inventions is a very tricky prospect (interesting is how often those very inventions were all pretty much accidents or at least their common uses were sort of accidents). So all businesses get caught trying to "manufacture innovation." Which then leads to all sorts of "goofy" processes such as 20% time, invention Friday, forced brainstorming, greenhouse, and so on. Most people that study the forced march of innovation would say that these are no more or less successful than chance. That might explain why there are so many books explaining how to innovate—you'd think someone would have written an innovative book on how to get the best ideas done.

Needless to say I am one of those people that thinks there is a lot more to innovation than the single idea. There's execution—just getting the idea done (having the idea doesn't really count if you don't ship it). There's timing. There's expressing the idea in the product. There's how we talk about the idea ("showmanship"). There's the quality of the execution of the idea (for example, Mac Time Machine compared to Shadow Copy). As a company you have to think about how the innovation might relate to other ideas we have going on or other current market conditions (the discussion of Exchange and different potential back ends). There's making sure we have the right people working on the idea (the right mix of experience, optimism, pragmatism, etc.). And you could go on and on. What I would say is that management is not about "fear of taking risk"; rather good management is looking at all the conditions that surround an idea and making a call as to what the chances of success may or may not be.

The challenge I always think is that we always have more ideas than we can get done. Just take this to one developer on any single project—even one intern for this summer. In one day of thinking about a problem you can often think up a whole summer worth of work. And that is before you even dive into it and begin to learn what you don't yet know. So given that, by definition we will always have more than we can get done. And that means we have to prioritize. It means that there are "winners" and "losers" in the stack of ideas. Does that mean we are afraid of risk or not taking chances? I don't think one could conclude that. Does it mean that everyone on the team agrees with the prioritization? Does it even mean that the decisions one person made on their own prioritization list would be the same decisions they would make a year later? Gosh, these are tough questions. I think we can safely say that this judgment is an important part of the process, but no one is psychic. All we can really ask for is that everyone at least put forth the effort to learn all the perspectives that go into a decision. In the end though "no matter what happens, someone always said it would"—good or bad, right or wrong.

Some technology changes are termed "disruptive," which I think is a tricky buzzword. We actually don't know if something is disruptive until it actually has caused disruption—but a lot of things get called disruptive before the disruption happens. And even then that isn't necessarily a bad thing for one company. People thought the automobile would put the railroad out of business 100 years ago. Railroads still are an essential backbone of the country, and even more so in other parts of the world. So were autos disruptive to transportation? I guess it all depends on definitions and what success or failure means. As people have really looked into this concept it turns out that more "damage" gets done to a company that constantly chases the next disruption—you stretch resources too thin, your teams get whiplash, people lose confidence that management has focus, and so on. So much like innovation a lot of what goes into "should we chase this" is really about taking into account all the known information at the time and then "reasoning under uncertainty." This is tough stuff. It takes guts to commit. It takes guts not to commit. For every manager that makes the bold decision to embark or bet on a disruptive technology who lies awake at night wondering "did I make the right call" there is another manager who lays awake at night wondering "did I make the right call" by not changing directions. Only time will tell. No matter what happens, someone always said it will. I know I've been on both sides of that sleep deprivation experiment. But "disruptive" is easy to throw around—it is like a neutron bomb in trying to get groups on board. It divides teams into those that get it and those that don't in the eyes of the speaker. I don't think that we need to do things that put distance between teams and people.

Finally, this month's HBR [*Harvard Business* Review] has an article that seems fitting to refer people to. It refers to an article sometime back that I didn't recall and was a good read. It is about how organizations need to think about being ambidextrous in terms of how they approach innovation. I'll let the article speak for itself—http://harvardbusinessonline. hbsp.harvard.edu/hbsp/hbr/articles/article.jsp?ml_action=get-article& articleID=R0404D&ml_issueid=BR0404 ("The Ambidextrous Organization" by Charles A. O'Reilly III and Michael L. Tushman). One caution about these articles—HBR articles are a bit like comic books for execs in that they always seem to be exactly what you want to read. That's the style. If you read enough issues of HBR you can pretty much prove or disprove any management technique you can imagine. That's because business is about people and people are pretty hard to predict and model when it comes to thought and associated behavior! That's what makes all this so interesting.

—Steven

Innovation is invention times impact. Innovation must accomplish something new, but must also have a real impact, on revenues, profits, company image, or on broader issues of value to society. Innovation without impact lacks integrity, like strategy without execution. Douglas Engelbart invented the computer mouse in the mid-1960s, while working at SRI International. The device was large, expensive, and unwieldy, and was not commercialized for more than 10 years. It remained a curiosity until it was introduced with the Xerox Star computer in the 1970s. If this had not happened, we would still be thinking of Engelbart's mouse as an interesting invention, not a major innovation. The innovation's impact increased further with additional implementations in Apple's Lisa and Macintosh computers, and with many additional DOS- and Windows-compatible versions.

Many can invent, but having significant impact today often requires scale. You may need scale in research and in development, manufacturing, customer service, or distribution. You may need scale in sales, technology infrastructure, or a massive number of data centers as with Google. You may need a well-known brand or simply access to a critical mass of customers or advertisers. Impact, in short, requires scale in execution, the ability to translate innovative ideas into significant actions. Scale in execution, in turn, often requires the resources of a large enterprise, which is why biotech firms work with traditional pharmaceutical firms, leveraging their scale in R&D, manufacturing, and sales, and why Linux only achieved real impact when the muscle of companies such as IBM and Hewlett-Packard started pushing its use with their scale in customer service and systems integration. Individuals and start-ups are a great source of inventions—large enterprises (or the partnership of ventures and enterprises) often present the greatest opportunity to translate the potential of the invention into substantial impact.

Large enterprises have increasing opportunities to innovate. However, many management researchers have argued that enterprises will fail in their innovation efforts because, in essence, organizations cannot be good at invention and execution at the same time.[1] This way of thinking drove management practice in the 1980s and 1990s, and created many of the organizational models that we use today for separating "upstream" institutions aimed at research and invention, from "downstream" operating units. The same mind-set shaped industrial research laboratories such as Xerox PARC, Bell Labs, and IBM Watson Research. These organizations were indeed extraordinarily successful in inventing new generations of technology. However, the same research laboratories that invented prodigious new technologies failed to translate these inventions into significant innovations for the companies that funded those efforts.[2] Beyond the downfall of the industrial research laboratory, these experiences led to a common prescription for executives: abandon doing innovation in the enterprise and create autonomous ventures or spin-offs to re-create the advantages of the independent, creative organization.[3]

Despite this last prescription, the reality is that the large enterprise lives on producing major innovations like the Wii and the Prius. The tide is changing and, with the growth of Google and the turnaround of Apple, a different and more realistic picture is emerging. The "ambidextrous" organization article, mentioned in the blog, is part of a more recent stream of thinking that argues that in order to survive in today's environment, an enterprise needs to be optimized for both innovation *and* execution—and the two are often one and the same thing. In fact, the simultaneous importance of innovation and execution for enterprise performance has been shown in a number of research studies[4] in industries such as automobiles, software, semiconductors, pharmaceuticals, and biotech. These studies show that some enterprises are actually quite good at innovation, and that their expected performance is dramatically higher than the expected performance of start-ups or spin-outs. Moreover, they show that capability in innovation is a significant differentiator of overall enterprise performance.

In sum, the notion that disruptive or architectural change drives the need to abandon traditional organizations and create independent ventures is just not consistent with the evidence. Innovation often can and in some cases must stem from the enterprise. The evidence shows that enterprises do differentiate themselves through innovative strategies. Moreover, the evidence also demonstrates that excellence at innovation implies not only achieving excellence at invention, but also translating the potential of the invention into actual impact. The innovative strategy must match the execution. Not only does strategic integrity require innovation, but innovation also requires strategic integrity.

The Innovator's Reality: Innovation and Integration

The issues in the previous section are front and center for the Windows team. As with most other large enterprises, Microsoft must drive innovation to execute strategy. Given past challenges, it is important for Windows to invest in the creation of new experiences for its users that energize its competitive position and image. Windows must also continue to innovate in the face of new generations of technological threats and opportunities, largely driven by Internet-related technologies. Windows benefits from the extensive and deep capabilities it has built over many years of investment. At the same time, Windows is also "burdened" by a valuable legacy of applications and devices that need to continue to work as the computers transition from one operating system generation to the other. This legacy is in many ways the core of the Windows business and any innovation must transition the legacy as well as push toward new boundaries. Microsoft faces the "innovator's reality" of optimizing both for invention and from impact, which means targeting both current trends as well as historical customers and partner relationships. The Windows team must create new experiences while being sensitive to the massive complexity of its operating environment, and to the needs and constraints provided by its extensive base of partners and users.

This innovator's reality means that innovation is increasingly complex because the complexity of customer needs increases with time.

Customers become more demanding with time, and most often do not abandon old requirements. As new technologies attempt to overcome old technologies, they must still solve old customer problems as well as provide new advantages. To be competitive with gasoline-powered cars, electric cars need to not only be more fuel efficient and environmentally friendly, but also achieve good handling, offer convenient filling stations, exhibit an attractive exterior, comfortable seats, and, of course, convenient cup holders. Similarly, Windows needs to continue to offer its customers the features they are accustomed to and Internet software will have to solve a range of problems traditionally solved by personal computer software. Innovation is complex because innovators must solve new and old problems at the same time, and provide a comprehensive, integrated solution to their customers.

Additionally, the time for innovators to solve old problems with a new generation of technology is less than it was in the previous generation. Customers simply do not have the patience to abandon needs that have already been satisfied. Car customers today are very used to great handling, front-wheel drive, cup holders, and leather seats. These features were implemented over decades of innovations and refinements in gasoline-powered cars. But in electric cars, customer demands made the time allowed to develop these same features dramatically shorter. This means that despite a radical change in car technology, design, and architecture, existing car manufacturers have had an enormous advantage over new entrants to the industry, since many critical capabilities carried over from previous technology generations. Similarly, Web services that are delivered in a new manner via the Internet still must solve the same problems that confronted Word, Outlook, and Exchange, but the services will need to do so in less time than was available for personal computer applications to surpass the functionality of older mainframe applications. If they manage to connect strategy to execution, established automobile and software companies will have significant advantages in confronting new generations of technology, no matter how apparently revolutionary or disruptive these technologies may seem at first.

The innovator's reality implies that it's not enough for a new technology to provide unique advantages to be successful. New technology also needs to solve old problems, and do so quickly. The innovator's reality implies that innovation is not just discovering new things, but also the creative integration of old things. Innovation involves the challenge of integrating new technology with all the other features that customers are used to having in a product, like we see with hybrid cars. Additionally, new technology must be integrated not only with old product and production technologies, but also with sales and distribution assets, and with partner applications and technologies. The innovator's reality implies that successful innovation is driven less by discovery and more by integration.[5]

The next blog focuses on the relationship between innovation and integration. It looks at the two traditional options for managing innovation, setting up and autonomous skunkworks effort, and merging innovation with existing development. The blogs examine the challenges and pitfalls of both approaches. This post was the first guest post on the Human Resources blog, taking an organizational approach to the discussion on innovation.

Innovation and Organization

Greetings,

Lisa invited me to post this week as a guest and I'm happy to join here (this is also cross-posted on http://my/sites/stevesi/blog). Let's pick up on the topic of innovation and talk about the challenges of taking on new development projects and how those challenges can also appear as organizational challenges.

The first thing to get out of the way is the perception that working on innovation is good and working on projects that already exist is neither innovative nor all that good. As a technology-centric company we do have a tendency to operate in the mode of "once something exists it ceases to be innovative and thus isn't as cool to work on." That's just silly (actually it sort of sounds like the dilemma faced by AI researchers). The reality is that most of us come to work every day working on some combination of innovative new things we hope to be used by [hundreds] of millions of people and innovation on top of our products already used by [hundreds] of millions of people. We have to be careful not to let the topic of innovation be an issue that divides our teams and, or our efforts.

Let's focus a bit on doing brand-new things outside the expected trajectory of an existing product (as a note, it is almost certain that down the road something fitting this description will end up as part of a larger existing effort, or will itself incorporate an existing effort, as it "matures"). There are two challenges.

- How do we decide, from a vast number of potential ideas and paths, what to pursue?
- Once we decide what to pursue, how do we pursue it?

The first question was posed by Lisa recently and discussed. I'd like to focus on the second.

The conventional wisdom is usually wrapped up in *Innovator's Dilemma* and says that a new venture a company wants to get into will get stifled by the big, slow, existing groups with all their baggage and near-term problems and will never see the light of day. So therefore the way to move forward is to create a new group, pick the "best" people, grant them a charter that allows full freedom to pursue the idea, use whatever resources (code, tools, techniques) they want, and tell the larger group to stop working on the idea. The theory even goes as far as to say, put folks in separate facilities, different badges, and in general full isolation from the "mother ship."

When this idea works you can write books about it. In fact the expression "skunkworks" defines this type of process. Unfortunately there are downsides that we (Microsoft) have experienced more often than not:

- Usually the first thing that gets done when staffing an effort like this is to "steal" folks from the nearest existing efforts, thus making it very hard to deliver on the plans in place (and goes a long way to creating a, sometimes bitter, rivalry). It goes without saying, but often the folks that move are not a random distribution but a subset that work well together (thus usually a subsystem), or the top of the performance "curve."
- Charter conflict is really hard to ignore. I know as a manager, I have spent a lot of time over the years talking about "overlap" or "conflict" across groups.
- New ventures are never 100% new. In fact, most new things tend to look a whole lot like existing things early on as it takes time to build up the infrastructure upon which to demonstrate the newness. Pretty much every innovation these days looks like something to organize photos, play music, watch videos. The devil, er um innovation, is usually in the details.
- Most of the time a bunch of groups were already doing something near the space of the charter, so the question becomes inevitably "can we depend on you" to which the answer is "we are just starting so no."

That inevitably leads to groups knowingly tracking each other. And of course those discussions quickly enter into the [difficult] realm or maybe the *technical buzzsaw* gets pulled out by some existing teams.

- New groups can attract a lot of attention, especially when as a company we are more transparent. That then has a compounding impact on morale, recruiting, and the like. Live.com lists over 4000 references to Microsoft NetDocs, for example, an old project that was adjacent to Office and might be described as fitting this mode of working.
- Showing immediate progress isn't all that hard relative to finishing something. As programmers we all know getting something to a state where it can be demonstrated is the "head" of the work and the task to take that to completion is definitely the "long tail."

So that can paint a pretty grim picture of these challenges. Do you just move ahead and let things fester? Of course we have to keep in mind that we need these projects to be successful. We also need the current products to have new releases and serve customers (and pay the bills).

Yet following this organizational approach, Microsoft has had some very visible and successful efforts such as Windows NT and Xbox, to name two.

Another path is to try to place the venture within the "scope" of an existing product development effort/team. The basic idea here is that we know we want to do something we *believe* is substantially different than the existing product but do so in a manner that allows the innovation to be created and delivered as part of the existing product. Efforts like this generally don't get enough credit because they lack the accoutrements of innovation described in books. In fact, often these look just like "features" no matter how much they might be cutting against the grain or causing "trouble" within the group. Spinning up these efforts causes a number of challenges, some familiar:

- Staffing these efforts follows a similar pattern as above. Ultimately we want to do something new and we need to start somewhere. So how we take from one side of the team to fund the other causes tensions.
- All eyes are on the new team. I promise that at the start of the project everyone, including the people on the new thing, expect the new thing to be the last one across the finish line. So while the team is already under a lot of pressure to "create" they now have double the pressure not to create problems for everyone else.

- Large projects do have processes and overhead that can be burdensome. Of course these processes like SDL [security development lifestyle],[6] multi-lingual UI, accessibility, and more are not things that can ever be ignored so it is just a feeling like "[H]ey, we are new and should be able to postpone these."
- While it can't be proven, one might conclude that the new thing will take on characteristics of the larger project, which might not necessarily be a good thing.
- Being connected to a larger effort increases the cost of failure, since presumably the effort is baked into the marketing plans and the resource trade-off feels much more real.
- Getting credit for innovation this way is difficult because even the delivery looks "incremental." I've received a lot of mail in the past 2 days about Vista features compared to competitive features announced this week, where some are saying "[W]ait a minute we had this feature but didn't make such a big deal out of it."

So it looks like this is a pretty challenging way to move forward as well. Do you tax a new effort with such overhead out of the gate? Will we get innovation credit for work delivered this way?

And again, Microsoft has had some very visible and successful efforts following this methodology such as Internet Explorer, SharePoint, and Outlook Web Access to name a few.

As a social science endeavor it is likely that this boils down much more to execution and circumstance than there being a specific methodology to follow (otherwise there would be a lot more successful innovation and [a] lot fewer failed efforts). What we need to do is become better as a team at knowing the patterns and what to expect so that we can manage through the inevitable trade-offs that any risk-taking venture will require.

To wrap up, let's share some experiences in this area. What has worked? What really doesn't work? Is there a model we should try to apply in general?

When discussing, let's keep in mind two things. First, that we have finite resources (even if that finite number is large) and so we can't pursue the full combinatorics of innovation—that is every combination of technology and people. Second, that the company and all that we stand for depends on both innovation within our existing products and innovation in brand new things. We need both.

—Steven Sinofsky

The blog describes two contrasting ways of setting up an innovative effort in an enterprise—we will continue to refer to them as the "skunk-works" and "internal" models. Both are described as having advantages and pitfalls. Skunkworks can especially be problematic because of conflicts with other efforts, and because they lack integration with the existing businesses. Internal efforts can appear slower because of additional bureaucracy, processes, and methods, and can be "perceived" to lack innovation by the rest of the organization because of their very structure.

The blog ends without making a universal recommendation as to one model being "better" than the other, although Steven's preference can be detected by reading between the lines. Despite some common perceptions, the internal model can work quite well. No method is perfect, but large organizations, properly managed, can indeed drive innovative strategies to successful completion, and do so better than skunkworks projects.

The differences between autonomous and internal innovative efforts have been well analyzed in management research.[7] The most important implication from the many studies is that neither model works universally well; but the problems encountered in an autonomous effort and in an internal effort are qualitatively different. The problems with an autonomous effort are more structural in nature—an autonomous team will experience a scarcity of assets and resources, and will by definition fracture the integrity of the existing organization, which causes the various conflict issues the blog describes. The problems with an internal effort are more managerial and organizational in nature, such as making sure that the processes and methodologies are not too burdensome and that the integrity is not hampered by the inertial issues described at length in Chapter 1. The implication is that good management can solve the problems with an internal effort—but despite the quality of management, the structural problems with skunkworks will remain. If innovation is primarily integration and recombination, a well-managed internal effort will provide the better results.

The challenge of running an autonomous effort is highlighted in an empirical study of over 60 ventures (see Exhibit 4.1). Each of the ventures shown spun out of a traditional enterprise (such as Wal-Mart or Toys "R" Us) to set up an autonomous skunkworks project, aimed at dealing with the "disruptive" threat posed by the Internet. The results are striking. After five years *none* of the autonomous ventures were still in existence.

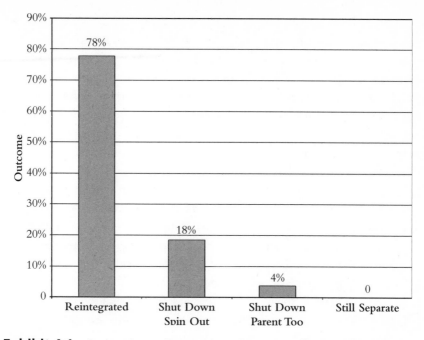

Exhibit 4.1 Innovation as Integration: Outcome of More Than 60 Enterprise Skunkworks Ventures Launched to Respond to the Internet

Seventy-eight percent *integrated* back into their original enterprise and 18 percent shut down. The remaining 4 percent spent so much capital they shut down the original enterprise as well.

The autonomous ventures did not work because of the innovator's reality. The value of an enterprise is in its assets and capabilities, in its ability to understand and solve traditional customer problems. When the enterprise spins out the venture, it is separating these assets and capabilities and damaging the integrity of the innovative effort. This may have some short-term impact on speed, but in the long term, the disadvantage of fracturing connections to the enterprise's most valuable properties is too much to ignore. Walmart.com is valuable because it has access to Wal-Mart's distribution mechanisms, Wal-Mart's customer lists, and Wal-Mart's capable organization. By spinning off a venture based in Silicon Valley and separated from the parent, Wal-Mart abandons what differentiates it without even embracing the full advantages of a real start-up. The research shows that if an enterprise has a strong, established business, innovating from skunkworks in a related area will lack integrity.

It's interesting to point out that the two examples in the blog that are considered autonomous successes are Windows NT and Xbox—in both cases, Microsoft had no existing operating businesses in these areas when the projects started. NT and Xbox were successful autonomous skunkworks at least in part because Microsoft had to develop everything from the beginning. In each case, the teams were seeded with key contributors that had established expertise in each of the businesses. In both cases, the businesses were eventually integrated with traditional Microsoft organizations.

These considerations imply that the Windows group, like many other enterprise-centered innovative efforts, *must* master integration. Windows has a powerful legacy of innovation that delivered generations of solutions to customer problems, creating a wealth of partner opportunities. Setting up a new skunkworks would mean redeveloping all of that foundation from scratch. The key is to drive an integrated effort in such a way that it benefits from being internal to the business, but also from some of the advantages of a skunkworks project. Central to this is the idea of participation.

Innovation, Participation, and Integrity

Participation provides a way to navigate the continuum between a completely independent and autonomous team and an effort that is fully tied to the characteristics of the old business. An autonomous team provides a way for team members to innovate with few constraints. A traditional, fully internal effort can bind the team to a full set of bureaucratic constraints. An empowered team, with each member actively participating in the development of new strategy, can feel motivated to break with past trajectories but also be cognizant of what it takes to make use of existing assets and capabilities. This is the topic of the next blog.

Empowerment in WWL (or the Allegory of the Cave)

As we approach the MIX conference where our team is going to have an opportunity to show off some great work (as promised http://blogs. msdn.com/ie/archive/2007/12/19/internet-explorer-8-and-acid2-a-milestone.aspx) it seemed like a good time to touch on the topic of *empowerment*. Empowerment—granting authority, power, or a greater sense of self-confidence or self-esteem—is a critical part of any successful development team, and creating an empowered organization has been a goal from day one of our organization.

Empowerment is the sort of thing that gets asked about in employee surveys and talked about in books about management, but at the same time few have a clear idea of what it really means or how to measure an empowered employee or empowered team. It should be clear that empowerment is not an absolute, since we are part of a corporation that has responsibilities to shareholders and a management structure where we are each in turn responsible to our managers. Therefore, even if we are empowered we are going to face constraints. For me that means an empowered organization is one where you are aware of the constraints placed on you and you feel these constraints are mutually agreed upon, rational, and in the best interests of all those involved including yourself. Empowerment must clearly be a state of mind. Sounds pretty philosophical to me and I am not really sure how to act on that.

In more practical terms, to work on an empowered team means that you own an area of the product and that you have the latitude to deliver great work to customers. That's much easier to understand. In the past few weeks as we get to the IE milestone, finished the vision Windows Live Wave 3, and as we successfully moved to the next milestone in Windows, I've had a lot of folks on our team stop me in the halls, talk to me at lunch, or send mail telling me just how much ownership and how empowered [they] have felt *relative* to past projects. I'm sure this is not yet a universal feeling, but considering the amount of real progress (code) we've made and the scale at which we need to deliver this is really good to hear.

Why are people saying this? In the conversations, what I'm hearing are things along the lines of the following (paraphrased):

- We planned on what to do in M1 and along the way had all sorts of decisions to make (adds/cuts, prioritization, architecture) and no one checked up on us. We just made the decisions and moved on.
- I thought for sure after the milestone we would have a big meeting and a VP would tell us what we did was wrong and we would have to reset our whole feature list.
- I am working on user interface and I'm in charge—no one is telling me what to do.

- MQ was wide open in terms of what we could do, so we came up with a plan and just did the work we thought made the most sense to improve our test infrastructure and coverage.

The general theme is consistent, which is folks are getting important work done and doing so in a way that affords the necessary freedom from interference.

The key reason why this works is because we are working with a strong sense of accountability and operating under a plan. The plan was developed by the very team that is doing the work. The accountability is defined by what the team said they would get done. Each member of the team is doing their part to deliver on the promise.

We are a learning organization and we are still learning how to make sure everyone shares these expressions of empowerment. I know we will get there, just as I know we are not quite there yet.

All would be well and good, except I'm hearing another consistent theme which has me concerned. When I speak with teams *outside* of our group or speak to folks who are thinking about working on our team, the number one concern I get is "I worry about how top-down and micro-managed I *hear* the organization is." I have to admit this question sort of hurts my feelings given how much emphasis we put on empowering folks on the team to do their best work. I posted recently about one of the most visible aspects of this, which is the way our team handles "reviews." And there have been a number of posts on how we go about coming up with feature lists, schedules, etc. So why do folks on the *outside* think that a "Sinofsky org" is one that is dis-empowering when folks on the inside of the team seem to be feeling pretty darn empowered? I do hate to admit it, but over many years in Office I've probably heard this same comment now and again as well. I never thought much about it until now because it has become such a hot topic of conversation. What is my answer to this observation or question?

As we talk about all the time, the focus of our growth as a team is on being the best engineering organization at Microsoft (in every dimension) and at the center of that is the mantra *promise and deliver*. We're making pretty bold promises (suite of live services, standards compliant browsing, shipping a new release of Windows) and we intend to keep them. And when we accomplish what we set out to accomplish, there's a natural tendency to assume we run a tight ship, or maybe even a really tight ship. And naturally folks assume that starts at the "top."

I admit it. I try to be pretty buttoned up. But I am just one person. There are a few thousand people on the team. Each of them acting independently, doing great work, and doing so without me looking over their shoulder . . . ever. It all seems like magic. :-)

I think folks generally assume that for any big project to deliver it requires some super human project management effort. And then by definition such effort must be one person in everyone's face all the time making sure they don't do the wrong thing or spin out of control (thus annoying them [at] best or disempowering them [at] worst). And for whatever reason, folks generally assume that starts with me. The assumption is that for a big project to actually finish on time, have a great feature set, and be successful the leader of the project must reign over the project with an iron fist—micro-managing, disempowering, and making the place un-fun.

The reality is there is a better way. The better way is creating a team where the high-level goals of the project are set from the start—not the features, but the business goals, the project end-date, and the underlying project assumptions around compatibility, system requirements, etc. Those are where senior management adds constraints to the project (and even those are done in an iterative manner with the team). The individuals on the team, working together deliberately fill in the details which lead to the vision. With those details filled in the work then happens. All along the decisions are the individual's decisions **within the very framework created by the individuals on the team.** Those details are the user experiences, the architectures, the tests, and interactions, the very richness of the work that customers can love. None of that was written down in the vision. Every bit of it was written by the individuals doing the work. In fact, we have dramatically reduced the number of project managers in WWL (and given the few that we have much clearer responsibility and accountability). We have also worked hard to reduce the processes and tools that feel like "homework" and do little to help people do their jobs (and of course we can do this because we have almost no one checking up on folks from outside the team).

Yes there are top-level constraints on the team. Some of those might seem onerous—like one group can't change the ship date; one group doesn't get to do its own private beta release; we strive for a seamless user experience (which means your features should fit in with other features); we do have performance goals, which means your features can't be bloated; we do have compatibility goals, which means you can't unilaterally break things; we do say if you sign up to build <x> you need to deliver it and not just change your mind to work on <y>, and so on. But that's not a whole lot and frankly no matter what you work on I think those are going to be hard to make your very own, since every project is part of a system somewhere.

There is a distinction between empowerment and chaos, a wise person recently emailed me. It is entirely possible to be empowered to do whatever the heck you want to do. But the minute you want to work with other people (because few efforts at any scale can really be the work of one person) you are going to need to get together, share some goals, establish a vision, create an execution plan, and follow through—all of which some folks might see as disempowering ("[W]ait, I don't believe in that goal" or "[W]e need more time than that"). Chaos might sound cool, but shipping great software to one billion people sounds even cooler to me, and experiencing that reality is truly empowering.

Perhaps empowerment is just a word and the real meaning needs to be experienced.

My hope in writing this was really to share the progress we have made in building an empowered organization and also to talk a bit about why folks might think the very opposite to be the case.

The blog shows how to drive a participatory model of innovation that takes the best of both the autonomous and internal models described above. As the blog argues, there is a better way than either extreme. The better way starts from an integrated structure, but creates a structure for empowerment and participation that defines a framework for autonomy. The approach involves creating an integrated team with high-level goals and constraints set at the start. All team members participate in an iterative planning process to fill in the meat of the strategy and create a framework that guides the execution of the project. This framework is detailed and includes user scenarios, architectural frameworks, potential design approaches, and testing strategies. This work is not only done by management, but by all individuals on the team. Empowerment is not a state of being but a full management system. Under the guise of empowerment, the blog effectively presents an abridged version of the strategic integrity framework presented in Chapter 2 and described at length in this book.

Exhibit 4.2 compares the Strategic Integrity Framework to other ways of organizing innovation. The traditional modes discussed in the

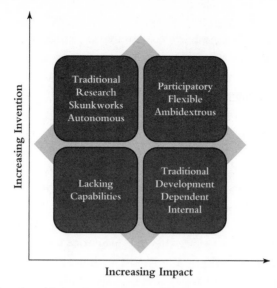

Exhibit 4.2 Combining Invention and Impact

management literature are captured by different terms. There are traditional "Research" organizations, autonomous teams, skunkworks, or organic organizational forms, which represent those modes that are optimized for invention. There are "development" organizations, internal efforts, dependent on the core business for resources, which represent those modes that are optimized for impact and execution. The goal of the participatory approach is to drive both simultaneously, by embodying some of the elements of both approaches.[8]

In the case of Windows, all projects are fully embedded within the traditional organization but also share similarities with classic skunkworks. Team members feel driven (and are expected to) to invent, examine, and implement new products, features, or technologies, and test past assumptions. At the same time, they are cognizant of project constraints and of the opportunities offered by traditional assets and capabilities. Team members feel part of the old business but also feel like they are sharing in a unique, tightly knit community, working together toward a clear goal. Team members are brought into the strategy of the project, since they drove its development. Implicitly, team members are working to match strategy to execution—problems are apparent so that the appropriate reactions can be taken. Team members are working hard to achieve strategic integrity.

This chapter has presented a vision for how an enterprise can drive the innovation needed to execute effective strategies in times of change, adapt its foundation of assets and capabilities, and create products that excite increasingly demanding customers. The innovator's reality implies that the enterprise's past is its greatest asset, not its unfortunate liability. A great strategy, a great plan, and an empowered organization will extend the past success of the enterprise. Rather than fracturing the company into splintered "autonomous" units, it is much more effective to create a good system for managing, empowering, and inspiring an organization to participate in innovative strategies, adapt its traditional constraints, and keep its structure whole.

This chapter shows that innovation, participation, and integrity go hand in hand. If the world is changing, innovation is the only way to match good strategy with effective execution, which means that an enterprise will need to fully participate in innovation to give strategies integrity. Innovation will allow new strategic directions, new approaches to execution, and track the changing relationship between them. Innovation is the key to integrity in times of change.

Not only is innovation the key to integrity, but the reverse is also true. Integrity will drive innovation. Integrity will reveal the problems, clashes, and inconsistencies that cause enterprises to make the wrong decisions when their environments change. Integrity will make participation work and cause organizations to detect problems early and react when things are starting to go wrong. Integrity will cause organizations to realize when their capabilities are inadequate or when their assets are insufficient, and make the changes needed. Ultimately, integrity will drive innovation and adaptation.

The first four chapters of this book have introduced the concept of strategic integrity, described a framework for its implementation, deepened its conceptual foundations, and developed its implications for innovation and adaptation. The next five chapters focus in on the planning, organization, and decision-making drivers of strategic integrity, and describe how the ideas described so far can be transformed into real impact.

Notes

1. The literature stream started with P. Lawrence and J. Lorsch, "Differentiation and Integration in Complex Organizations," *Administrative Science Quarterly* 12,

(1967): 1–30, and continued with many contributions, including R. Henderson and K. Clark, "Architectural Innovation: The Reconfiguration of Existing Product Technologies and the Failure of Established Firms," *Administrative Science Quarterly* 35 (1990): 9–30; and C. Christenson, *The Innovator's Dilemma* (Boston: Harvard Business School Press, 1997).

2. See Henderson and Clark, "Architectural Innovation: The Reconfiguration of Existing Product Technologies and the Failure of Established Firms"; and Christensen, *The Innovator's Dilemma*.

3 See, for example, C. M. Christensen and M. E. Raynor, *The Innovator's Solution* (Boston: Harvard Business School Press, 2003).

4. See, for example, K. Clark and T. Fujimoto, *Product Development Performance: Strategy, Organization, and Management in the World Auto Industry* (Boston: Harvard Business School Press, 1991); M. Iansiti, *Technology Integration* (Boston: Harvard Business School Press, 1997); and G. Pisano, *The Development Factory* (Boston: Harvard Business School Press, 1996).

5. See M. Iansiti, *Technology Integration* (Boston: Harvard Business School Press, 1997).

6. For a Microsoft whitepaper on SDL, see "The Trustworthy Computing Security Development Lifecycle," March 2005, http://msdn.microsoft.com/en-us/library/ms995349.aspx.

7. See, for example, M. Iansiti, F. W. McFarlan, and G. Westerman, "Leveraging the Incumbent's Advantage," *MIT Sloan Management Review* 44, no. 4 (Summer 2003): 58–64.

8. P. Lawrence and J. Lorsch, "Differentiation and Integration in Complex Organizations," *Administrative Science Quarterly* 12 (1967): 1–30.

Chapter 5

Planning

Innovation, Risk, and Agility

Planning is key to integrity, as it links theory with reality and creates a foundation for managing innovation, risk, and agility.

The subject of planning has been the topic of endless debate over the last couple of decades. Traditional schools of thought have long emphasized the value of a good plan. Proponents of traditional product development methodologies, for example, have long argued for the value of top-down planning and defined detailed processes for translating a plan into execution. Others have argued that formal planning is a thing of the past. With speed to market being so crucial, competition fierce, and technological change so rapid and unpredictable, planning is not only a waste of time, but also an unnecessary constraint to innovation. Development projects, they argue, should be run without the "bureaucracy" of a planning process, eliciting customer feedback through many product iterations. The sooner you can throw something together and show a customer, the better it is—you can always fix it later . . . [1]

Together with several colleagues, this author performed research on hundreds of development projects to try to shed some light on this debate.[2] In software, they investigated the development of traditional personal computer applications, internet software services, enterprise software applications, and "cloud" software applications. These studies point to intriguing results. When the characteristics of the project (process, organization, tools, and so forth) are related to its performance (time, quality, productivity, and innovation), two factors appear particularly crucial. The first factor is the resources invested in planning and architecture. The second factor is the resources aimed at managing prototype iterations (driven by inputs such as user feedback, competitive and market responses). In essence, *the two schools of thought are both right and both wrong.* The best projects exhibit both the structure of an extensive planning process *and* the flexibility of (carefully structured) iterations.

The research shows that a great plan executed without iterations is almost guaranteed to generate products that miss their mark. However, lots of iterations without a good plan are almost guaranteed to produce products that are shallow and lack real substantial innovation. The now famous example of Google trying out 41 shades of blue can be thought to take iteration absent innovation to an extreme.[3] It is the combination of deep planning and carefully structured, analysis-driven iterations that drives performance. In the best firms, planning and structured flexibility go hand-in-hand to produce real innovation. Other research, performed in industries ranging from automotive to semiconductors, confirms these results as well.[4]

This chapter focuses on an approach to planning that can drive both innovation and flexibility. The chapter is divided into two parts. The first part focuses on "the theory" and examines the general characteristics of a good planning process and its impact on strategy, innovation, agility, and risk. The second part of the chapter focuses on "the practice" and describes the Windows planning process in action.

Planning Theory: Essentials

The concept of planning has a complex set of meanings. *Random House Dictionary* defines a plan in different ways, including the following:

> A method of doing, developed in advance; a systematic arrangement of elements or important parts; a program stipulating a benefit; a proposed course of action.

Each of these definitions provides an important perspective. The value of thinking through "methods" and implications "in advance," the parsing of complex tasks into "a systematic arrangement" of simpler tasks, the articulation of customer and competitive "benefits," and the clear statement of "proposed actions" highlight different points of view discussed in this chapter. Planning is not simply about writing down what you are going to do. Planning is a complex process that links goals to actions by articulating and analyzing the approach for getting the goals done.

For the purpose of this book, we will define business planning as the process of matching strategy and resources. As such, it is not the same as what many companies define as their planning process, which may be aimed at defining budgets for individual units, with special focus on resource allocation, and much less systematic thinking about strategy. As with the dictionary definition, the business planning process should involve thinking through business goals and their practical implications, formulating approaches for achieving these goals, articulating these into clear customer and competitive benefits (scenarios), partitioning the approach into clearly defined elements (e.g., features or tasks), assessing risks and opportunities, revising goals as needed, and translating approach into action. At the end of the process, strategy and execution should emerge as clear, shared, and consistent perspectives.

The business planning process for a large organization can be divided into different components, as shown in Exhibit 5.1. Portfolio strategy development is aimed at framing the business challenges for the organization and setting the overall business direction. The portfolio management process is aimed at matching projects to these business priorities, developing a clear project resourcing scheme and a focus based on the transparent analysis of opportunities, challenges, risk, and resources. The project planning process, in turn, matches project strategy to project resources. As we shall see in great detail below, the project planning process is based on the analysis of user and partner scenarios, as well as on the assessment of the feasibility and challenges involved with a desired set of product features.

Improving the planning process is often one of the greatest opportunities for impact in organizations. The definition of a balanced project portfolio, the structured analysis of risk and opportunity, and the systematic (and honest) allocation of resources, so important to business performance, is often harmed by ad hoc discussions and political processes, and left incomplete. The analysis of user scenarios and the systematic assessment of project challenges are also frequently left undone.

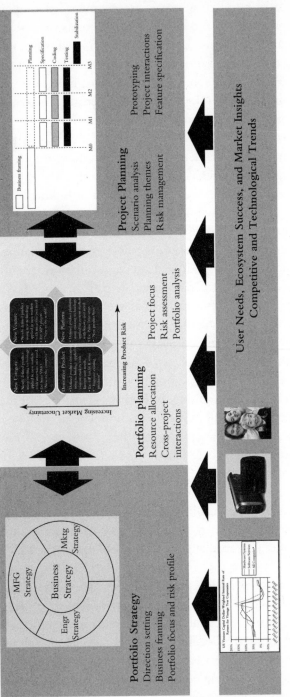

Exhibit 5.1 The Business Planning Process

What features (or projects) get done at any particular time all too often is decided by a small group of people (sometimes even a single executive) leveraging their power in the organization without accurate data or a transparent assessment of market needs and technical feasibility. Data from hundreds of companies focusing on product development portfolios shows that the norm is having way more projects than it's possible to execute, with development resources significantly overcommitted, and no hope of matching portfolio to strategy. Many organizations have so many projects in the portfolio that it would take more than twice the resources available to get things done.[5]

A good business planning process should systematically examine the objectives of different projects, the risk and opportunity profiles, and the resources required, to make sure that the resulting portfolio optimizes the impact of available resources on strategy. It should encompass a deep understanding of user needs, ecosystem requirements and trends, competitive challenges and opportunities, and include detailed scenarios of what the organization should be able to achieve. As the process evolves, it sets strategy and puts it in action by integrating the activities of all relevant levels in the organization, matching business opportunity to technical challenges, possible innovations to new user and partner scenarios, working top down, bottom up, and middle out. As such, business planning and strategy development are one and the same thing.

Planning Theory: Innovation

Few will question the fact that a good planning process will provide much needed structure in translating strategy into action. However, one of the most common arguments against planning is that it restricts innovation. The next blog addresses the issue in the context of Windows. During this time, the industry had grown enamored with a rapid release or update of products, some maintaining the industry label "Beta," indicating a product still in testing, well beyond the traditional testing phase. The implication was that rapid change can be equated with innovation. Many, both internally and externally, were expressing concerns at the pace of change possible with Windows and as such Windows would inherently lack innovation.

Q: Innovation and Planning . . .

Does planning hinder innovation? Or "what if I want to do something that isn't in the plan"?

One thing I am asked about quite a bit is the intersection of planning and flexibility (trying to avoid saying agility these days). This is a good question. If you haven't worked from an upfront plan before—one that fits the description of what we've talked about—but you have a lot of experiences in changing paths while software is developed, then it is logical that one might worry about planning bringing a certain rigidity to the product development experience.

Nothing could be further from the truth. If you have a plan and change your mind on the way to the destination, then it is flexibility. If you don't have a plan and change your mind, then it is pretty random. In other words, if you know you want to go somewhere warm for vacation and your flight to Hawaii is cancelled but you end up in San Diego—well, at least you got somewhere warm. But if you just want to be somewhere else it is tough to know when you got there. The hallmark of a good plan is one that can also be changed—that's because the plan is not about the minute details but about the overall goal.

There is reality, which is you can't plan innovation. We can't come to work in the morning and say, "[O]k time to innovate." Innovation, on the one hand, just means introducing something new (often the same as invention). But in reality innovation is introducing something new that has a big impact and is recognized by others (i.e., whoever is ordained as the recognizers at the moment) as having big impact. Innovation can be thought of as invention + impact. It is the impact portion of innovation that makes it rather unlikely we will just "plan" innovation.

However, if we have a clear view of customer "problems," partner opportunities we want to create, and other "success factors," then we can develop a plan where we align our resources against a finite and prioritized set of these. We can balance the investments in a way that recognizes where the harder challenges are going to be or where we want the most potential for innovation. In other words, the more developers we have on something, the more likely the work represents something super difficult, but known, or super important to one part of our success factors.

With that plan in place and execution beginning a few things can happen along the highway of engineering:

Oops, we tried to do too much. This always happens. It happens 100% of the time. This will happen to us. That's ok. An incredibly important part of the plan is to break the execution up into chunks where we can take a step back and evaluate where we are and see how to scale the work to the remaining time. Now this is a big thing to get right. We can pick a problem that has no hope of scaling, or if we are so wildly off on our estimates, the only option will be to completely cut the work from our plan. That is why good plans have understood ways to scale them before we begin execution. This is not the same as having a list of things we "must do," "want to do," and "wish to do." Our plan, from day 1, is the list we plan on doing. If we do less, then that is ok so long as the spirit of the plan is in place. If during execution we lose the spirit of the plan, then we lose the feature. One thing to keep in mind is that our software does not come with a list of features we thought we'd get done—just the features we do get done. So finishing with high quality and depth is way more important than having breadth of things not done well.

Oops, we thought of something cooler. This happens all the time. We will do many things in the product that were not in the original prototypes or in the vision. Perhaps something that will become clearer later on as we progress is that we expect a lot of this to happen in the depth of the work we choose to do, rather than in expanding our breadth. If you're on the Apple or Google discussion groups or follow their work, what people seem to often say is that they "get it right" or they "add that last few percent that make it very cool." These touches are things that you do not spec upfront because they require flexibility in the schedule after you have most of the system working—these are the fit and finish elements. In Office schedules when we knew we were doing something really big we only planned on using 2 of 3 development milestones and the third milestone was for "finishing what we learned about." OneNote, InfoPath, graphics, and much of the UI work in Office 12 all followed this. If you're doing something new and plan on using all the time, upfront, there is a 0% chance you will accomplish the goal I think.

Oops, the market changed. Perhaps the most challenging area of product development is when you are going head to head with a competitor and the competitor announces something or comes out with something new that we aren't planning. This doesn't happen as frequently as we remember, but it does happen lots. Most of the time since we're all sort of studying the same types of customers and have the same inputs we often think of similar new things to do—it is the execution that is different and sometimes the competitors are more compelling. Of course I think this is a lot about "thinking of something cooler" even if we didn't think of the original idea. I believe we should always have the time to polish in a way that makes our software as competitive. Also remember, rarely does competition hinge on a single feature and so it is important to look at the whole picture—even though your area might have a deep competitive issue, perhaps the whole project all up will remain very competitive and probably surpass the competition.

We thought of something completely different. This one is always the toughest. From the day we start a project we will see new cool things that we think we should be doing. That is by definition. The world is expanding and software can always do cool new things. We can't do everything. Sometimes we might choose to try to get a head start on a new idea—as a company—and do work in our labs, MSR [Microsoft Research], or start an incubation. But since new things are always coming up if we always try to go after them then we will never finish the thing we are working on. It does take discipline and focus to finish—it is a lot harder to finish than to start. Probably the hardest part of "waiting" is when it feels like we are not creating but "just finishing." My feeling is always that anyone can start something, but the people that get paid (by customers) are the ones that really finish and the real value to the marketplace is the finish work and getting something done with world-class quality.

The other aspect of planning that folks have asked about is "[W]hat if we want to do something that doesn't fit in the team structure." This is a bit of the chicken and egg [problem], but also something that takes a bit of a leap of understanding [about] how we are working.

We are in the midst of picking our team structures now based on the top-level inputs to the process that were outlined in June. These were, hopefully, not random or nutty ideas. These were based on the top-level goals for the business that are basically the framework arrived at working with a lot of leaders in the company and also in hearing what is exciting and interesting to you, marketing, sales, and the press. At the same time if you look at the areas they are very broad—super broad and not even clear what features we will do. What is clear is a base set of potential technologies and a broad customer problem space (whether the customer is an end user and we are talking about "my stuff" or the customer is a developer and we are talking about "graphics APIs [application programming interfaces]," for example). These represent the ingredients we have selected for the plan, if we were cooking. But if you watch *Iron Chef* you know even with those ingredients you can end up with pretty different meals!

The next step is to put leaders in place. That is going on now. Once we know we have the "framework" we are going to use, we are going to go off and learn and understand the way to bring the framework to life. We need this framework so we can have depth of planning. If everyone goes off and plans the same high-level goals, "do cool UI" or "do cool social networking, " then we will end up with 15 groups with the same ideas expressed differently. If you're ever wondering why Microsoft has several mail programs it is because in 1995 when you wanted to do something "internet," you first ran off and created a mail client which could serve as the basis of showing off [your] internet idea (which mostly people didn't get to). So we break up the org and the planning into groups that have relatively clear boundaries. The planning process is about identifying where those areas come together in scenarios and with partners to deliver an end-to-end solution that builds software with few redundancies. At this point we've picked the type of meal we're going to make based on the ingredients we picked. But we still have to cook and we might figure out a lot along the way :-)

By definition at this point we have decided what to do. And because of the way we planned we have a strong combination of top down and bottom up. We're in execution mode. If we plan on serving dinner, then we probably don't want to come up with a new course or meal in the middle. A bunch of our success will depend on presentation and having a meal that hangs together.

The goal of the planning process is to mix the top-down framework with the bottom-up creativity in the use of that framework. That way we end up with a coherent product at the end but also one that taps the creativity of all the *sous chefs* on our team!

To many people, planning invokes connotations of bureaucracy. Many plans and planning processes indeed can reinforce this notion, because of their lack of flexibility, their top-down nature, and their narrow set of inputs. But a great planning process, one that is broadly shared, integrates creative inputs from the entire team, aligns resources for maximum impact, and is managed to adapt to changing conditions can have the opposite effect and drive innovation. A great planning process, that mixes a "top-down framework with bottom-up creativity," will encourage invention and enable maximum, aggregate impact.

The planning process does not end when execution begins. The preceding blog highlights important considerations that can help guide planning and iterations during the course of the project itself. It emphasizes the importance of discipline in considering the changes, since finishing "with high quality and depth" is important to maximize the impact of all innovation. Nobody likes a software product that is imperfectly finished, that lacks the polish and robustness we have grown to expect. A highly innovative product in one dimension, which fails in traditional dimensions such as quality, reliability or user interface design, would lack in integrity.

Planning Theory: Agility

The next blog extends the discussion on planning, flexibility, and agility and examines the process for managing iterations of the plan.

Agility in the Context of Planning

I had a drive-by conversation today about agility—a drive-by conversation is what you get when you send me mail with a question or comment and I show up in your office to follow up :-). The question was from a member of the Windows Live Platform team, but I think it applies broadly—"I hear we are going to schedule our releases to be something like a yearly schedule. That seems like a rather long time and in our space things can change dramatically in a short time—look at YouTube that didn't even exist 2 years ago."

The question is pretty straightforward but it brings up at least three points about our development methodology and process worth highlighting. So to answer this I will just jump to a few points that popped into my head during this drive-by.

The short answer is that I am confident that for all of our engineering areas (Live, Windows, IE, Search) we are deliberately picking a timeline for planning and development that we believe is right for the business and for our engineering capabilities. We have spent a lot of time upfront determining the best balance of time to market, depth of engineering, and making sure we can do a differentiating amount of work in a predictable manner.

1. If you have a plan, then how can you be agile?

A lot of times there is a core belief that if you make a plan, then it becomes a drone-like exercise to slog your way through it no matter what, and therefore you are unable to adapt and make changes. Our projects are complex—we are delivering software to be used by [hundreds] of millions of people. And the uncertainty of our environment is relatively high—things in technology change and assumptions sometimes don't hold true forever. But we are not at the extremes of those. For example, we are not building a new Alaska Way viaduct, which would be a very complex project that needs to be accomplished by a very rigorous plan attacked in a very firm stepwise manner. We are also not working on something like drug-discovery where there are total unknowns at every step. So we develop a planning process coupled with an execution process that is a balance of structure and rigor along with flexibility and organic decision making. We will frame the areas we work on (as we have seen in the memos from DHach in Internet Explorer and ChrisJo/BrianA on Live Experiences and Platform—note these have been distributed appropriately to those teams already). The specific features will come from the feature teams, with the scheduling being owned by them.

The question is how we will react if something shows up that we didn't plan on. The something can be self-inflicted (like a service we are running gets into some operational trouble) or it could be a competitor in the market does something that substantially changes our competitive situation (for example, if someone delivers a major innovation in email). The bottom line is that the plan is our plan, so we can change it anytime. Unlike building a big road, we can actually change our minds. The only commitments we have to unwind are the ones we wrote in the InfoPath form (note to self, this means we have to be careful about what we say in public since that means being flexible implies a big public announcement). Changing is not zero cost—unwinding the partially done work involves cost, not shipping a planning feature involves cost, and then spinning up new work involves cost. But we can easily make these trade-offs and decide to do it.

The only requirement is that we make these changes in a completely honest manner. If we are 4 weeks into a dev schedule the changes are really easy—we just need program management to develop the specifications and testing to make sure we can get the work validated while we develop the architecture and approach. If we are 80% through the schedule, then you really need to ask if we will get to market any sooner if we ditch everything rather than wait for the next software wave.

A lot of this also depends on just how much change we are talking about. Sometimes folks could be asking, "[H]ey, this whole new concept appeared so what's our answer" or sometimes it is, "[H]ey, they added blue to the choice of colors for flagging messages" and sometimes it is, "[W]ell we thought we'd have 4 choices but really we need 6." Generally the items that are incremental should be handled by a well-functioning team. Having a plan makes this super easy since we know what trade-offs we are making.

Deciding to enter a whole new area is something best done at release boundaries. This is one where I think the "time to market" argument is one that is often very tricky to discuss as a practical matter. Let's say we're working away and someone introduces a whole new service for managing projects on the web that is integrated with web-based mail. It gets a lot of blogger attention and is the next big thing because it is exactly what students need (just to make up a fake example). Imagine we are halfway through a 12-month development cycle. If some part of the team drops everything, it will take us perhaps a month or so to undo the work we did and make sure the partially done stuff doesn't break anything, and we need to figure out the other parts of the code that depended on that. So even though we might free up 5 developers, it is likely at least 1 will need to help out the other teams. So we might only gain 3 months of calendar time. Now we start coding like mad. One of the things that the competitor did was cool integration with web-based mail, but we can't really do that right now because the web-based mail team is sort of busy finishing for the next few months. So we could punt on that feature, or continue to unravel the work of the mail team. This cascading effect is pretty normal and in the end you only gain a small percentage of the time over just finishing what was going on. In the meantime, we also get to learn about how the new offering was received. The notion of "first mover advantage" is well-known to be provably not much of an advantage (Yahoo was around before Google, Friendster was around before MySpace, and Napster was around before YouTube). It is why I think sometimes being patient accomplishes two things—you get done the work you thought was valuable to do in the first place, and it allows you to learn from the market and do an even better job—after all, we have to face the fact that we weren't first, so we need to do a great job being not-first.

2. Isn't 12 months a lifetime? YouTube wasn't even around 24 months ago.

This is a tough one to answer because 12 months can be a lifetime—if 12 months go by and we only got 2 months worth of work done, then for sure when we finally get around to RTM/RTW [release to manufacturing/release to Web] that will look like a whole lot of time has passed and we didn't get much done. On the other hand, if we get 12 months worth of work done in that time and we picked well, no one will ever notice how long it took.

It is important not to generalize success of one company to a development methodology. To attempt to put a number on it, in the US every year about 650,000 new companies are started. And every year about 600,000 companies go out of business (the net is growth in the economy, spin-offs, etc.) At a more micro level, there are about 10,000 new information companies (NAICS classification) and about that many "corporate deaths" (on a base of about 125,000). So we have quite a few data points to analyze when we look at companies. If you think about the over 1.3M companies started in the past 2 years and that there was one that made it like YouTube (and one Facebook—though actually those are 1 in the past 5+ years) and think about all the failures (Friendster is a great story), there are some staggering odds (I think you are about twice as likely to get dealt a Royal Flush, if you just consider the relative number of companies started and You Tube [YT]). So we probably don't want to make the statement that 12 months is a very long time if the baseline comparison is "YT started and we were caught off guard." One of the perils of business, because it is a social science, is that humans often generalize from a single data point and leave out all the conflicting evidence. We also tend to leave out a bunch of calendar time that did happen. Again, YT is a Royal Flush, but if you look at something substantial like the AJAX mail client on Yahoo, this has been in beta for over 9 months and when it went to beta it was clearly the work of at least that much time before that. And it still isn't released. That seems like an eternity. I think they are doing great work!

The real issue is that you have to pick a timeline that allows you to get substantial development done. Again, this is where the YT example skews perspectives, but it generally takes some substantial effort to make an asset that endures (the Friendster example is also quite salient here). If you want to do something that is worth a lot of money in the marketplace, then it will take a lot of effort, probably more than 5 people, and that means you need to plan and execute effectively. You want something that can't be cloned by 3 other people in short order, which means you probably want something that takes 25–50 developers to make, and that takes them time to do and build a sustainable competitive advantage.

We want to have enduring impact with what we do—we want to create billions of dollars of market cap. While it would be great if it was as simple as doing a few YT's, but I think I would rather bet on doing so more deliberately since that has a higher chance of being repeatable.

3. Are we signing up for releases every 12 months?

Nope we are not. We are signing up to get the next release of Live Services done when we say we will (in the memo from Chrisjo/BrianA this week). (Note: we have also said the range of timings we expect for IE and Windows in other communications.) We are being deliberate in not signing up for "yearly releases" right now. I think we all know why that is the case—the road to yearly releases is littered with failed attempts. Our intentions are right, but our planning and execution failed us.

Every project that has signed up for clockwork releases has hit some snags and the schedule rapidly unfolded. There are as many reasons for failure as there are attempts. With Live 1.0 a main challenge has been the cascading of dependencies and the unknowns that became "must solve" that hit each of the separately spinning development teams. This caused the schedule that was supposed to be complete over the summer to stretch out until spring 2007.

As a result, our WWL philosophy for signing up for schedules is that we will schedule one release at a time. We will do a great plan. We will be excited about what we will do and confident in how long it will take us to get that done. We will work super hard and be honest with ourselves along the way, ultimately achieving the date we set out to achieve.

Once we accomplish that we will plan the next release.

This holds for Windows and IE as well. We don't want to get ahead of ourselves and start to pre-announce our committed releases before we get more predictable at one commitment at a time.

I just wanted to touch on our hallway conversation a bit. I hope this was interesting. I know all this talk of planning can sometimes sound like we have some big master plan that means we spend a zillion days upfront talking about every line of code we will write and then we just mechanically go through the development process. Nothing could be further from the truth. That type of process is one you would use for building a bridge. We are also more structured [than] "a few folks in a garage making stuff"—not just more structured but we have a bigger responsibility because we're running services for so many, building Windows and IE for a huge set of customers. So we will balance those two extremes.

I think we have a pretty flexible path we're on. Our ability to be flexible though depends a lot [on] each of you—the more we are clear on what we can do and the more we plan the work and work the plan, the more flexible we can ultimately be. **With a plan, we can plan to be flexible!**

The blog makes a strong argument that a structured and thorough planning process can be a great driver of agility. Going through the discipline of the planning process, and defining a framework, a structure that links strategy to execution, possibilities to realities, and different organizations to each other, provides a great foundation with which to evaluate and drive the necessary changes. Additionally, the planning structure provides a much quicker way to recognize and focus the capabilities necessary to make successful iterations to the plan, making the necessary and appropriate trade-offs.

> The bottom line is that the plan is our plan, so we can change it any-time . . . Changing is not zero cost—unwinding the partially done work involves cost, not shipping a planning feature involves cost, and then spinning up new work involves cost. But we can easily make these trade-offs and decide to do it . . . The only requirement is that we make these changes in a completely honest manner.

The tie to honesty in the quote is particularly noteworthy. If one divorces the ability to make promises from the reality of execution, it is easy to promise the moon, add more features, expand project scope, cut costs, and also claim that the product of service still ship on time. The reality of project execution will likely make these broken promises and lead to significant problems downstream. Integrity in planning and integrity in changing the plan are crucial to success.

These considerations tie the planning process to the management of iterations and to the overall flexibility of the project. The research studies we summarized at the beginning of this chapter show that a good planning process makes it easier to manage project iterations and drive project agility. This blog also ties back to the arguments made in Chapter 3, arguing that a good planning process is a sound bridge between the traditional skunkworks and integrated forms of organization, that enables the creation of something that reflects the best of both models: "So we develop a planning process coupled with an execution process that is a balance of structure and rigor along with flexibility and organic decision making."

Planning Theory: Risk

The next blog considers the impact of planning on risk.

Risk-Taking in the Context of Planning and Agility

As a follow up, I was asked about how we should think of risk taking in the context of planning and agility. I think this type of question also starts from the premise that if you have a plan and are executing, then you are not taking on any risk. Nothing could be further from the truth—the question is what sort of risk are we talking about?

Of course once you have a plan and then you have a schedule, we all know that it is very difficult to deliver on that schedule and that set of features. Yet somehow we are quick to discount that risk—the idea that we might not finish with the software we said we would finish with, and even worse, we might not finish on time. In fact, I think we can change "might not" to "probably won't" and capture most software projects. If you're the customer, sales, or marketing person that is expecting a set of features at a certain time, then this type of project seems to have a ton of risk. I am not willing to discount that risk to the overall project, or to classify this risk as "execution risk." I think that trying to run our team responsibly needs to consider that we are pretty risky every time we commit to a product plan—that seems inherent in the software industry. I believe our job is to reduce this risk substantially, but historically (even those Office schedules I posted recently) we could say that we've been flying by the seat of our pants for quite some time.

But I am sure that the question I was asked was not about the risk of executing on the plan, but was about taking risk in terms of "breakthrough" or "high-risk/high-reward" development activities. These are terms that are used to sometimes bifurcate product plans into "been there done that" and "cool." It depends a lot on who you ask as to whether a project is risky. Sometimes we can make a project look very risky even though the technologies are relatively well understood and the primary risk is around engineering (say, like Windows NT) but in reality from a business perspective the risk is enormous. Sometimes we can do a project that is really risky from a customer perspective but we feel like we have done a very good job containing the risk (the new user interface in Office

2007). Sometimes the risk is just because we are entering a space that is not one we have historically been in (Zune). One nice example of risk taking is doing the .net framework—we essentially reset our position in the market for server development to 0% and started on a major project to architect from scratch a new way of building internet-scale applications. We know the success we have had there as well as the remaining opportunity. Across the board, Microsoft is a company that has consistently taken very big risks that could have major downsides if we fail to execute or the product is not adopted. So from my perspective we are constantly putting our core assets at risk (Windows, Office, Developer) with major, major risky bets.

At the same time, not a week goes by where I don't get mail from someone saying, "[H]ow can I get this cool idea into our products? It seems like Microsoft doesn't take any risks on getting these ideas done. At Google, I would just do the work and check it in."

There's a lot to this comment. I will put aside the idea that you can just release stuff at Google—I really don't know and it is hard to prove or disprove that from the outside. I do know as a public company and one under the spotlight I would imagine they are rapidly going through the learning and having conversations about "[U]h, oh we can't just throw stuff out there." Microsoft went through this in the late 1990s when we used to allow anything to be put out on Microsoft.com for use/download.

The real interesting thing is how to talk about this issue in the face of risk? Just because we don't do something does not make us risk-averse or unable to take on risk. However, I can really see how in the eyes of that one person not executing on their proposal makes us seem stuck in the mud. We hire passionate people. We hire people with ideas. We hire people who are super creative. And we hire people who are risk takers. How do we mix that with a culture of planning? How do we take on the risks we want to take on, but make sure everyone is a big contributor even if we're not doing every idea that every individual has? This is a tough management challenge. How tough? Imagine that since March I have gotten about 50 pieces of mail saying, "We need to do this thing . . . " (actually it is not about 50 since I keep them in a separate folder). Say we, ultimately, as an entire company, end up doing 2 of those. That means there are 2 super-duper evangelists for how agile and risk-taking Microsoft is as a company. That's great. We also have 48 people who think we are not risk takers. We can most certainly pick the wrong things. We can even pick what to do for the wrong reasons (someone might be great at making the pitch). But we can't pick everything. Yet the very act of not picking everything creates a large set of people who might feel we are not taking risks. Yikes.

One way to help is to make sure the planning process is very inclusive and open to ideas. As I've said a lot of time—the role of the planning process and program management's role in that is to "make sure the very best ideas make it into the product." It is not that all the ideas of the one PM on a team make it into the product. Or that my ideas make it into the product. I know I ask a lot of PM to get out there and get all these ideas. I expect them all to be considered and in conversations about what we chose to do be able to defend gracefully the choices we are making. For example, this week the WEX team had an awesome offsite where each feature team presented the "here is what we currently know" sorts of information— this is the very first step and just one source of input about what we might do. We have much work to do and by the time we have a plan, I am confident we will have explored a large surface area of ideas. At the same time, my hope is that we also involved a large set of people and that many of those with ideas will see that all the ideas were given their fair shot as being part of the plan. I read this week that Google has a "200 person" alias you send your ideas to. We have way more than that, but we don't do it with a star-chamber sort of vote. Rather the process is iterative, focused on customers, and done in a way that we can remove the "politics" from it because it is based on a decision-making framework. I've seen many companies where ideas get a thumbs up/thumbs down at a technical "hearing" and I've never met anyone happy with those results—even those who get approved ideas feel like they just went through too many hoops.

I like to think about the product development process as one fraught with risk and uncertainty. These are two very different concepts that we often mix up:

- **Risk.** The possibility of suffering harm or loss; danger. A factor, thing, element, or course involving uncertain danger; a hazard: The variability of returns from an investment. **Quantifiable and measurable.**
- **Uncertainty.** Not known or established; questionable. Not determined; undecided. Not having sure knowledge. Subject to change; variable. **Property of nature that defies measure.**

I believe that there is a general trend that confuses these two, which means we should be clear about what we're talking about when we talk about risk. The role of the planning process is to reduce the risk in the development process. We cannot reduce the uncertainty—you don't know what you don't know. We can embark on projects we don't know if the market will like, but we need to do so with an execution plan that removes all the risk. If you think about the architect Frank Gehry designing EMP [Experience Music Project] (or any other building), these are very impressive projects. There is a lot of uncertainty over whether they will look nice and people will like them over time. But he hardly throws caution to the wind and just assumes, "[H]ey, because this is an uncertain project we should just start working." In fact, a big part of the success he has is being able to make these projects happen at all—making them safe and reliable and maintainable for example. This happens because he is also a great engineer and because the projects are well planned. A counterexample might be Rem Koolhaas, who had a very uncertain design for the Seattle Public Library, but also did a relatively poor job of risk management in the engineering process (not unlike the people who did our kitchen!).

While you cannot explicitly reduce or quantify uncertainty, you can definitely understand the levers you have to control the downside. We can understand the cost to develop. We can understand the customer problem we want to solve with an approach and decide if there are alternate approaches. We can look at surrogate measures like the amount of pain the solution we propose will get rid of. Or we can look at the opportunity cost relative to other ideas.

For risk, it is all about being great engineers. The best way to reduce risk is to have a well-understood and repeatable engineering process. That is, we know how to make things. We know how to make them well (stable, performant, reliable) and we know how to make them on time. The better we are at reducing risk in engineering projects, the more uncertainty our team will be able to absorb.

The crime is when you make a big bet and then you see both risk and uncertainty compound each other. Some might say some of the early Longhorn bets were of this variety. We certainly didn't know what we didn't know—we didn't know if people would really use these technologies. At the same time, we did not [have a] totally clear view of the risk associated with the project along engineering dimensions we know we should understand. I do know this is a good learning experience and that is how engineers learn.

Another way of looking at the dichotomy is the difference between an incubation project and a development project. When uncertainty is very high you want to incubate. And once you have some of the unknowns known a little better, then you can decide if you want to move to a development project. This incubation does not have to happen in a different building on a different schedule by different people—it can be happening right now, for example. There is plenty of time to incubate. The trick is to be sure we are incubating what is truly a new idea, rather than building something we already know about for a long time just to get to the point of trying out an idea (mail clients used to spring up routinely inside Microsoft just so we could incubate ideas for information management or even code architecture).

- **Incubation.** Overcoming the challenge that a technology might not work
- **Development.** Overcoming the challenge that a product might not be successful

I will leave this post with the way that I will look to think about the "portfolio" of products and technologies we develop. We will have a spectrum of technologies along the following risk matrix. The idea is that some technologies are risky and some are uncertain. So you can think of them something like the following figure [see Exhibit 5.2]:

This is just a framework for looking at things and I'm sure that we can define intermediate conditions or other ways to cut the data. The point I would make is that while our products overall might be in one quadrant, features and technologies within those products will be in all four quadrants. The question for management is how much of what we do is where—and what is the right distribution across these quadrants. It is not as easy as it might seem :-).

—Steven

The management of "unknowns" is a key concern in the execution of any strategy, particularly in turbulent industries like software, and should play a prominent role in both portfolio and project planning. The blog takes on two different schools of thought. Some have argued that any unproven technology should go through advanced development to achieve demonstrated feasibility before being incorporated into a project. Others have argued that when competitive pressure is high, people should be encouraged to experiment with aggressive technology and business models directly in projects.

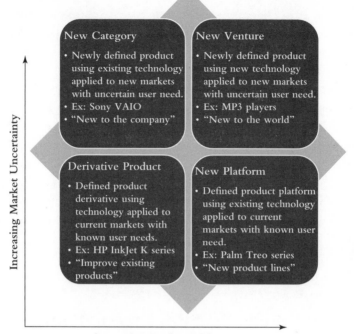

Exhibit 5.2   Managing Risk and Uncertainty[6]

The blog first differentiates between uncertainty ("property of nature that defies measure"; un-measurable unknowns) and risk (quantifiable and measurable variability; measurable unknowns). The blog then argues that a great planning process can drive the assessment and management of risk, which has important consequences for portfolio planning. If a project contains uncertainty, it is better to isolate the uncertainty by incubating that component as a separate project in the portfolio, minimizing interdependencies with other projects until the uncertainty is resolved. But when the project only contains risk, detailed planning and extensive experimentation can be used to manage potential negative consequences, and the risky component can be integrated with the rest of the project. This integration has significant benefits in speed and productivity. In a study of the development of high-end servers, for example, this author found that projects that integrated the management of risky technologies outperformed projects that separated them by a factor of three to one in productivity (and where 30 percent faster to market).[7]

In sum, our planning "theory" expands on the empirical evidence we discussed at the beginning of this chapter. A sound planning process can drive innovation and help manage risk in the enterprise. Additionally, the right planning process should be integrated with project iterations to drive flexibility and agility.

Planning (either at the project level or at the portfolio level) is the place to start. The right planning process can improve product development productivity by a factor of two or more, as well as significantly shrink development lead time. If the planning and resource allocation process is broken, heroic project leaders will not be able to make a project converge. You simply cannot have positive impact if resources are misallocated and misaligned. On the other hand, a great planning process can provide the structure and integration necessary to dramatically increase the predictability and impact of a project.

The next section lays out the Windows process in detail and discusses how these important objectives can be achieved in practice.

Planning Practice: The Anatomy of the Windows Planning Process

While Steven had planned many projects before as a developer or program manager, the process for him was "organic"—placed in his engineering DNA by the managers he was fortunate to work for early in his career. To transfer this DNA broadly and quickly, without turning it into an overly prescriptive tool required some thought—overemphasizing the mechanics would be a disaster as the team would naturally focus on "checking off" the steps for the new management, rather than seeing process for what it was, a tool. Steven created the picture shown at the start of this chapter, as a way to visualize the process—and the picture took a life of its own. Still, many saw it as a linear and rigid description, not as the overlapping and interlocking steps—the iteration and consensus. So within that context, efforts were needed to further define and refine the "process."

The next blog describes the Windows planning process in action. Written a few months after Steven moved to the Windows organization, his dialog with the Windows team arguably represents the moment that the organization started to gain real coherence, working together as an integrated and transparent organization. The planning framework memos had

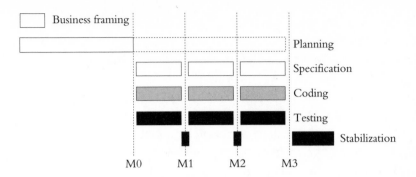

Exhibit 5.3   Windows Development Process (High-Level View)

just been finished, and the teams were working on specific features and scenarios. The blog shows how all of this comes together in a unified effort.

The planning process fits as part of the broader product development effort, as sketched out in Exhibit 5.3. Planning is kicked off with a top-down effort at business framing, follows with several bottom-up, middle-out iterations, as described in detail in the blog, and continues with a structured approach to evaluate and react to changes during the course of the project. What in this context appears focused on an individual project can also apply to complex project portfolios. Windows is a broad organization that not only includes Windows development, but a variety of other Windows Live products and services. Moreover, Windows itself can be thought of as a portfolio of dozens of projects, each focused on a product feature—each of these needs to work seamlessly with the others and ship simultaneously.

Next Steps for Planning

This is a post that is primarily for the teams working on Windows and Windows Live, and COSD [Core Operating System Division]. On Friday the Windows folks received the planning memo from Julie Larson-Green outlining the planning process and next steps for the next Windows release. This memo is the fourth for the Windows and Windows Live planning work, as we have already published the planning memos for Internet Explorer from Dean Hachamovitch, Live Experiences (with Live Platform) from Chris Jones and Brian Arbogast, and Live Search from Christopher Payne. While I recognize these are memos and not code, the collective work they represent is significant and it represents team-wide progress towards building the next wave of software for customers and the market. We do have a lot going on in the near term (especially with respect to Longhorn Server and SP1 in Windows), but this memo focuses on the planning work going on in parallel. I thought I would take this milestone to just reiterate a bit about the process we are following.

The purpose of the planning memo is to pull together our best of two broad themes—the state of the business and the intended focus of the next release (release means the next big bucket of innovation beyond servicing the in-market products). That means these documents document the business and competitive challenges and help set us in the direction for what we want to accomplish in terms of building software that we can sell effectively (and thus enabling the appropriate sales organization to sell what we can build). The planning memo (about 30 pages) is not itself the plan—it is a framework to use to figure out precisely what we will do at feature, architecture, and business levels. With a planning memo we get the whole team (all the contributors to the release) on the same page so we all are at the same starting line at the same time. You can think of this as an invitation to ask questions, propose ideas, and to contribute to developing the features that will go in the release. Over the next phase (each organization will spend a different amount of time on this part of the process) as we develop the plan we will make the hard choices about what we will do and won't do. Visually you can think of this phase as the opening to a funnel and the output will be a steady stream of features.

But the process is more than just a memo and an invitation to brainstorming, as those are part of everything development process; rather this process also introduces a big change in how we will work together to come up with the ideas, to decide what we will do, and to execute. For me this is the biggest change and the one that I know will be challenging. We will all feel a bit out of sorts over the next months as we go through the process. The big difference is really a significant shift from "top down" to a combination of bottom-up and middles-out planning. The planning process is not about me telling you what to do, or worse, you trying to guess what I might like. What we have done as a management team is put out there the business problems and the broad themes we wish to focus on (along with some big bets, which I'll mention below) and "pass the baton" to the Feature Teams. In many ways people say, "[W]e want to be accountable and to be empowered" and I would say, "[H]ere are the keys to the car." When you want to know what we are working on for the next wave of software, you don't have to ask me (or any other VP); you have to ask yourself, your GPM, your Dev Manager, and so on. I mean it.

In an internal blog post, Jon DeVaan described succinctly what is really different for members of the team. I loved these points and thought they were worth repeating:

> I really do want you to speak up if you or your team cannot meet the expectations laid out in this mail. I am asking! Please help me out.
>
> The overlapping work, with the exception of SP1/LHS is not "ship a product" work but rather tasks around planning and improvement.
>
> We are setting aside time to improve how we work.
>
> We are setting aside time to plan so we can identify the most valuable ideas, understand the cross dependencies, and make simplifying and focusing decisions before writing code.

Now of course this is a big leap—not just for individuals, but for the team as a whole, for management, for marketing, for everyone. It is easy to see how we could have total chaos, warring factions, failed "dependencies," and pretty much a complete meltdown. How do we avoid that? Well that's the point of the planning process. As one example, the planning process lays out relationships between teams on certain technologies. If through the process we reach a consensus about investing in a shared technology to be used by groups, then we also make a few other decisions, such as making sure the groups are staffed appropriately, that we are not also hedging [our] bets (otherwise known as betting against ourselves), making backup plans because we don't believe in the plan, and so on. We use the calendar time ahead of us to iron out these issues and agree by consensus before we start down the execution path. And that way we don't have to have arbitrary reprioritization happening down the road and we don't have to deal with fire drills when "the truth" comes to light. But all of this means we need to achieve a new level of discourse during the planning process. What we are asking from the feature team leaders is a lot:

- **Sharing.** We need a lot of information to be shared. The mechanism of sharing is not as important as making sure the sharing is happening (use Groove, email, SharePoint, hallway posters, smoke signals, or whatever works for your team). We need people to share customer learning, insights, and perspectives. We need people to share their most current thinking in an ongoing basis. We need teams to be full participants in the forums that get set up for offsites, demos, team meetings.

- **Writing.** If it isn't written down at some point, then it is really hard to know if it is a solid idea or not. Writing is thinking, and the act of writing down an idea will push you to think through more details than writing down 5 bullets on a slide.

- **Prototypes.** A picture is worth a 1000 words, but you do need both the words and the picture. We really need people to prototype ideas during this phase. Again, this is not about salesmanship—it is about piloting ideas and deciding if they have enough value **and** can be implemented. As with Sharing, the mechanism (PowerPoint, Flash, Visual Studio, Paper) is not as important as the concept.

- **Listening.** A lot of time we (as in "we Microsoft people") tend to think that getting things done means being sure to be the fastest with the memo, with the argument, or with the deck. But the most important part of the planning process is listening—listening to all the disciplines (dev, test, pm, planning, product management, user experience, execs) and doing the legwork to walk a bit in those other shoes and becoming clear on alternate perspectives. We want our plans to reflect inputs from many different and valuable perspectives, not to be entirely one-dimensional (great design but wrong feature is just as bad as great feature but no customer, which is just as bad as high quality but poor architecture for scale, and so on). A good write-up will reflect listening from a broad set of constituencies.

- **Consensus.** The team should not expect escalation and executive tie-breaking. The way you "win" in terms of your ideas being part of the product plan is to convince a broad set of people that support the idea. In the end, unless you plan on designing, coding, testing, and selling the feature yourself you will need to win these folks over. If you can't articulate the idea enough to win people over who have to help, then the idea needs more work or a different perspective. I will comment below a bit on something you are probably thinking about right now—so hang tight.

- **Cross-group collaboration.** Oh, everyone dreads this of course. But the truth is we work on systems of software where no one is "self-contained" and it is a bit of folly to try to structure things so that everyone can work in isolation. The planning process is designed to take the pain out of the process by *forcing* the discussion of these issues upfront rather than creating an environment where they are ignored or optimistically planned with the hope of a miraculous late-stage recovery. A big part of creating the actual plan will be to then create solid interfaces (both in code and across teams) so that we can work like a large number of small teams with clear touch-points and expectations.

The planning memos each lay out two main focuses of work in Big Bets and Planning Themes.

- **Big bets.** These tend to be technologies that cut across a product and represent concepts that will require a platform shift or platform support and significant engineering by a broad set of people. An example of a big bet might be something like Continued Componentization.
- **Planning themes.** These are customer scenarios that also cut across the product. We intend to look at what to build from the customer perspective. An example of a planning theme might be "Making It Easy to Add or Replace a PC."

There is a lot of "across the team" and "cross-group" in what we do. The reason for this is simply because customers value this type of work. I have never met a customer who wants to use a dozen unrelated things and hope they work together. Whether in the rich client or web service space, integration is how customers can expand the set of tools they use and explore and benefit from the breadth of software we offer. Even (even!) Google has recently been talking about developing more integrated features and fewer discrete products. And of course Yahoo has spread itself thin on discrete efforts as well and is struggling with how to get things done.

If I were to put on a cynical hat right now there are a few things that folks are probably thinking to themselves that are less than flattering about what I wrote. That is ok—like I said, this is new for many and so along with us learning together we will also talk through the changes. I am pretty sure at least a few of you might be thinking:

This is slow and bureaucratic.

- This seems like design by committee.
- This is just more integrated innovation.
- All good products need a single leader.
- Innovative ideas are always squashed when they have go through a process.

- Building software is iterative so you can't just follow a "waterfall" approach.
- Planning sucks.

I have to be honest and say that I am just as worried about those things happening as the next person. However, I also have enormous faith in our team that we won't let the process become the goal and that we will truly rise up to work together on developing amazing product plans. Inherently developing products is highly uncertain—you have an idea and you just can't prove or disprove whether it will work. Anyone who says they "know" that something will be a good idea is just overconfident, but certainly not psychic. Ideas take time to develop into products and along the way you learn a lot and, even worse, the market is changing. Back on October 19th I did a post about risk-taking in the context of planning that I would refer you to (sorry to cite myself).

But to directly address some of these I might say the following:

- The process takes time that is non-zero. There is no doubt about that. When you're building a house, you can let the architect draw plans for where every nail will go. That will take a very long time, but it won't materially improve the house or save you money. On the other hand, you can't just grab a pile of wood and get going. You do need to do some pre-work. We will work to find the right balance—about 25% of the time of the project is a rule of thumb here. Those on the team who have started to plan have also started to say "we need more time" so usually this part of the process looks slower from the outside than the inside.
- This is not a bureaucracy. There are no rules and regulations for how to vet ideas and share information and prototype. Each feature team will find what works on their own. The outputs are clear (lists of proposed features).
- We are very clearly not designing by committee. This one is tough because in many ways my experience in the past 9 months has been one where I have learned about how many things have been decided and designed by series of committees of 1 (the escalations through the management chain of multi-disciplinary managers). If the Feature Team works to deliver on the planning themes and creates exciting plans with reliable execution, then that is what was decided. The only time others have to get involved in the design is when the Feature

Team proposed something that is beyond our execution capabilities or the team didn't do the legwork accounting for the relevant constituencies. Even then, the next step is not a committee decision, but a back to the drawing board.

- We are not trying to integrate everything. We are, however, trying to define the right places for integration and, more important, plan on doing that work and making sure that we all know it is important and reward it accordingly. We will not schedule ourselves at 200% of capacity.

- Many great products have been conceived by one person. Very few products have been actually delivered by one person. It is true that organizations can be built around a single hero. But those products usually have a complexity limit or a scope that is truly manageable by one person. The iPod is a great example of this—the product is relatively finite (and some might say that much of that single-minded focus was not brought to iTunes). I think we will find during our planning that big ideas will ultimately get championed (though certainly not necessarily thought up) at the lead level.

- Yes, many ideas are squashed during the planning process. In fact more ideas are squashed during planning than we ultimately go and execute. There you have a management challenge. If 10 people propose 10 ideas and we do 1 idea, then we have one happy and creative person and 9 people who clearly have to find a reason for their idea not getting done. Usually it is easier to blame the process rather than the idea. My experience is that the primary reason ideas don't make it through the pipeline is because they just haven't been thought through enough—the boundary conditions, the relationship to existing ideas, the breadth of applicability of the scenario, the performance characteristics, etc. My suggestion is that if your idea is not gaining traction with your peer group, then really ask yourself what you could be doing better, who else could you talk to, what other groups are in the same space that you should hear from, and so on. The process is here to help us build great products, not prevent us. Yet I know that if we're not doing what you want then it is the process (and ultimately me) that receives the blame.

- Absolutely. This process is about continuous refinement. We are developing a plan. We will write it down, but not carve it in stone. We will learn along the way. Things will get added. Things will get dropped. But we will create a very solid foundation for the cycle and work forward from that.

- Yes, writing code is way more fun than thinking about writing code. And for some, even rewriting the same code again because [it] didn't have a plan beats not writing code. Some might even enjoy rewriting code for the second time rather than not writing code. But I have to admit, I do believe in measure twice, cut once. We will have a plan. Too many people, starting with our shareholders, depend on us to have an idea of what our outcome will look like and how we plan on returning value to shareholders before we start using the shareholder resources at our disposal.

I am sure there might be some other concerns. By all means drop me a note. It is really important to me that folks reach a level of comfort that allows us to move forward as a team. This process is new—it is a combination of best practices from Microsoft and the industry and represents the effort of a lot of people. We are not reading from a playbook so things will adapt and we will make changes to how we work, even while we're in flight.

To conceptualize the process, the picture below [see Exhibit 5.4] is one that we have used quite a bit. Whenever I talk about it, the first thing I say is that everyone wants to read this picture as a linearization of the process into a "waterfall." That is not the intent, but there are only so many ways to represent iteration in one graphic. Within each of the phases below there is iteration, regrouping, and re-assessment.

We have just made our way across the first row and are now working on the plan within feature teams (the mini cycle). Even within that you can see that we were making some progress forward while iterating on some areas (like inventories of assets, organization).

We have different timelines for each of Live, IE, Windows/COSD, and Search. But the next big step will be a product vision document. This document will describe the features of the product and the high-level goals of what and why we are building what we are building. You can think of this as the product guide before the product is built. You can think of the main themes in this document as the rough draft of how we will market the software. We will know the value propositions for each of our customer segments. We will have prototypes for each of these themes. We will have schedules. We will understand "dependencies." All

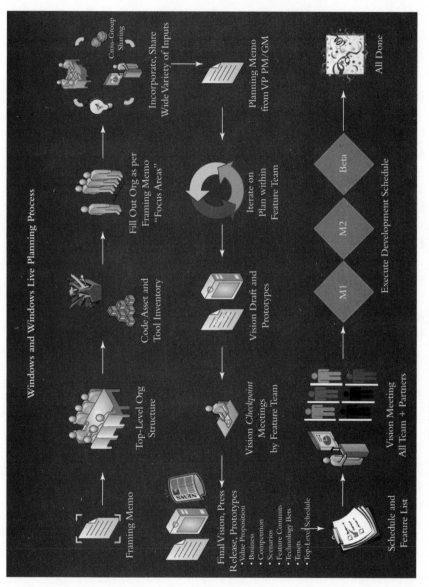

Exhibit 5.4 The Windows Planning Process

in all, the next few months are all about getting that work done. At the feature team level, the primary intermediate work product will be feature team vision documents, which are mini versions of the vision focused on a feature team's contribution to the planning themes.

As a team we will then get together by Feature Team and make sure we are in sync as we release the vision. The vision will also include a Press Release—that really says how signed up we are to the product. We will work with marketing who will author the release as though we are really about to RTM/RTW.

From this we will have a full-blown schedule. A big part about working differently is that this schedule will be based on the estimates of each developer. We will not just take what they say and change it. If we can't get the work done in the time we have for the overall project, then we cut the feature. This hurts. But it is better to cut it before we start than to try to drag things out. We also will not have schedules that bet against each other. Every team will schedule as though the goal is to be the first team to finish, not just the second to last ;-). If we don't know enough to have a detailed schedule, then we clearly don't know enough about the proposed feature yet. Doing the prototypes and thinking/planning the architecture during the past six months was supposed to educate you on these topics. If the work is still unknown, then this does fall into the category of "features squashed by the process" but I would say there was more you could do. Every feature can be broken down into knowable chunks. The classic of all classics is landing a free man on the moon. Yes, there was a 10-year goal, but the first thing was get a rocket up, then get a rocket with a man, then circle the earth, then walk outside the ship, then dock with another ship, then get to the moon, and so on. Each of those steps had a schedule and was made up of knowable things. We can do the same, even for the biggest, hardest problems. And if we want to work on problems that span releases then this is the time to componentize the work into deliverables on a per-release basis where each release delivers something valuable to customers. Just like the NASA folks did.

The mechanics of the development schedule will be different— milestones will be different in length and number. But the key is having the total development time broken down so there is time for regrouping and reassessing. And also time to make sure we are making progress. For our services, the integration at the operations side is super important as well. While we have talked about the feature planning, in parallel the Dev organizations have been (and are writing) Engineering Guidelines for the projects that outline these and other topics as well.

Then we have a big party. We will deserve it.

This post was about the planning process with a focus on feature planning and the work we have as a team ahead of us. It is very exciting. I would just remind everyone that we need to continue to fly under the radar and not get ahead of ourselves in terms of public comments about what we're up to.

I hope everyone is energized. I am very excited to move to this next phase of work.

—Steven

This blog post describes the heart and soul of a participatory approach to strategy. No topic that was part of the development of Windows 7 had more discussion, more debate, more e-mail threads, more concerned glances, and more excitement than the Windows planning process. This is the essence of the effort. This is how projects are resourced, priorities are set, resources allocated, and timelines decided upon. This is how strategy turns into action.

The Windows team just "lived" the planning process for many months in order to establish a coherent foundation for the future of Windows. The organizations involved in this planning process were set up in mid-2006, before Vista's release to market, which was in October 2006. The first framing memo dates back to November 2006, just before the date of the last blog post. The framing memo was followed by the Vision document in July 2007, and by the official schedule start date of September 2007.

The Windows planning process (see Exhibit 5.4) thus starts with the Project Framing Memo, which is written by senior management and establishes the business foundation for the effort. This is circulated among the organization to elicit and incorporate a broad variety of inputs and discussions to discuss and define the most important "focus areas" for the project. These areas are captured in a series of additional memos, each dedicated to a specific area of project focus. This drives a more detailed planning effort, which encompasses bringing in input from literally everyone on the team, and drives to the development of a comprehensive final vision document. This includes feature requirements, user scenarios, resource requirements, risk assessments, prototypes, and other analysis.

The iterative and all-encompassing nature of this planning process is almost unique. While most other planning processes are driven down from the top, in this case there was a truly iterative process, with everyone participating. Everyone was involved in providing ideas, driving estimates of resource requirements and risk, engaging in the development of mock-ups and prototypes, brainstorming about alternatives. The team was fully engaged for months debating and analyzing, researching and prototyping. When the process was done, the strategy was shared by the entire team, since everyone contributed. The whole team was aligned, driving the strategy, and the strategy is grounded in reality.

Planning Practice: A Focus on Scenarios

The creation of user scenarios is one of the most important elements of the planning process. This blog goes in some detail into what it takes to define scenarios.

What, No Dilithium Crystals? Delivering on Scenarios

Success at scenarios is hard. Really hard. It is way easier to try to define the problem to be solved as something that takes only your efforts and then get that done and call it a day. Sometimes we think we can define a scenario to just be a small thing so that one person (or 3 people) can get it done—that is always a beautiful thing. But in reality doing anything substantial is going to take a range of expertise and contributions from a set of people on the team, and more importantly, from a bunch of different pieces of code. How can we get that done? I had lunch today with the Windows & IE Test Managers and this was a big topic of conversation.

Delivering on complete scenarios to customers is another place where accountability really comes into focus—the only way to deliver scenarios is for everyone to feel like they are working towards making them happen. That's the big change we are making with respect to planning Windows 7. The model of "butt on the line" doesn't work—it doesn't scale, it isn't accountability, and it requires a lot of effort by force and none of those are the style we want for our team. Rhetorically, I asked the test managers if any could recall a person tagged as "BOL" [i.e., butt on the line] getting "fired" (or 10'ed) for not delivering and the answer seems to be "not really"—that's because this model is less about actually doing the work and more about reporting what isn't getting done. We aspire to deliver on complete scenarios because it is a natural outcome of the work we are aiming for—none of us will feel successful if we don't execute on the scenarios. That is, either we are all successful or none of us are successful. That's really all a customer wants from us anyway—either you can automatically switch from work printers to home printers when you switch networks or you can't, not that networking can switch networks and default printers can switch, but the magic doesn't happen in the middle. That magic in the middle is what makes scenarios come to life for customers.

This reminded me of something that happened to me growing up. When I was about 10 I got a copy of the Star Fleet Technical Manual and I loved it. I loved that it had blueprints for how to build a phaser. I talked my father into taking me to the electronics store to get all the parts so I could make a phaser, having tired of building the Revell model for the 10th time (remember that 3-pack of the phaser, tricorder, communicator!). We had the parts list and schematics and I was marching up and down the aisle getting all the parts. I was mostly done and then I realized I needed a dilithium crystal to finish off the design, but surprisingly (remember I was 10) the store did not seem to have any. I was really bummed. I felt ripped off.

Of course what I learned was a valuable lesson in how important it is to complete scenarios for the highest level of satisfaction! This sort of magical part is really what brings magic to customers with our software. While we all want our software to do what we expect—that's too low a bar for Windows. What I think our software needs to do is surprise customers by getting the right thing done at the right time, but doing so in a way that just makes sense for customers—makes sense to the degree that people don't need to think about it and try to rationalize it or spend time understanding it. The satisfaction is so high they just accept it for normal and thus the bar is raised. In literature, the device *deus ex machina* is one authors use and when used effectively that special MacGyver tool is plausible and satisfying to use and it just works for the story.

Our job in making scenarios come to life is to think about the connections from one part of the storyline of using Windows to the next. Our job is to make sure that people are not left holding a bag of parts waiting for dilithium crystals. Our job is to make sure that our users have just the right tool at the right time to get themselves out of a computing jam. This is entirely achievable. It just takes focus. It takes shared goals. It takes everyone realizing we are working towards these goals.

But it won't happen by magic—there is no *deus ex machina* that will appear and make the scenario work before code complete. It will take the work of everyone on the team.

The tool we have as a team is the product vision. Within the vision are scenarios. At our team meeting we illustrated the scenarios with sketches that show how we plan on making Windows 7 great for customers. It is important to note that the vision and the illustration start from these scenarios—success is delivering on the scenarios, not on the component features or technologies. If we don't deliver on the scenarios, then the release is not successful. Sometimes when people rave about Apple what they often rave about is the complete picture—that is what we are focused on.

We can turn this vision into practice by thinking about the layers of the scenarios and thinking about the unique contribution each member of the team can make. At the highest level we have 5 thematic areas. Each of those represents 8 or so scenarios. At the scenario level it is clear which of the 35 or so feature teams (across WEX & IE, COSD, eHome) will contribute to each scenario. That is the first step of turning wishes into execution—the themes of the vision can be divided and conquered. And then within those scenarios we are at a finite number of teams that will contribute. The next steps are management—actually management 101. We have a goal. We have an org. We now need to align resources to the goal. The goals are supported and consistent across the team so there is no separate channel where "other" goals are added. So the first reason we often fail at delivering is no longer a failure point.

Now we are at the place where our dev managers, test managers, and group program managers across the teams can write down the scenarios (and we clearly know which of the feature teams have the most invested in the success of each scenario—that is not that they are "BOL" but that realistically they have the most number of people working on something). There are a few things that need to get done:

- **Write the script.** This can be words or pictures or both. But the basic idea is that we need the sequence of steps that defines the scenario.

For IE 8 planning these were done with a low-fidelity UI toolkit in PowerPoint. That's tool enough.

- **Identify the features.** We need to break down the steps in the scenario into features. What are the specs that will need to get written?
- **Identify the dilithium crystals.** Every scenario when told from the perspective of one team requires a magic step where other teams will need to be doing work. This is always the case. But since this is a shared goal the other team is also supposed to be working on this scenario and is likely thinking, "[H]ey, we need a magic step from you, too!"
- **Communicate.** Don't do all this in a vacuum. We need people early on to be working together across the organization. This is how we will be successful.
- **Plan for validation.** What does success look like and how will we be sure we have reached it?

If you're looking at this list, you can see the different roles that jump out. Each of our engineering disciplines has a unique role to play:

- **Product design and user research.** For user-centric scenarios the skills and attributes this team brings are critical to being able to "storyboard" or draw out the scenario. The scenarios from the team meeting represent the design team working with program management (and product planning) to illustrate the goals we have. Design is there to be a partner at the table and so bring them into the fold.
- **Program management.** Of course the specs are owned by PM but so is the need to reach out and bring together the other groups. Rather than view this as "dependency management" the idea is to create the virtual team that is required to get the work done. There's no top-down process for doing this and it can be as light or as "heavy" as the team agrees to. It is critical that before we start coding we get this communication going because we need to make sure everyone is part of the scenario that needs to be.
- **Development.** Development needs to write the code of course. But at the scenario level, development needs to identify the ordering that the work needs to get done—you can draw a picture in any order but the code can't be done that way. Since development owns the schedule, failure to include them early on (or failure of dev to participate) is sure to reduce our likelihood of success.

- **Test**. Test is there to validate the scenario. Bringing test in from the start lends a valuable perspective of completeness. Test is often the first to recognize "[H]ey, there's a big magic step missing."

The key work that needs to happen is in writing down all of the above. Design needs to create the sketch. Program management needs the list of specs, then the specs. Dev needs to translate that into work items in a well-ordered schedule. Test needs to have a plan to validate this.

Everyone on the team has the job of making sure that the scenario stays whole throughout the product cycle. That is the goal. There's no bonus points for a team that gets "their part" done if the whole scenario doesn't get done. There's no congratulations if a team said, "[W]ell, we thought this idea was cooler than the scenario in the vision" if they left their partners hanging. We can change our minds and we can adapt the project, but it needs to be done thoughtfully and globally—optimizing locally is how scenarios get botched.

As we approach M1 coding, the role of the feature team group managers is to make sure that the balanced dev schedule represents the right priorities and that the scenarios will be getting done by the team. Dev managers will look at how many dev hours are going to which scenarios. It will be a warning sign if too much of the team is focused outside the goals of the team. PM needs to make sure that the specs are complete and the scenario well-understood enough to be the "booked plan." And test needs to sign up to validate the progress throughout the milestone.

At the end of M1 we will have a demo day where each feature team will be showing off their work. Of course the full scenarios won't be done but we will certainly be able to show progress and more importantly everyone contributing will know their efforts are part of the scenario.

So let's go out and make sure we're not left waiting for the dilithium crystals to show up!

—Steven

This last blog provides detail on the scenario development process, which is in many ways the real meat of the plan. Scenarios are the way that the Windows organization figures out what the strategy really means in practice and understands the resources and dependencies that are involved in getting strategy done. One can see the value of the scenario development process, as it provides a means to not only determine user requirements, but also understand interdependencies between functions and group and create precious alignment between them.

Planning Practice: Vision Rollout

This next blog underscores how planning is not just about figuring out what to do or even how to do it. Planning is also about aligning and integrating the organization for maximum impact.

Vision Rollout—What to Expect . . .

We are getting close to the completion of the planning phase for the next release of Windows—that's a big deal. A huge number of people have worked an amazing amount since we kicked off planning about 6 months ago. For some, it seems like forever ago and others still wish we had more time to dot i's and cross t's. Such is planning.

I am really excited about where we are. I know that sounds like a cliché, but as a team we've come a long way and we are all signed up to build a great release and make big improvements in the engineering, decision making, and overall process. While planning can be fun, the next steps are where everything kicks into gear and we really see what we can do as a team as specs are done, test plans in place, and code gets checked in. Many, many people have worked on the vision, but that isn't every single person in the team. Some folks might have been on MQ, SP1, Server full time and still others might have been working on some prototypes or planning related work but aren't sure what the GPMs and planners have been up to in terms of writing the vision itself. That's ok!

As a reminder, the vision is the framework for the product plan. It provides the key business drivers, competitive landscape, main scenarios, technology big bets, and engineering tenets along with the schedule. It represents the performance review commitments for the organization as a whole. It is our commitment to Microsoft to deliver the next release. It also represents the very best combination of bottom-up, top-down, and middles-out planning that we could accomplish. It is critical that we internalize that the vision dictates our release goals, the spirit of the release, and our priorities. When people ask about "non-goals" it is easy—anything else you can possibly think of is a non-goal. The only goals are the ones listed. The vision defines the minimum bounding box for the release—we can and will do more, but only after we accomplish the letter and spirit of what we signed up to do.

As a team our next big step is the vision document—this is a big new step for our team working as a team. Live Experiences has gone through this work and so [has] Internet Explorer. So as a group we are developing a shared experience. But for many this will be the first time where we collectively author our shared "organization commitments" and sign up to execute on a plan we all believe in. I don't take this lightly and know there are some tough questions. It is worth thinking about three of the most common observations/questions that come up at the time the vision document is complete:

1. Where's my feature? Which is my feature?
2. That's it?
3. I don't agree.

There could be a lot of other questions about the specifics, but I think this covers the most primal reactions to the vision. (Oh, by the way, we will be getting together for an all-team meeting for the vision, the prototypes, and the overall view that supports the document.)

Where's My Feature?

Generally, when people look at the vision they are looking through the lens of trying to find the part that is "closest to home" or the feature they know they want to work on. If you've been directly involved in planning, then you know where to look (which pillar, tenet, big bet, etc.). But if you are seeing this for the first time you might have to read the whole document and you might wonder why your feature is not listed or why it seems to be listed "in the wrong place." The vision is designed to be a customer view of the release—not a perfect customer view, as product management will take time to really hone the messages—and so the organization of the document does not just reflect our engineering team organization. There might not be a section on wireless networking, but there might be a section on "Laptops" that includes major improvements in ad hoc wireless as it relates to the fact that over 40% of all PCs sold are laptops and 100% of them have wireless networking. So it is important to read the whole document and to view it through the eyes of a customer.

But even after all that, sometimes you just think, "[H]ey, my favorite feature is missing." That might actually be the case. It could be that after all the upfront planning, the thing you thought we should do isn't in the document. It could be that the specifics are just too specific for the 30-page document (you can't put the work of all of our SDEs on 30 pages, no matter how hard we try). It might also be that the feature just isn't on the schedule. There was no audit committee or exec approval, so the GPM and the Dev Manager for your feature team are the place to go—they own the feature list and can tell you all the trade-offs. Once we publish the vision, we stick to the scenarios and the features there. We can add more but removing things will alter the spirit of the release and the commitment to the business, so that is really only done with broader discussion (and not just within a team prioritizing).

There are many features in the product that won't be mentioned in the vision, but will be in the reviewer's guide and in demos. But when we start the product we use the vision to write down the things we know we must get done. And we know this should account for the bulk of our developer schedules. But the vision is not all-inclusive because our knowledge of the situation will evolve as we develop the product.

There is plenty of time for creativity, still. In fact, not only is there time but the success of the product requires that creativity go into overdrive about now. That leads to the next observation . . .

That's It?

Almost universally the first time someone reads a vision document the reaction is one of a modest shoulder shrug as if to say, "[G]osh, is that all there is to it." If you take a moment and consider the alternatives, visions come in two forms. There is the ho-hum vision that sounds like "[Y]ep, another turn of the crank." Most visions are like this. There is also the vision that sounds like "[O]h my gosh, I can't wait to get this done it will be amazing." My experience has been that visions like that are prime examples of "if it looks too good to be true, then it probably is."

There are going to be very "hot" features in our vision. But the reason the release will be "hot" is not because of the vision. The vision picked the areas of innovation, but not the details. The details are left to each and every person on the team being creative, opportunistic, agile, and above all committed to making the scenarios great. We've been fond of using the comparison between Windows' Shadow Copy ("Previous Versions") and

Apple's Time Machine as a way of thinking about the difference between inspired and technically superior (and first). The vision document just has a scenario [that] "users should be able to restore their files after accidently over-writing or deleting them." The end result can be as headline grabbing as Time Machine or as technically nice as Shadow Copy. The difference between the two is really in the execution by the individuals in dev, test, [and] pm working together.

This type of effort cannot be captured in the vision document because we don't know yet what inspired decisions will get made by the team. That is why we don't keep planning and planning until we have every detail known, but stop when we have a very solid framework for the release and a set of "musts" in terms of scenarios. We really need each of the members of the team to turn it up a notch and really find creative and trailblazing solutions to the problems at hand. Some of these might have surfaced during planning (no examples here on purpose) and that is great. But overall, we have a reasonable number of investments so there is room to have some do better than we expected, most do as we expected, and a couple might not come together. That's just smart portfolio management. Those that do better might end up being "demo features"; those that do as expected are exactly what we need and when done well they still exceed our expectations. Those that don't come together are things to learn from, but it is part of the risk taking of product development.

And even after all that work we still have a ton of work to do with product management, who will really refine our message to different customer segments, look at the results we are getting in Main, and clarify and finalize how we will demonstrate, position, and communicate the product. All of that goes through an iterative process.

I Don't Agree.

Of course there are going to be folks who disagree with the chosen priorities or think, with or without the first two observations/questions, that the vision just doesn't have the right stuff in it. We have a few thousand people that contribute to building the product and we all come from different perspectives. Yet we do share a common goal, and with the vision in place we need to use this as a chance to get on the same page as an organization and move forward.

The overall goal of the vision remains to define the minimum bar for the release. There will always be folks who think we are signed up for too much (even though it is the minimum bar). There will be folks who signed up for too little (please contribute your creativity to these scenarios and make them even better). And there will be folks who think we should have a totally different set of ideas. To those folks, what I can say is that over the past 6 months the team of leaders—group managers in WEX, COSD, and product management—have considered everything brought to the table by everyone in every group that works on Windows. We have worked (and will continue to work) with OEM, the field, support organizations, customers of all sorts, and even us executives. The vision represents the best mix of attainable and stretch goals, of customer expected and customer unarticulated, of addressing past problems and forward-looking innovation, and above all it represents the bringing together of all of those views in a cohesive set of priorities that when implemented well represent a product we can bring to market effectively.

We have about another 3 weeks of work—the vision is coming together rapidly. The end of planning always happens quickly. It is exciting and I hope everyone is as anxious to get started as I am.

—Steven

PS: Many folks ask, "[W]hy not share the vision or post it somewhere," which is a perfectly reasonable question. My view is that the vision is a "working document" for the product team and that the disclosure of our plans represents the first "marketing" we will do of the next release of Windows. I expect our product management team to move forward in disclosure as they would with any other information we want to disclose—putting it in the right format, offering it in the right forum, and so on.

This blog focuses on organizational alignment and highlights a crucial second role of the planning process. Planning at Windows is not only a way to create a powerful and detailed framework for how to operationalize strategy. It also serves to drive coherence in the organization so that the entire team truly "lives" that framework, and is aligned behind it. The process of discussing and socializing the plan is an integral part of the effort.

This chapter shows why planning can be the central mechanism that joins strategy to execution for each member of the organization. Planning is crucial because it serves as a key process to connect strategy to action, and the management team to every corner of the organization. Planning is the process that makes the team drive the strategy of the business and participate in its definition. More than understanding the implications of strategy for execution, and more than making sure that a project's objectives fit customer needs and competitive realities, planning allocates and aligns the many and disparate resources in the organization to achieve coherent impact. As such, the planning process can provide the central nervous system of an integral business.

The chapter provided a discussion of both planning theory and practice. It started relating planning to strategy and continued by discussing its impact on innovation, agility, and risk. The second part of the chapter enriched the discussion with a detailed description of the specific planning process used in the Windows organization, its scenario foundations, as well as the work done to create alignment and coherence in the organization.

As we move from planning to organization in the next chapter, we reach from the nervous system to the organs. If planning provides the central framework for what to do, the organization defines the resources available to actually do it.

Notes

1. See "Repair Shop" blog.
2. See, for example, M. Iansiti, *Technology Integration* (Boston: Harvard Business School Press, 1997).
3. See Douglas Bowman "Goodbye, Google," *StopDesign.com,* March 20, 2009, "http://stopdesign.com/archive/2009/03/20/goodbye-google.html.
4. K. Clark and T. Fujimoto, *Product Development Performance: Strategy, Organization, and Management in the World Auto Industry* (Boston: Harvard Business School Press, 1991); M. Cusumano and R. Selby, *Microsoft Secrets* (New York: The Free Press, 1995); M. Cusumano, A. MacCormack, C. Kemerer, and B. Crandall, "Software Development Worldwide: The State of the Practice," *IEEE Software* 20, no. 6 (November–December 2003): 28–34.
5. See, for example, S. Wheelwright and K. Clark, *Revolutionizing Product Development: Quantum Leaps in Speed, Efficiency, and Quality* (New York: The Free Press, 1993).
6. Drawn from C. R. Davis, "Calculated Risk: A Framework for Evaluating Product Development," *MIT Sloan Management Review* (July 15, 2002): 127.
7. Iansiti, *Technology Integration*.

Chapter 6

Organization

*Matching Capabilities
to Strategy*

S trategies should match the organizations that execute them.
Setting up the right organization, with the right capabilities and the right structure to execute on a specific strategy, is essential to achieve a high-integrity result. Organizations mirror themselves in the output of their work. Indeed, a new car, with its styling and features, subassemblies and components, will mirror the organization that developed it. Gaps between components in the dashboard will indicate a lack of communication between departments and suppliers. Consistency and coherence, in both form and function, will instead indicate tight integration between different functions.

This mirroring phenomenon has been studied at length. A number of studies have shown that organizations will reflect the characteristics of their environment, such as uncertainty and complexity, and that this in turn will be mirrored in the nature of the work that they do.[1] Empirical studies have also shown that organizations that are more "integrated" produce products with measurably improved integrative performance—the whole indeed was comparatively more than the sum of its parts.[2] These studies (and many more) point to an important finding: The output of an organization is related to ("mirrors") its structure. On the other hand, a large organization must choose a reporting structure that scales, and so designing the organization is an important step that goes beyond deciding who manages which code or which members of the team should manage which other members of the team.

The mirroring phenomenon has important implications for strategy. For a strategy to work, organizational structure and capabilities must match the nature of that strategy. A dispersed organization will not produce a tightly integrated product. A fractured organization will produce a fractured outcome. An organization paralyzed by inertia will not respond to an innovative strategy. No great strategy will achieve its desired output if it is not matched by the right organization. And for a strategy to achieve integrity, the organization should have that quality as well. It is hard to hide a lack of capabilities or organizational fissures with a coat of paint. You can see it in the awkward gaps between dashboard components or between the front bumper and the body of some automobiles.

Organization and Strategy

The next blog examines the relationship between strategy and organization. It breaks up a strategy into its "architectural" components and discusses the organizational implications of each architectural level.

Thoughts on Mission, Vision, Planning, Tactics

When organizing an effort it is easy to get caught up in the extremes of the work—the very big long-term picture or the details in front of you at the moment. For an organization to be predictable and manageable, it is important for all members of the team to be on the same page with respect to timescale, perspective of detail, and connections between those and connections between members of the team. Without this consistency (and constancy) of view the disconnects and frustrations will mount. These frustrations will cause members of the team to avoid working together and to ultimately work against each other as a side effect. Equally important is the role of management with respect to this alignment, as different levels of management are ultimately responsible for the alignment within and between each part of the organization. Taxonomy is necessary for this coordination and alignment, and it is helpful for an organization to outline how the work of each "layer" of

Exhibit 6.1   The Architecture of Strategy

the team contributes to such a taxonomy. This can be thought of as the *architectural diagram* required to implement a strategy.

A taxonomy that is often found to be helpful is to consider one composed of 4 elements of a continuum of effort that represent the strategy: mission, vision, plan, and tactics. Each of these represents a different level of abstraction that is applied to the work and a different timescale. [See Exhibit 6.1.]

Mission

The mission of an organization defines the reason for being. We've all gone through the Dilbert-esque process of defining a mission statement. The frequent problem is that these mission statements become the product of group authoring or trying to appease all aspects of a team. There are several books that outline sample corporate mission statements. There are many fantastic mission statements from eras of government, some long and some short (Declaration of Independence), some prescriptive and some proscriptive (Magna Carta), and some that at first glance seem tactical but are really quite abstract (the Emancipation Proclamation, or Fundamental Declarations of the Martian Colonies; oh wait, that was from an episode of *Star Trek: TOS*). In the modern corporate world, perhaps a very famous vision statement is Microsoft's "a computer on every desktop in every home." Another way to look at a mission is to just define it as an abstract concept and not worry too much about authoring a specific document. Sometimes a mission can be a collection of strongly held beliefs—the United Way has a mission that is understood by the organization through collective learning and understanding of the *helping hand*.

A good example to work with is a mission that the US Military has to defend the United State of America. It is clear. At first glance, though, it would seem to allow for anything and everything you can imagine. Yet it also establishes the scope of the efforts and defines what success looks like. The mission is further refined by subsequent levels of the taxonomy.

In terms of the organization, the President, Joint Chiefs, and most senior officers would often define their roles relative to this overall statement.

The timescale for a mission is long. Many believe a mission should span generations. In a business the mission is often the founding principles of the company.

Vision

The vision of an organization is often the view that many people talk about on a routine basis and represents the way that one connects to the organization in a concrete manner. Whereas the mission feels inspirational, a vision will appear aspirational—visions feel achievable, represent a goal that can be written down, and most people think of as operational.

The word vision (in English) is sometimes a tricky word to use, but [it] is also commonly used outside a taxonomy so we'll carefully use it here. The reason for the challenge is that many believe a "vision" should be what we have classified as a mission. The desire expressed herein is to provide a further refinement of the taxonomy so that it can be operationalized at the organizational level.

A vision is usually the reason a major part of an organization exists and thus the vision defines its purpose. In a government such as the United States, the *Constitution* outlines the vision for each of the three branches of government. As you can imagine, members of the legislative branch end up with a pretty good idea of what their role is, and equally so for the other two branches. Even within an organization such as the military, you could look at branches of the military or at the unified command model to see how a vision could be used. The vision for NATO is to further refine the defense of the United States by securing allies in Europe and defining the boundary between the west and east (at the formation of the group).

A vision further defines the kinds of roles in the organization and brings the first look at specialization. That is, at the mission level there is no real notion of specialized roles, but rather it is the organization as a whole. A vision defines some subset of the overall team contributing to a mission and provides more detailed views of how they will work in a roles and responsibilities model. The NATO command structure as it relates to the Armed Forces, or the members of Congress. In a business organization, a vision would tend to cover a product line or the sales force, as two examples. The vision for those might be "build the Windows Operating System" or "revenue collection for the company."

Since a vision represents part of an organization, the leaders of each of these parts of an organization might often comprise a sort of "leadership team" that must routinely coordinate and measure success toward the greater mission. A very important point is that there is a distinct difference in abstraction between the leaders of the mission overall and the leaders of a vision. As we move through the taxonomy, it should be clear that while there might be personal experience at each level (no doubt because the leaders moved up the organizational structure) the level of detailed knowledge at the operational level thins quite a bit. While some CEOs have been both sales people and engineers, it is not likely that a CEO is current on the latest engineering practices or for that matter also an expert in finance, law, or other aspects of the organization that would report to her. Thus the bridge between these parts of the organization becomes an important place to focus management and communication energies.

The communication for the current state of the organization rests with the leaders of the contributing teams such that the leaders of the mission are well-versed in what is taking place, how resources are being allocated, and how the mission is progressing. At the same time, the leaders "above" will need to recognize that there is enormous complexity in undertaking a vision—the President could not hope to know all the things going on in the military and thus "stepping in" at any given moment comes with the risk of looking somewhat disconnected to those below. A well-functioning organization has the tools in place to enable investigation without these kinds of risks. A poorly run organization does not properly equip leaders to engage in an effective manner should they choose to "step in," which as a leader is always their prerogative.

The timeline for a vision can be long as well, but generally shorter than the mission. In the context of business a vision is the lifetime of a product (a patent on a drug, a product line, etc.).

Plan

Many believe that the plan is everything and often confuse the plan with the strategy, so again it is worth considering the way to represent things in a continuum. Perhaps nothing has occupied more pages of ink, more PowerPoint slides, and more consultant hours [than] the pursuit of strategy. In the 1990s this went as far as to define strategy as the end unto itself with the influential paper *Strategy as Revolution*. In the context of this taxonomy, the plan defines the framework for execution. That is, when you know the plan, those skilled in the art also know the types of tactics that will be employed.

Too often the plan is a high-level view that cannot be operational-ized. This is where the overall strategy fails. If one skilled in the art can look at a slide deck (as is all too often the case where the plan is rep-resented) and not define the next level of execution as it relates to the vision and mission, then it is almost certain that the plan is going to fail. Experience has shown that plans put in place have built-in deficiencies "left to the reader as an exercise," which simply cannot be if the overall strategy is to succeed. That is not to say there will not be execution chal-lenges (there will be); nor will you learn about elements of the plan that were missed by all (as that is precisely how an organization will fail), but the goal of putting a plan in place is to define a decision-making tool such that execution can proceed.

The plan is not only for senior management. Through our planning process at Windows, everyone participates in creating, refinement, and validation of the plan. And the plan, once set, provides empowerment through the organization. The plan allows for the "middle management" of an organization to move forward relatively un-tethered to upper man-agement. This is the key element that distinguishes plan from a vision. A vision is an abstract concept that requires ongoing work to maintain. Through a plan, the strategy becomes a tool of execution and manage-ment. Taking an organizational view, the plan is where the rubber meets the road. People building and executing a plan are defining what an organization will actually do and are actually accountable for getting it done. The communication between this level of management and the level "above" is one focused on rigor, execution, and rhythm. As with the "seam" between mission and vision, the seam between vision and plan is one that should be considered with care—what is the communication, what are the "rules of engagement," and what defines helping v. hindering.

If the NATO treaty represents a vision and the NATO command represents the organizational unit charged with that vision, the plan for NATO, in the 1980s, for example, included the decision to deploy Pershing Missiles in Western Europe. This initiative clearly said what needed to be done, was defined to support the NATO mission, and had implications (proscriptive and prescriptive) that could be understood. In a business, a plan would be a fiscal year, a product cycle, or the decision to enter a new business with a specific new product.

The timeline for a plan is measurable. The plan represents what will get done by the organization in support of the vision and mission.

Most importantly, the plan creates opportunity for creativity. This is often counterintuitive for folks, within or outside the organization. Having a plan is not about having the prescriptive lines of code we will write, but about the achievable set of scenarios we will commit to. Will these be exciting? That depends on the tactics employed to build them. Will they be brilliant or pedestrian user interface? That's up to you? Will these be breakthrough or just feature bloat? It depends on how the solution is created and evolved. We have a great example from Windows 7 around the area of performance. The plan for the release contained in our tenets was precisely:

Performance breakthroughs for key scenarios. We will achieve great base-level performance by tuning the system in accordance with our performance and benchmarking reports and by actively fixing performance bugs during the development cycle. We will measure our impact in terms of the overall performance of user actions throughout an end-to-end scenario.

The reality was that the plan was achieved and exceeded by an awesome collaboration of teams across Windows and across dev and test to turn performance from a pedestrian feature to a winning feature. The right scenarios were picked and the right way to measure and execute was critical to exceeding the expectation of the plan.

Another common misunderstanding about the plan is how "exciting" it is when it is written down. Executives always want to see a plan that "pops" or to see a plan that "knocks back" the competition. The reality is that if you could write down in a paragraph the reason why we would "win" we should just do that ASAP. We should do that "one thing" and be done with it. A corollary is that if we can write down the plan, but it takes 10 years to achieve success and presumes an entirely static environment, then of course we don't have a plan. Plans are rather pedestrian. Plans are a step in the process, not the end result. Senior management has to be comfortable with the reality that a plan "enables" success, but does not define it. If you hold out for a "killer" plan, then you will be waiting a very long time and likely give up when you finally have a plan that can't be achieved.

Tactics

While through most of the latter part of the 20th century business literature was focused on strategy, the 21st century saw a rise in the interest in and focus on execution (in fact, a book was even published, *Execution*). All too often in leadership the tactics defined and employed by the organization are a level of abstraction that is not thought through enough and as the writings on this topic point out, failure is almost always a failure of execution rather than strategy. The reason is simple, which is that execution involves the delivery of work products outside the organization and that is really where another party gets a "vote" in defining success or failure (whether that is competition, customers, enemies, etc.).

Tactics are really the implementation of the plan. In the Pershing Missile example, it is one thing to have the slide deck extolling the value of the missiles. It is quite another to design, build, test, and deploy the missile and requisite support organization to keep it running, and of course actually use it should it be needed.

The resources, labor, and potential for failure at the tactical level of just about any endeavor are massively greater than those required to establish the right plan, the right vision, and the right mission. It is why in the initial picture these are drawn in a pyramid shape. That is not to say it is easy to define the areas above, but those areas are more often defined by one great moment, a spectacular invention, or new technology, or just an insight. In business, the notion of innovation is often defined as invention + execution (or sometimes impact, which to achieve requires execution). The mere presence of the idea is not enough. It is why all too often the business press is filled with stories of companies that had the "idea" first but for any number of reasons their execution was not the right combination (Sony Betamax, Microsoft Virtual Earth, Replay TV to name a few recent ones). It is also why being first is not sufficient to being the long-term winner.

At the organizational level, tactics require extensive efforts by most of the organization, but at different types of contribution. Most importantly, this is where empowerment is the most critical organizational asset, merely because it is impossible to effectively tell everyone what to do every day. Thus the tools of tactical execution are training, documentation, and communication. The collaboration across an organization is also key, as the organization must deeply understand the decision-making framework imposed by the plan. In military parlance this is known as "commander intent" and in the current military environment of unclear enemies, urban warfare, and constant threats it has become an incredibly important (and empowering) tool for troops. In business the tactics are the account plans, specifications, and marketing plans. And we also see at this level the extreme depth of knowledge required to execute on the tactics—not just knowledge of how to build state-of-the-art tools, but actually putting those tools (and their flaws) to work.

At the tactic level, senior management provides support, resources, and removes organizational (bureaucratic) obstacles to completing work. Middle management provides the support for measurement, collaboration, and the critical skills training and coaching required to be successful. And the 80% of our team that is "doing the work" needs to be able to focus on the work at hand, not on wondering if the work items, plan, or overall framework will shift under their feet.

The timeline for a tactic is short relative to the timeline of the plan— you can think of this as the milestone plan. Often a plan is broken up into some measureable milestones or logical dividing points (quarters, milestones, campaigns). A big part of the plan is also developing an understanding of how to break up the allocated execution time and how to utilize available resources.

This has been a pretty abstract view of the elements of coming up with a plan. It wouldn't be unreasonable to assume this was a *Dilbertesque* tour through subtle definitions of common words. I would accept that. On the other hand, we all too often expect magic answers or silver bullets for a "strategy" and those simply don't exist. Anyone who says there is such a magic answer probably hasn't thought through what it will take to really get done all the elements required for success.

Building Windows, Windows Live, and Internet Explorer are responsibilities of our team and we're responsible in turn to an enormous set of constituents—the business we are in, 500 million LiveID holders, advertisers, almost a billion people running Windows, developers, ecosystem partners (IHVs [independent hardware vendors] and OEMs [original equipment manufacturers), standards bodies, partner teams within Microsoft, our field sales and support, and many more. Having a clear view of strategy and how we arrive at what we are doing is critical to doing our part in this enormously complex arena.

The four levels of the strategy architecture create a framework for matching strategy and organization. *Mission* is the first and highest level. The mission should not only inspire the organization, but also real substance. A mission should also have diagnostic power to gauge organizational fit. Does the organization truly fit its mission? If the mission is "a computer on every desktop in every home," do we have the kind of organization that will get us there? Does the organization have the kind of potential for customer reach and innovation that can make this happen? Is the mission a real inspirational goal or is it simply a neat but unrelated idea (which is not useful for alignment and easily forgotten). Is the organization right for the mission? If not, the company should reinforce the organization or change the mission, but force-fitting one to the other is not a good idea.

The second architectural level is the *vision*. The vision defines the purpose and focus of an organization—it is aspirational and more concrete. The vision plays a major role in the alignment between strategy and organization, and begins to define the key building blocks in reaching the long-term strategic goals. In this architecture, vision works at a lower level than mission and defines the specific resources necessary to work toward the mission. It provides a long-term look at the steps necessary to converge toward the mission.

The combination of mission and vision roughly corresponds to what Prahalad and Hamel termed "Strategic Intent" in their 1989 Harvard Business Review article by the same name. In that article the two authors questioned traditional top-down views of strategy and argued that consistency between strategic intent and organizational competences is crucial—and that without consistency, strategy is virtually useless. However, the authors did not detail the tools and processes needed to achieve consistency. The strategy was defined independently, and the organization was supposed to separately figure out the right way to translate the strategy into action.

In this view, there are two additional architectural levels, the *plan* and the *tactics*. The plan and the tactics are where the real work is done and where the entire organization contributes to strategy development. First is the plan. The plan, as described in great detail in Chapter 5 is the detailed, iterative process of matching strategy and resources, and describes the essential framework for execution. Planning is the heart of a collaborative process of strategy development. Planning is how each member in the organization determines how the mission and vision can be consistent with practice.

Next are the tactics. The tactics take over where planning stops and defines the decisions involved in getting the plan done. Tactical success has roots in functional excellence, project management, and in the level of consistency and detail put forth in the planning, mission, and vision levels. This is when failures all too often occur, as specific decisions and features are criticized by customers and partners. What is often less obvious is that tactical failures may have roots in problems at the mission, vision, or planning levels. A well-thought-through and sound planning process, as described in Chapter 5, is crucial in detecting these failures early and driving the necessary remedies. What is not covered in the planning process is often covered in shaping decision-making value systems, which will be discussed in Chapter 8.

In sum, the four strategic levels form an important architectural model that is useful in matching strategy to organization. We described each strategic level and described the implications for organizations. In the next section, we use the framework to get more specific, since we actually describe the Microsoft organization and examine the implications for Microsoft strategy.

Microsoft's Development Origins[3]

Microsoft's organization was not built overnight. Let's take a step back and examine the history of Microsoft's development process and the various organizational roles that shape its characteristics. Microsoft was founded in the late 1970s, during the very early days of microcomputers. Early in the company's history, its main strategic challenge was capitalizing on the vast opportunity created as the personal computer industry went through its formative stage. Microsoft wanted to provide the tools, technologies, and operating system products that would help build the nascent but potentially vast personal computer ecosystem. As such, its focus from the beginning was on building deep technical excellence. Microsoft was built, from day one, as a technology company.

The main challenge in managing Microsoft R&D in the early days of the organization was finding qualified programmers. Very few colleges or universities offered degrees in computer science, and those that did so taught very little about software engineering methodologies. The programmers that were recruited by Microsoft had very little, if any, formal training in software design. The work environment in the company was very informal; the programmers basically all worked together on the same or similar projects and didn't have the benefit of development timelines or software development methodologies. Jon DeVaan, currently Microsoft Senior Vice President for the Core Operating System Division, who has been one of the most influential engineering managers in the company and a great mentor of Steven's, once described this environment as the "development herd":

> There was one central team which was in charge of developing all our applications. Once a project team finished developing the latest release of Word, they'd jump ship and start working on Excel. And then on to PowerPoint, and so on. So everyone worked on everything. It was fun for a while, but eventually we realized that we needed more focus if we wanted to produce leading-edge products.[4]

There was also an emphasis on individual star performers within the development team who could showcase impressive skills:

> There was one guy who could type 80 words a minute. That's pretty impressive, but what's really impressive was that he actually wrote code at that speed. He'd write a 10,000-line application in two days, then if it didn't work, he'd throw it out and start again from scratch.[5]

As the strategy evolved, its projects became increasingly complex, and the connections between separate projects became increasingly important.

The Microsoft organization no longer matched the strategy. These star performers presented problems when it came to working together as a team and maintaining firm development schedules, for example:

> I design user interfaces to please an audience of one. I write it for me. If I'm happy then I know some cool people will like it. Designing user interfaces by committee does not work very well; they need to be coherent. As for schedules, I'm not interested in schedules; did anyone care when *War and Peace* came out?[6]

One longtime Microsoft veteran summarized the problem in this way:

> There are a lot of problems with relying on individual super-stars: they are in very short supply; someone has to maintain and update the software they've written (which doesn't interest them) and often other people have difficulty understanding their code; sometimes they don't understand what the market wants; and finally, if you try to put several of them on the same project, you get real problems with design decisions—"too many cooks spoil the broth."[7]

Ultimately, this kind of development system works for small projects (and is still found in start-ups) but can't scale to manage the complexity of a real software enterprise, with a diverse project portfolio, complex requirements, and significant schedule pressure. Microsoft had to grow up.

Building the Microsoft Organization

During the late 1980s and 1990s, a different approach was established to create a more effective organization and a more structured working environment with a focus on stemming the reliance on individual superstars, while at the same time motivating creative developers. In August 1988, the applications division was formed under Mike Maples, who championed a more structured, process-driven approach. Microsoft was divided into an applications group and a systems group (which included languages and operating systems). Each of these groups was further divided into a number of specialized business units, each assigned to specific product areas. Examples include the Office Business Unit, responsible for all of Microsoft's business word processors (PC Word, MacWord, and Word for Windows) and the Excel Business Unit, responsible for Microsoft's spreadsheet products. This more structured organization allowed specific teams to focus their time and energy on just one product line and also to develop a unit-based camaraderie.

The role of program manager, which had been slowly developing within Microsoft's organizational structure over time, was formally created and a Program Management function was added to each of the business units to join engineering and testing functions. The program manager is responsible for the vision of the project as well as the integration and coordination of everyone involved. Jabe Blumenthal, the first program manager at Microsoft, described the evolution of this position since the mid-1980s:

> In early 1984, we began to work on a spread sheet for the Mac. I got involved and became a sort of service organization for the development group. I helped document the specifications, do the manual reviews, and decide what bug fixes were important and what could be postponed to a later release. While I didn't make the design decisions, I made sure that they got made. The process worked out really well, so they decided to call it something and institutionalize it.[8]

As Microsoft's organization became more structured, and as the disciplines of development, testing, and program management grew deeper, Microsoft became increasingly able to develop, grow, and sustain a complex and innovative product line. Product launches became more predictable, and the products themselves more innovative. In the applications group, the development organization produced an array of successful products, such as Office 95, 97, XP, and 2007, and crafted a variety of truly innovative applications, such as OneNote and Sharepoint. Similarly, the Windows team created a sequence of breakthrough releases, such as Windows 95, NT, and XP.

The Windows Organization in Action[9]

The Windows development organization consists of thousands of people and closely matches the requirements defined by its mission vision, planning and tactics (see Exhibit 6.2). The resources for any project are

Exhibit 6.2   The Windows Organization
Photo by Steven Sinofsky © Microsoft Corporation

dedicated to that project—these resources include development, test, product planning, usability, and product design, in addition to program management. Each role brings a unique perspective and a unique set of skills to the product development process. While you can often be someone who has an affinity for another discipline, rarely can any one person bring all of these skills and experiences.

The first role is development. Developers write the code. They are in charge of the code's architecture, the performance, the reliability, the security, and getting the functionality into the product or service. Of course, development is at the core of what Microsoft does as a software company, but it cannot stand on its own.

Testing is next—software design engineers in test ensure the quality of the product or service but, more important, that the product or service ultimately meets the needs of the customer. Testers review all specifications as respected members of the team and use their perspective and experience in working with program managers and developers to ensure that the product is not going to be fragile and that it will be possible to insure a successful implementation.

Usability engineers validate the designs of Windows software and incorporate the statistical understanding of customers into the process. Microsoft was an early pioneer in integrating usability in the software development process. Many usability team members have Ph.D., master's, and bachelor's degrees in human computer interaction (HCI) or related areas such as anthropology or psychology. These team members design mechanisms to test and validate designs and design assumptions.

Product designers work in partnership with program managers to develop the interaction model for the products and also own the overall look and feel. While many companies use design for "graphical design," Microsoft designers are experts in computer interaction— many have studied at universities like Delft or Carnegie Mellon, where they have targeted programs in this discipline. When you look at the new user interface in Office 2007, for example, what you see is a strong collaboration between the program management experts and the design and usability experts.

Finally, Windows planners are experts in understanding the market place and understanding what customers need from software. Planners own market and customer research. They also own communicating that research to the product team, to program managers and to the executives deciding the overall goals of a release. Planners are assigned to broad technology and business areas (collaboration, business intelligence) where they become experts in all the products, services, and solutions on the market and in how Microsoft can offer customers improvements over what is in the market. Many planners have a business background and have worked in marketing before becoming planners.

The Power of 3

The Windows organization (and other development groups at Microsoft) relies heavily upon a "triumvirate of success," which includes the program manager, the developer, and the tester. These three roles form a critical peer group, whose consensus drives the decision-making process. This creates a unique set of relationships that creates multifaceted views on important issues and ensures robust decisions. These three disciplines represent the engineering disciplines required to build the software features. There are technical disciplines that are shared across all features that are equally responsible for the development of the product and these include product design, content authoring, operations, and others.

The program managers shepherd the creation of a vision for the product while working closely with executives, managers, and customers. They then translate this vision into a plan, including specifications that outline what is needed for the addition of new features to each application. This specification document describes the way that the developer writes the code for these new features. Every time a specification evolves, the central information sharing web site is updated to reflect this change and the associated developers are automatically notified.

Developers are responsible for actually writing the software code. As Antoine Leblond, the Senior Vice President of the Office Client business, has said:

> There's a little bit of a fighter jet pilot attitude [with developers] … they're kind of the F–16 pilots of the product development . . . [T]here's this sort of power you get from being the one who actually writes the code . . . [A]nd some of them maybe abuse that power a little bit . . . [O]ne of the things that we're so much better at now is actually understanding how to have a good relationship between developers, program managers, and testers and how to get that dynamic working in a really productive way.[10]

He continued to describe some of the tensions that had occurred within developers, testers, and program managers:

> Historically, it's been more of an adversarial relationship, especially between developers and testers … [I]f you think about what their job is, a tester, it's all about annoying developers . . . [F]inding out what they did wrong . . . I mean, how insulting! O my God! So, actually it takes some amount of maturity as a developer to understand that those guys have the same goal as you do . . . [Y]ou know what's the old joke? That program managers are not smart enough to be developers and that they're not good looking enough to be in marketing, so they make them PMs . . . [A]nd the testers, they're just the psychos; they're the ones who just love breaking things, they just have devious minds.[11]

The testers are responsible for validating the code created by developers to the specifications created by program managers. Jeanne Sheldon, longtime Test Manager for Microsoft Word and the current Corporate Vice President, Office Authoring Applications, equated the role of the tester to that of a scientist. The testers might run experiments that are based on the hypothesis that a bug with certain characteristics exists. When a successful test finds a defect in the code, the tester's hypothesis has been proven valid. As she further explained, a tester can never prove that the product or service is perfect—he or she can only prove the existence of any defects. Also, as in the case of a scientist's log, careful records are kept of the bugs that may be found within the code.

Grant George, the Corporate Vice President of the Windows Experience Group, leading the charge on Windows testing, previously summarized this relationship between the program manager, the developer, and the tester as follows:

> [T]hat partnership with those three people has to be tight. They have to understand exactly where each other is and they have understand exactly what they have to deliver and when they have to deliver it because if the three of them don't agree no team structure or bug data or e-mail is going to fix that relationship not working.[12]

This "power of 3" is described in the next post from the blog.

Power of 3 and Working Together

This weekend I had a chance to see the new film *21*. I only mention this because there was a great scene that established the numeracy of the central character of the movie, Ben, played by Jim Sturgess.

In this scene, which takes place in a lecture hall for some sort of advanced math class, the professor, Micky Rosa, played by Kevin Spacey, offers up the classic "Let's Make a Deal" (or "Monty Hall") test. There are three curtains; behind one is a "brand new car" and behind the other two there are goats.

Ben chooses what is behind curtain A.

Prof Rosa, then says, "[G]ood news, behind curtain C is a goat"; thus it increases the chance Ben will win a new car. The professor then offers Ben the opportunity to keep curtain A or switch to curtain B.

Ben says, "I will take curtain B."

Prof Rosa tries to talk him out of it—"I know where the car is so maybe I am playing games with you."

Ben replies, "I will gladly take curtain B and thank you for the additional 33.3% chance I have to win the car."

He's right. It is just statistics.

Today in talking to someone on the team about the notion of having dev, test, [and] pm working together on solving problems it sort of struck me how there is also a statistical element to our working relationship—the power of 3 "choices" adds to our success. By just having the different perspectives we are more likely to achieve success. Overall the process is less prone to a single point of failure and more likely to yield the desired outcome. Of course we're already ahead of the math because more often than not we agree and 2 out of 3 of dev/test/pm are not "goats." :-).

OK, I know this is a stretch and an inverted metaphor, but I thought I would give it a shot.

It is not a simple trade-off—the benefits of working together has a non-zero cost. But I think it mathematically increases our success rate, especially when we work together throughout the product cycle.

See: http://www.nadn.navy.mil/MathDept/.courses/pre97/sm230/MONTYHAL.HTM.

—Steven

PS: Congratulations to everyone who worked super hard on the ISO standardization of Office Open XML!!

Development Process and Organization

An organization whose mission is innovation depends critically on its development process. The process performs two functions. The first output should be innovative products. The second output should be an improved development organization.[13]

The Windows Experience, or WEX, division is representative of the broader Windows group. The development organization for WEX starts with Steven's direct reports, each managing a particular discipline, including development, test, and program management. Reporting to each of these discipline leads there are approximately six managers, one for each of the major groups in WEX. Each of these managers has, in turn, another half a dozen direct reports, each once again, with a similar number of direct reports.

After all disciplines get together to decide which features will go into the next release, these same features are assigned to feature teams, or feature "crews." Each crew is built off of a program manager, and a small number of developers and testers. Each of these feature crews develops the feature in its entirety, in all its aspects and functionality, until it is fully functional and tested, and is then integrated into the primary Windows code base.

The development process is broken down into different milestones, known as M1, M2, and M3. Each milestone will exhibit a fully functional product, virtually ready to ship, albeit with a smaller set of features than the final product. No feature is integrated into the primary code until it is fully functional and tested. If a feature is not completed in time for a given milestone, it is not included in the primary Windows code.

Deciding which features are ready for prime time is determined by a clear and transparent process, driven by extensive test data and expert opinions.[14] Decisions to include features are conservative. It is considered to be wise to leave a given feature out of a particular release rather than have that feature impair the quality of the release or even slow the release down.

The transparency of the process works not only top down, but also bottom up. Information about the quality and timeliness of individual features is communicated across the organization and drives frequent and accurate updates to project plans and expectations. Each feature crew will communicate project updates at least once per week.

A Design Funnel

The design of features is done in several stages. The Windows product overall obviously provides unique challenges. Apart from the complexity of the existing code base, and the diversity of applications that are compatible with it, Windows is used by over a billion people, each characterized by unique needs and habits.

Bringing together the information in the blogs we can create a conceptual model of the design funnel. The first stage in the design funnel (see Exhibit 6.3) is the generation and organization of a stream of *new ideas*, ranging from major changes (changing the user interface paradigm to touch) to refinements (such as improvements in multimonitor support). Designers will work with program managers and other team members to "bake" the ideas, and expand to development and testing as the approach becomes more thought through.

In the second stage, the most promising ideas drive extensive information and *data gathering* efforts. These can draw from a vast amount of information, ranging from market research and user needs studies to the extensive data base of customer support incidents, to blogs and articles written by industry experts and pundits. The emphasis is on pushing

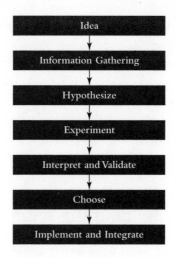

Exhibit 6.3   The Windows Design Funnel

the team's thinking and going beyond the data to also reflect potentially unarticulated problems and needs.

The data gathering stage is followed by a stage aimed at framing hypotheses. Each clearly describes an improvement to user experience. The hypothesis stage not only frames what to improve, but also why it is important, as well as a first cut as to how the improvement could be achieved.

At this point, the process moves to the *experiment* stage, in which the goal is to cast as broad a net as possible to explore various options. This includes sketching, scenario writing, storyboarding, html, and Power-Point prototypes or even what is known as "wireframes" (a basic visual guide to user interface). By conducting experiments, the team will not only identify the best alternatives, but also learn about the very essence of the problem it is trying to solve.

The next stage is the *interpret and validate* stage. In this stage, the team examines the variety of options generated in the experimentation phase, fleshes out the implications of each and validates the original conjectures with additional experiments. The emphasis shifts from the local to the global as the system-level impact on the overall product is considered.

The next phase drives the *choice* of which features will be included in the actual design. The phase involves the creation of detailed implementation plans, which inform the choice and prioritization of each feature. These materials roll up into the overall "product plan" for the release, which lays out what the team requires the product or service to achieve in terms of business goals, scenarios, and schedule. The product plan is complemented by the "principles of design" document, which delineate the core design values, language, and vocabulary that the team will use in its efforts.

The final stage is *implement and integrate*, which focuses on building, iterating, and refining the chosen solution. The design finally becomes reality as the design process merges into the development process described in the previous section.

Building the Team

Even if one is successful in creating an organization and a development process, how does the structure learn to function in the right way? Not only will the characteristics of the team drive the nature of the process, but so will the nature of the process drive the characteristics of the team. Teams deliver projects and projects build teams as the next blog discusses. (*Note:* RTM means "release to manufacturing" and signifies the completion of the development effort.)

5 Ws and H of the Product Cycle

We talk a lot about shipping code, but there's something that we build during a product cycle that is even more important than any single release, and arguably more important to Microsoft, and that [is] the team. Along with building the product, each release gives us an opportunity to build our team. Like building the product, building the team is something that is never "done"—building the team requires the same focus on the long-term, consistency of purpose, and commitment to greatness that we normally ascribe to building our software. Product cycles allow us the chance to go through the whole "story" from beginning, through the middle, to the end. Like any good writer (or good actor in the theater) practice leads to perfection and so we should think about how we get better each and every performance. And like any good story, we should have a strong structure in place to tell the story.

So it might help if we treat a product cycle like a news story and think about the 5 Ws and an H. This structure is an appropriate way to think about the product cycle since we are after all creating a story, or narrative, for customers which they experience by purchasing [our] product (a great example of this can be seen in the current *BusinessWeek* article "Building the Perfect Laptop," which also happens to be a good story about innovating with a plan and clarity).[15] As I was reading this story I was reminded of the narratives we have been developing for Windows Live, IE 8, and Windows 7.

In future posts I hope to return to this metaphor but for now let's have a brief look at these six components of a great product cycle:

- **Who.** It all starts with who will build the product. The qualities each person on the team brings and the values each member of the team represents. We want diversity of thought and background combined with a consistency of execution—maximizing the contribution of each and every member of the team. Who also starts with the tone and style of the senior leaders of the team (Aleš, Arthur, Chris, Dean, Grant, Julie, and Steve, and me). As we've talked about many times, the importance of our group managers in how they represent the best of the qualities we wish to have as a team and how they run the team is really paramount.

- **What.** Choosing what product to build is where the planning process guides us. I think it is fair to say that historically we have focused nearly all of our energy on this question. Most of the "fights" and "disagreements" happen over what we will build. Most of the tension happens over wanting to build more than we have. Of course what we build is insanely important, but I am also a believer in the role of the planning process to bring out a very solid set of ideas that we commit to. The idea of the planning process is to front load the "conflict" so we can execute smoothly, and more importantly so we can focus our execution on execution, which is itself super hard.

- **Where.** Certainly some could consider where to be the location of the team, but for me where represents the business proposition of "channel" (commonly referred to as "place" in the 4 Ps of [the marketing mix]). Every product must meet the needs of different customers (individuals, enterprise, developers) who acquire the product through different channels (retail, OEM, solutions providers, VARs [value-added resellers]). As we develop a plan, it is keenly important that we clearly understand this aspect of the plan. This too is often the source of tension and challenge. Microsoft has dedicated field and business folks for a plethora of channels and segments, and each one wants an entire offering for their area. Often this feels a bit like slicing up a pie, and more often if feels like our pie just isn't big enough. So like all aspects of the product cycle, this is another one where front loading the discussion allows us to execute against a plan we know by definition is not perfect for everyone.

- **Why.** Why will customers like the product we will build? We need to know this of course when we start, but we also learn a lot along the way. The key thing we must establish at the start of a product cycle is a clear sense of purpose for the release. This is expressed in the vision, but more often than not when we tell the story of a product we will lead with, why did we build this product? It is especially important when customers are satisfied with the product they have or at the other end of a spectrum when customers feel like there isn't much of a reason for Microsoft to update (or customers to upgrade) to a new product. It is important that this be an emotional connection with customers and not just restate the features (what we built), as that does not reflect the context of skeptical customers.
- **When.** Clearly all product cycles have a schedule. Like many news stories, the when is pretty straight forward and I think the schedule is straight forward too. We pick a date and get into execution mode on the planning and the plan. Also like news stories, the place we don't want to spend creative energy is on the date. I was recently on a mail thread with someone asking when will Windows 7 ship (someone who does need to know). In a pretty vicious while (TRUE) do {} loop, I kept referring to the vision statement, but this person was convinced there is another schedule with extra buffer time hidden away. Believe me, that definitely isn't the case!
- **How.** The processes and organization we use to build the product represent the how. Like the song in *Gilligan's Island* "and the rest," *how* is often the forgotten aspect of a story. How is complicated and detailed. How requires domain knowledge. How isn't often very fun to talk about. On the other hand, how can also be distilled down to an over-simplistic view that leaves out details just so the story can be told. Without a great understanding of how we will build the product, the other questions don't matter. In fact, a great how can often make up for missing story elements. But missing the processes and organizations, the best you can hope for is a non-sustainable burst of success (a super creative idea that requires heroics to get out the door,

leaving a trail of bodies along the way, so to speak)—the essence of repeatable success is knowing how to build an organization, processes, and procedures.

That is why I believe when we RTM/RTO [Release to Operations] we certainly celebrate accomplishing what we set out to accomplish. But we have also shipped a version of our team. Teams are built release over release, just like software is built.

Building our team and working to improve how we build our services, browser, and Windows has been about trying to make sure we have a fantastic 5 Ws that our customers, partners, and the press (and bloggers) will care about, first and foremost. But focusing on the [h]ow is the real test of growing our team and growing our capabilities. I feel that without our deliberate efforts at improving how we build our software we will not ship a sustainable engineering organization. We are here for the long term and that means building an organization that has the skills and capabilities that go beyond any single product release.

My simple view is that if we can RTM a great team, then we will be able to take on even bigger challenges, harder technical problems, bolder competitors, and more sizeable business goals. Having the ideas and strategies to do those are necessary, but without an always improving team, those ideas are just trees falling in a forest that no one hears.

Our team should feel super proud of the work we've done to develop the story behind the release and should feel very good about the progress we've made on improving how we engineer our products.

Stay tuned for MIX 08 and the first chapter of the public story of IE 8 . . .
—Steven

Who, what, where, why, and how: As the blog discusses, the "how" is usually the forgotten part. Microsoft is a culture that assimilates and generates ideas, of technologies, and products. For that reason it is sometimes more difficult to get credit for creating an innovative and effective organization, processes, or procedures. But these "how" factors are essential, "Without a great understanding of *how* we will build the product, the other questions don't matter." The how is about building a great team. A great team will ship a great product. A great team will improve and ship an even greater product next time. "The essence of repeatable success is knowing how to build an organization, processes, and procedures."

Beyond the how, the four Ws are also important. Well worth highlighting is the "tone and style" of the leadership team. We have found that "diversity of thought and background combined with a consistency of execution" are an important part of the "who" philosophy. The "what" debates are traditionally fraught with passion and argument, which is one reason why the planning process described in the previous chapter is so important. The intent is to frontload the arguments to enable smoother and more consistent execution once the planning stage is completed. The "where" aspects focus on the needs of customers and partners, which are often in conflict with one another. Again, the planning process should define a framework to resolve these disputes. But beyond the facts and features, the team is strongly encouraged to form a personal, emotional connection with customers and strive to represent their perspectives during the development process. Finally, the "when" aspects must be considered. The "when" can traditionally be a sore spot, with software projects often shipping late. The philosophy of "when" should be one of honesty. No hidden schedules. No padding and no hidden issues.

Beyond great products and services, what is being built is an organization that has the capability to develop and deliver on the strategy, in a sustainable fashion, release after release, and year after year. This is an organization that is empowered to think strategically about problems, that has the creativity to examine novel issues and technologies, and the structure to execute for maximum impact.

Microstrategy

The philosophy of strategy development is to share the load across the organization. Clearly, leaders have greater responsibility for vision and mission, but contributions (and many opinions, both positive and negative) are offered across organization on a daily basis. Team members are passionate about the direction of their business, about the scope of activities in their group, and about a variety of other considerations, ranging from mission to technical details. Planning and tactics are where the broader team is most active because of the vast number of decisions that must be taken. This distributed activity represents a "microscopic" approach to strategy development and execution and makes a big difference in shaping a great strategy, achieving integration and coherence, and obtaining a result that is innovative and reliable. When this is done correctly, features will meet and exceed customer needs and where product and service performance exceeds that of competitors. The contribution of the entire team becomes absolutely essential. The following blog describes the process for contributing ideas and evolving the strategy.

From Brainstorming to Plan to Feature—Selling Your Ideas

Over the past few weeks as we progress through our various projects, I find myself involved in a typical conversation:

> **PERSON ON THE TEAM:** Say, I really can't believe we're not doing a feature I thought of.
> **ME:** Yeah that sounds like an interesting idea. Did you talk to the folks on the PM team that seems closest to the work?
> **PERSON:** Absolutely. I pitched this idea months ago. It seems so obvious to me that we should do this and the way it should work is straight forward.
> **ME:** So why aren't we doing this feature?

After that question there can be any number of replies. Some of them are not very nice and involve calling the members of the team names. Most are constructive, pointing out that the team said there wasn't enough time on the schedule or it wasn't a high enough priority. Some folks also point out that the feature might not have fallen within the scope of the release of vision. But the general theme of all the answers is that the "fault" for not doing the feature rests with the team that was supposed to do the work, specifically not with the person suggesting the feature. That piqued my interest . . .

It is important at this point to remember a few things. First, the list of features we are not doing in any given release is infinitely long—it is way longer than the list of features we are doing. That means it is pretty darn easy to think of something we aren't doing. Second, any given feature might seem more important than the features we pick—certainly for any given member of the team there might be a different view of priorities. It might also be the case that after the release is said and done, even years later it, it might become totally clear that we should have zigged rather than zagged. No matter what happens, someone always said it would.

Third, the essence of putting together a product plan is that it has a holistic set of features that represent a coherent whole. This means we might not do some things because they don't "fit" within that coherent whole. They might not fit because we want the release to be relatively short and the feature takes a long time, or because the release is about being compatible and the feature might break from the past, or any number of other reasons. Above all, the planning process is just a process and as we have talked about the plans **never** look like "[H]ey, this will be a breakthrough and knock it out of the park." It is only after development actually progresses and every member of the team focuses their creativity on execution do we really have a strong sense of what will really be the breakthrough features in a release. Planning is a tool for professionals, not a "breakthrough product Wizard."

With that as background, let's return to the question at hand and try to offer a tool for getting your ideas through the planning and development process. I hesitate to use the phrase "selling your ideas" since that conjures up a ton of negative images. It might suggest that getting things done requires a plaid jacket and loud tie like a used-car salesmen. It might suggest that getting a feature into the product is less about analytical proof that something is good and more about who you know or how fancy your slides are. In reality, getting anything done in an organization larger than just you requires you to convince someone of something—and so let's call that skill *selling your idea*. We don't hesitate to invoke "selling" when it comes to getting someone to join the team, and yet it should be clear that getting people to work with you to get something done or to run with your idea is really exactly the same as "selling" someone to join the team.

Everyone has to sell their ideas all the time. A dev needs to convince test that a given check-in/RI is ready to go. A PM needs to convince dev that a feature is worth doing. PMG needs to convince PM that a given feature is key to marketplace differentiation. And so on. The part of the job of trying to convince someone to embrace your feature idea is just a natural extension of the overall dynamic of working as part of a team. Selling ideas is not just a PM skill (or job requirement) and it should not be looked at as a "soft" skill that "if people were smart like me then this wouldn't be a necessary step."

Assuming that your feature idea fits within the overall goals of the release the skills required to get from idea to booked feature are important skills that everyone should learn to master. When it comes to selling your idea, there are a few things that you should think about doing before you start trying to convince people of the virtue of the idea. At the same time, talking with others is also a way to develop these ideas fully (which is why they say great ideas are usually the work of the team and no single person). A few things you should think about doing up front:

- **Define the problem you are solving.** This sounds silly, but before you start talking about the feature it is probably a good idea to have a crisp definition of the problem being solved. Sometimes this is an end-user problem. Sometimes this is an ongoing "fighting the code" architectural problem. Sometimes it is enabling a new hardware device. But overall if it takes too long to even explain the problem to people then it is going to be a steep uphill climb from the very start. A good example of defining the problem solved might be TiVo's "pause live TV."

- **Educate yourself on possible alternatives.** A great trait of Microsoft people is that when presented with a problem and a solution, there is a good chance the next solution will be forthcoming. As you talk to people you will educate yourself on lots of alternatives. A good thing to do is stay focused on solving the problem, not implementing the specific solution you initially proposed.

- **Describe your solution.** Of course you have to get good at describing your solution. Again this sounds pretty basic but you would be surprised how many times the solution is unclear to people. This should not take away from the brilliance of the feature idea but should be a warning if folks don't understand the solution.

- **Connect the problem and solution.** Another Microsoft trait is that we often describe a problem and then dive into the solution (often the architecture) and then along the way the connection between the problem and the proposed solution is "lost." One way to do this is to "circle back" and make sure to reinforce the connection.

- **Think end-to-end.** When proposing a feature it is often the case that someone will think of the feature in the context with which they work and then assume the rest will be pulled out of the oven at the end of the show. More often than not this is the spot where you "lose" people who might support you. So you have a great idea but didn't think through the performance characteristics enough to win over folks who spend their days working on perf. It doesn't mean you need to be an expert in every area, but it means when you are proposing your idea you need to do the legwork and become educated in the full spectrum of "issues." If you ever need a list of potential issues, the average template for a specification provides a pretty exhaustive list of things to consider.

- **Know the competition.** Never, ever propose an idea (to me) that does not come with a complete understanding of how the competition accomplishes this same task. A corollary to this is never, ever propose an idea where you define the idea to "navigate" around a competitive offering—that is don't define your idea to be your competition but slightly different. The gist of a competitive offering compared to a new feature is "[A]re the features going after the same problem." I hate to bring it up, but this is a great place to insert OS X's Time Machine compared to Shadow Copy.

- **Visualize the idea.** Probably the most compelling way for anyone to understand an idea is through visualization. This does not need to be a "prototype," but it does help to convey the idea visually. You can use a bitmap done with paint. A PowerPoint slide. But take the time to work out the visual representation of the idea—not the visual representation of the code (architecture), which is important but not always what the customer will appreciate (sometimes it is though). Sometimes it is appropriate to get help from a member of the design team who might be the first partners you enlist in helping you.

While this seems like a bunch of "homework" to get your feature into the product, one way to think about this is to cost this relative to how much we will invest in delivering the feature. We will spend 1 to 3 years developing the feature. We might spend 10s of millions marketing it. We will support it for 10 years. And of course there are the opportunity costs. So this could be a pretty big [$]100M decision. So take it seriously.

The legwork in selling your idea is what comes next. This is where you have to hit the pavement and really talk to folks and work to convince them. Here are a few tips for "working it." We'll call the folks you are talking to "stakeholders" even though that word sometimes has a very specific meaning—I just mean "someone who cares."

- **Make a list of the stakeholders.** You have to start with a list of folks you need to work with. There will be program managers, developers, testers, maybe planners, designers, product managers. You might also want to enlist the support of people who represent the customer point of view strongly (Customer Support, Field) or developers in other groups or companies. This list will likely grow longer as you begin to talk to folks. Obviously this is potentially unbounded but the biggest and most important thing you can do is make sure that you generate the "buzz" around a feature and you can only do this by talking to people.

- **Walk in the stakeholder shoes.** When you're talking to someone you really want to make sure you know what is going on in their world when talking to them. One of the most obvious things that is going on during planning is that, well, everyone is planning. That means when it comes to partnerships you are by definition "competing" for resources with all the ideas (both "internal" and "external" to a team). So knowing the priorities or focus of a potential partner is really important. Demonstrating that you understand this perspective can also help you—you can make sure your idea fits with the partner's efforts or resource allocation, for example.

- **Look at the proposal through the eyes of the listener.** Closely related is also making sure that you are taking a look at your solution through the eyes of a stakeholder. This is important as you talk to different disciplines or even different areas of the product. When you're talking to a person who cares lots about performance you don't say "I know the perf issues need some work but trust me." If you are talking to a person who cares about global perspectives don't say "I'm sure that there might be a whole different way of doing this in <country>." Instead, use the time with a stakeholder to broaden your views and make sure you begin to see all the facets required of the solution.

- **Listen actively and adjust based on feedback.** When talking with a stakeholder the goal is not to "check them off the list" but to make sure you genuinely understand their perspective. One way to do this is to make sure you play back what you are hearing. Along with that recognize that people do not want to spend their time talking to you if you are not really listening or adjusting. You obviously would go crazy if you put in everyone's conflicting views but you do need to know that those views aren't going away, so making sure you hear them and making sure that the stakeholder knows you heard them is a critical step. This is often the hardest part—knowing how and when to help someone see that maybe there is a better way!

- **Don't go for the close.** Often people want to rush and get a "commit" on a feature. There is an element of consensus building (after all, that is what this is) that requires a much more delicate touch. Like the annoying salesperson at the department store that says "[S]hall I wrap this up for you" before you have even looked at the price, you want to let stakeholders lead you to the close, not the other way around. This often flies in the face of our tendency to think our ideas are brilliant and people who don't see this brilliance immediately as being deficient. So be patient.
- **Don't escalate.** The biggest cultural issue we as a team are trying to change universally is that "escalation=failure." Escalating is a word that drives me nuts. Because no one ever means "escalate to affirm"; they always mean "escalate to reverse." So if you don't like what you're hearing, you are far better off thinking about what you could be doing better—is it you don't understand the context, the constraints, is the pitch unclear, is the solution too complex[?] But you have to admit you hate it when someone goes over your head to reverse your work, so "do unto others." When it comes to selling features, going in for the kill by getting someone in trouble is never going to bring the best out of them.

After all this you might still be saying to yourself, "[W]hy don't people see the brilliance in my idea[?]" The whole point of taking this time and doing this sort of work is to help people see the brilliance in the idea. Since by definition we have way more ideas than we can possibly do, there are in fact going to be brilliant ideas we do not do. Making these decisions is not a perfect science, or even a science. We trust a large set of people to be thoughtful, professional, open-minded, and customer-focused in pulling together a product plan. This is tough stuff. It if were easy then there would be one successful product in every category and very few product failures.

I chose "selling your ideas" for this title because it sounded so cliché. But this is a skill that we all need more of. We can all get better at helping people to see our brilliance. Conversely, and more importantly, we can all get better at seeing the brilliance of others and using that to make our ideas better.

—Steven

This blog showcases the participatory nature of Windows's strategy development process. More than just being encouraged to provide ideas (or even submit ideas to some generic "idea bank," as some companies do), the Windows organization is actually driving the development of strategy through an explicit, high-impact process. Not only are all engineers invited to make real contributions, they are even coached on how those contributions can have the most strategic impact.

Once the steps above have been taken, the organization is in a position to deliver on the promise of strategic integrity. For example, the team is grounded in a deep base of specialized capabilities and a variety of passionate and knowledgeable team members are available to pursue new ideas and challenges. The teams are able to integrate these contributions, to spur and support a broad set of innovative opportunities. Inspired by new scenarios, prototypes, and customer needs, energized by the creative work of product designers, balanced on the engineering, testing, and program management triads, and weaved together by process, method, and milestones, the Windows 7 organization weaves its many inputs into coherent, high-impact, responsive strategy.

From the mission to the tactics, from the vision to the plan, the organization is empowered to set and drive strategy, as thousands of individual micro contributions build into a coherent whole. From myriad individual decisions, the strategy evolves to accurately mirror the organization, and the organization the strategy.

This chapter has examined the relationship between strategy and organization, the second driver in the strategy integrity framework. The chapter shows how strategic integrity can be achieved by aggregating the inputs of the many members of the organization, subject to a clear framework defined by the plan.

Setting up the right organization and process is not enough. Once in motion, the coherence of a strategy is challenged by countless unexpected issues, and the right structure needs to be complemented by the right management behavior. In the next chapter, we dive into the impact of management, which completes the linkage between strategy and organization, and helps maintain coherence between the two.

Notes

1. P. Lawrence and J. Lorsch, *Organization and Environment* (Boston: Harvard Business School Press, 1967); and R. Henderson and K. Clark, "Architectural Innovation: the Reconfiguration of Existing Product Technologies and the Failure of Established Firms," *Administrative Science Quarterly* 35 (1990): 9–30.

2. M. Iansiti, *Technology Integration* (Boston: Harvard Business School Press, 1997); and A. MacCormack and C.Y. Baldwin, "The Impact of Component Modularity on Design Evolution: Evidence from the Software Industry," Harvard Business School Working Paper, 2006.

3. This chapter borrows heavily from several Harvard Business School case studies, including "Microsoft: Office Business Unit," HBS Case Number 691-033; and "Microsoft Office 2007," HBS Case Number 607-015.

4. Marco Iansiti, "Office 2007," Harvard Business School Case #607015, p. 5.

5. Ibid., 6.

6. Ibid., 6.

7. Ibid., 6.

8. Ibid., 6–7.

9. This section draws heavily from one of Steven's external blog posts, "PM at Microsoft," *Steven Sinofsky's Microsoft TechTalk*, December 16, 2005, http://blogs.msdn.com/techtalk/archive/2005/12/16/504872.aspx.

10. Marco Iansiti, Office 2007, Harvard Business School Case #607015; p. 8.

11. Ibid., 8.

12. Ibid., 9.

13. This section draws from a blog by one of Microsoft's most experienced developers. See Larry Osterman, "Engineering 7: A view from the bottom," *Engineering Windows 7,* October 15, 2008, http://blogs.msdn.com/e7/archive/2008/10/15/engineering-7-a-view-from-the-bottom.aspx. For additional information, see Steven Sinofsky, "The Windows 7 Team," *Engineering Windows 7,* August 18, 2008, http://blogs.msdn.com/e7/archive/2008/08/18/windows_5F00_7_5F00_team.aspx.

14. See the "Cutting Is Shipping" blog post.

15. See Steve Hamm and Kenji Hall, "Building the Perfect Laptop," *BusinessWeek,* February 14, 2008, http://www.businessweek.com/magazine/content/08_08/b4072042350389.htm.

Chapter 7

Organization

What Managers Do

Throughout their daily behavior, managers translate strategy into execution.

In previous chapters, we discussed developing strategy, planning frameworks, and organizational capabilities. But experienced executives know that any strategy is only as effective as the daily behavior of the managers who are responsible for its execution. The myriad details that must be reinforced, the many team members whose actions must be aligned, and the many views that must integrated all demand constant management attention.

This chapter focuses on what strategic integrity means for management practice. It focuses on the crucial role management plays in ensuring the kind of organizational alignment and responsiveness that makes strategic integrity possible. (See Exhibit 7.1.) The chapter complements the discussion on organizational structure and processes that was the focus of Chapter 6.

The Manager as Team Lead

The first blog frames the role of managers within their organization. It was written for new hires and dates back to the time before Steven joined the Windows team—the blog, therefore, refers to the Office organization.

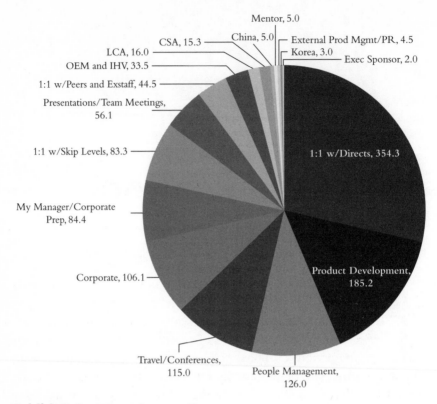

Exhibit 7.1   What Managers Do

However, it provides a great description of the management responsibilities that made the Office team tick and that established the foundations for the Windows team.

What Do Managers Do and How Big Should My Team Be?

> The first thing we do, let's kill all the lawyers.
>
> —BUTCHER, IN SHAKESPEARE'S KING HENRY VI

> The first thing we do, let's fire all the managers.
>
> —JUST ABOUT EVERY EMPLOYEE AT ONE TIME OR ANOTHER SINCE THE 1911 RELEASE OF FREDERICK TAYLOR'S PRINCIPLES OF SCIENTIFIC MANAGEMENT

Today I thought I would talk a little about a topic related to how we manage *feature teams* in Office. For those of you considering working at Microsoft this is a pretty important topic because the management environment and the management "system" (to the degree something that involves people can be called a system), the management structure will play a key role in both your success and your happiness with work. For the most part, if you're in college and going out on your first job you focus on job content (i.e., what you will be doing, what code you will write, what features you will design, etc.) and probably a little bit on the work environment (what your office is like or what the buildings are like). It is more difficult to focus on management, especially since even if you've had internships or other part-time work, your first full-time job will also be your first experience in being managed full time.

The first thing to note about management is that it is not a science. But it is not an art either and it is wrong to just assume that having a good manager is either lucky or rare. Management is like most things, in that with practice, coaching, and training, people can acquire the skills to become a good manager. And it is just as important to realize that employees comprise [edited] 50% of the manager-employee relationship, and thus have a significant contribution to make. In other words, being a good employee is a critical component to having a good manager. One way to think of this is that while there might be some classes with great professors where you received bad grades, most of the time there's a pretty high correlation between classes with good professors and classes in which you earned As.

So let's look a bit into the management structure of an organization like Office at Microsoft (of course all organizations, inside Microsoft and even specific teams in Office, have their own variation so what follows is a generalization). It is also worth saying that some readers might be people that have had a less than positive management experience (even within Office), but it would be wrong to indict all managers or management in general because of your experience. After all, managers are people and like all people are not perfect and are trying to improve. Some might not make it, but think of baseball—even the very best of the best might get a hit only one out of three times they go to bat, which seems pretty pathetic when you consider that the whole point of the game is to get a hit and players receive immense compensation just to get hits.

One of the first things that people always do when they think about their place in an organization is count how many edges there are between their place in the org structure and the CEO. When I started at Microsoft in 1989 and the company had 3000 people, I was a new hire from school and there were 5 people "above" me. Today a new hire from college in Office is probably going to have 7 people above them to get to the CEO and the company is a bit bigger :-). This is an interesting number and one that can either impress you if you have experiences with large organizations or maybe cause you to pause if you think that the number of hops to the CEO is a critical number. It turns out that balancing the height and span of an organization has a lot to do with the ability of an organization to be nimble and to also train and grow you in your career.

The typical organization in Office development is one where there is a group of about 5–8 developers (we'll use developers for this post, but the discussion is just points of the dev/test/pm triad) managed by a *lead developer*. That is the first level of management called a *feature team*. There are then 3–5 leads that report to a *development manager*. That is the second level of management, usually called a *group*. The development manager reports to a general manager or an executive manager that represents the place that development, testing, and program management come together. This structure is matched by development testing and program management (where there are about equal numbers of testers, and about half that number of program managers). The general manager or executive is where the *product* or *technology* comes together (think SharePoint, or Excel, or the new Office "12" user interface). In some groups, if there are a lot of products or a very large team there might be one additional level of management. I manage these general managers. My boss manages the overall Office P&L, so marketing, finance, HR, etc. as well as other products report to him.

To give you an idea, Microsoft Office "12" is built by about 30 product groups, each with about 3–5 feature teams, each with 5–8 developers. The whole point of a feature team is to have your immediate work area be a small, relatively self-contained "unit." When you consider the size of the business and the amount of revenue generated by Office ($10 billion dollars), it is rather astounding that the entire product line is created by such a relatively small organization. Many of the feature teams work with other feature teams directly, so it is not a series of independent silos. In fact, our customers demand this from us—they want Excel and Word and Outlook and SharePoint to work well together and not just be taped together in a box.

What made us pick these numbers: 5–8 developers reporting to a lead, and 3–5 leads reporting to a dev manager, and the three discipline managers reporting to a GM? That's a great question and the answer provides the evidence of our very strong commitment to management.

The first line of management is where you have the most interaction with your manager. This manager is someone who has experience in the product cycle and has probably (in Office) gone through shipping at least 2 full product cycles. During their career they have proven a consistent ability to write good code, meet the schedule, and their code withstood the rigors of testing. They have also fostered strong relationships with their counterparts in program management and testing. They have also mentored interns and had that experience managing. Like your professors in college who never really took courses in teaching, managers did not get sent off to "management school" or anything, but are assumed to have mastered the fundamentals as best you can given that the skill depends on firsthand experience. This manager has a number of specific responsibilities:

- **Know the code.** First and foremost the lead knows the code for the project. The lead is going to be your source of skill and experience. The lead will be the one to code review your code. The lead has the experience necessary to insure that the work of the team is of the architecture and quality necessary to get the job done for customers.
- **Help you to know what you need to do.** Your lead is like your coach. He or she will be the one to walk through your proposed architecture and implementation and make sure that it fits within the timeframe and that it meets the needs of the project. This is especially important if you are new to the code, team, or Microsoft. For example, conceptually it might seem straightforward to understand a new feature area, but the demands of security, globalization, performance, compatibility, accessibility, programmability, and a host of other issues to consider mean that you are going to need another set of eyes when you are just getting started.
- **Determine the tasks to be completed by the team and balance the work across the team.** The team works with program management to determine the scope of the work to be done. The dev lead works with the team to come up with a schedule and work list for the group. The individuals on the team own their own estimates and they work with their lead to get the estimates as accurate as possible. Under

no circumstances will the lead arbitrarily override your estimates. But if you need more time, the discussion that happens is with program management to scale back the feature area. If you and your lead have done lots of projects together, the lead might have enough information to help you estimate better :-).

- **Assist in skills development.** You might never have written C++ code or used XML or worked in Word's table code or something. Your lead is there to help you to learn and to get the tools to learn about the project you are about to embark on. As a company that develops intellectual property, most of our knowledge is actually held in the brains of our employees, so this type of knowledge transfer is super important.
- **Communication to/from the feature team about the feature team.** The lead is responsible for making sure the rest of the overall project knows what is going on. This could mean working with the test lead and program manager lead or it could mean working with the lead of another feature team that your team depends on (for example, if you are Outlook working with Exchange server).
- **Performance evaluation.** Your lead will ultimately be responsible for evaluating your performance (I am explicitly not getting into this topic here, but might in a future post). The reason I mention this is because you really want your lead to know you well and to know your strengths and weaknesses well and to have spent enough time working with you directly to be well-informed about your work.
- **Hiring the team.** Leads are responsible for getting folks on the team since they don't just show up. You might think recruiters are the ones hiring you, but the leads are the ones making the decisions and deciding if you might be a good fit for the work and the team. It takes a lot of time and effort to build a team. When I was a lead, I easily spent 4 or 5 hours a week hiring and recruiting. Today that time is spent in different ways, but it is still just as critical a part of my job.

So as you can see, your lead is going to have a lot to do in order to insure success of the feature team. In fact, the lead has a lot to do just to insure your success. You might be a programming deity and hit the ground running and never need a single bit of help, but still your lead is going to need to make sure that the work you do is lining up with the broader goals of the product and that you are working on the most critical needs of the feature team. And all the while, since the lead has so much experience and is such a proven developer he or she is also expected to be checking in code, fixing bugs, and making sure the architecture is holding up.

A lot of companies will tell you that the best organizations are "flat" and what they mean is that they want to have the fewest number of managers possible because "managers are evil" or "managers create more work than they get done" or other such comments. You don't see a lot of people out there defending managers and of course whenever an organization is not doing well the first thing folks want to do is get rid of all the managers who must be gumming things up. I will say that if a team is performing poorly, then there is a management problem. But that is quite separate from a problem manager. There might be a performance problem with a specific manager, but there is definitely a problem with the management process (even if that problem is just having the manager continue without improving). Both can be fixed, but this can definitely be a case of tossing out a solid principle just because of one problem area if you indict the idea of having management structure.

To illustrate this just consider this simple picture:

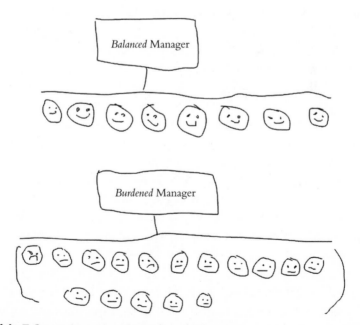

Exhibit 7.2 Balanced and Burdened Managers

The balanced manager above is a lead with 8 employees. This is the structure described above. You can imagine how straight forward it is for each of the 8 to interact and work together—they can sit at the same table at lunch, they can take two cars to a pizza place, they can bowl on 2 lanes at a bowling alley, and chances are you can easily remember everyone's name and what they are working on in detail. This is an effective team. If you need an analogy or comparable, the Navy SEALs are organized into 16 person groups with 2 officers (i.e., leads). In the Army, the smallest unit is the squad and it is 9 or 10 soldiers lead by a sergeant. I mention those examples, because the military has been studying organization for a few thousand years and because manpower is everything [and] is very motivated to have the maximal number of troops doing the work they need to do, and not have a lot of bloat.

Some leads might not be as effective as they would like with 8 and can work best with 5, or maybe 3. This is what we call "scale" and it is something that the dev manager needs to evaluate and take into account when building the team. And it is quite possible that some leads are very comfortable with as many as 10 employees, though that is certainly only the case when some of the team members are very experienced or the work does not require a lot of connection to other groups.

Now consider the aptly named burdened manager above. In this picture, this manager has 16 employees. You can imagine that it sounds pretty cool—they are a lean, mean, coding machine. There is no overhead for this team and they are ready to go into action. On the other hand, just imagine how much attention you would get from that manager in the course of the week. In Office, the expectation is that you have a scheduled weekly 1:1 with your manager (to work on the above issues, in addition to significant amounts of interrupt driven help and email). This manager would lose half the week just trying to have scheduled time with those employees and because of all that scheduled time the chances of having a successful interrupt driven event with your manager are near zero. In fact, if you just go through the list above of lead responsibilities you will see that most of them become impossible with such a "flat" organization.

Another issue to consider in the burdened feature team above is how on target the work is going to be. The lead is so burdened that the chances of every one of those 16 people being on the same page are very low. In fact, the dynamic you will see in that sort of organization is that the team will naturally "bunch up" or "silo" into two or three groups of manageable size. In other words, the communication and leadership will be partitioned in a path of least resistance, not necessarily in the path that is best for customers. The downstream effect of this is inevitably a project reset or reboot, since eventually "management" will figure out that the team is not doing what needs to be done and corrective action will need to be taken. This is a classic case where the individual employees are not at fault, but the structure is to blame. It is unrealistic to expect the employees to be psychic or all-knowing and so the person who needed to stitch together the work and make sure the right things were getting done the right way at the right time was failing you. And that person was failing you because there simply wasn't enough time in the day to pay attention to everything that was going on and to effectively tap the skills and energies of each of the members of the team.

A lot of times in start-ups or young companies there is a flat organization and it is touted as a benefit because there are no "layers" and no "bureaucracy." This does not follow logically from the role of management and is much more *testosterone* speaking. I've seen start-ups with 100 people that have more management than 100 people on the Office team. I've also seen start-ups with managers that oversee 30 people each. I've also seen teams of 10 people come up with so much process and bureaucracy that they could not get anything done. There is no correlation between layers and bureaucracy, though layers might make it easier to gum things up. There is no correlation between being a start-up and requiring a flat organization. And finally, there is a high correlation between a flat organization and managers that do not have time to spend managing. For the most part, my experience is that it is easy to rationalize not having managers since showing disdain for management is easy and on the outside and on the face of it few would disagree with you.

If you're a developer you might also be wondering what all the "other" people do—what is it that all those program managers, usability engineers, etc. do during the day since we're all here to write code, right? This is where experience in other disciplines really helps, because until you have actually had to do the job of another discipline you only see the places where they are not doing things to help you :-). Remember that an Army platoon or SEAL unit are about the size of a feature team, but what was not described were things like where all the supplies come from, who gets the tanks from one place to another, who figured out what mission the team should go on, and who trains all the soldiers in the first place. Organizations need all those support functions in order for the primary mission to be as effective as possible. If a developer had to go out and talk to all the end users requiring accessibility support, or had to talk to all the ISVs who want to use extensibility support, or had to figure out the compatibility testing, or how we would automate the release of service packs through testing, there would be a lot less time to actually work on the mission at hand. That is not a blanket excuse for anyone who does not pull their weight on the project, but just a caution that if all the organization did was write code there is a very high likelihood that the code would not be a great product or business—just like if all the SEAL unit just arrived and starting demo'ing what it thought looked like a good idea to demo.

Your first management experiences are a very important part of your career, much like the first two years of college when you're mostly taking required classes. We work hard to make this as good an experience as we can within the limits of human beings and the normal distributions of skills and behavior. We're a learning and introspective culture so we use the feedback from employees about managers to improve things. I would encourage anyone considering their first job out of college or moving to a new job to spend some time asking questions about how the organization works and what the relationship will be to your line manager.

—Steven

This blog reminds us all that managers are real people and have only limited capacity to do things. Their ability to process information is bounded, just like the time slots on their weekly schedules. As such, if strategic integrity is treated as some sort of perfect state, it will never work. The practical implementation of strategic integrity in an organization must conform to the real constraints of managers and employees. Working within these natural bounds, however, managers perform a crucial role. Managers produce the planning framework, work to integrate the plan, internalize it, communicate it to their team, and react to inevitable contingencies. Moreover, they also work to shape their team, building the values, processes, and capabilities that improve effectiveness over time.

The description of the manager's role emphasizes content and depth, business, and engineering substance, as he or she creates and internalizes strategy and translates it into specifics for members of the team. This is not a shallow administrative role, but rather true "technical leadership" contributing strategic perspectives, mentoring individual contributors, and coaching the team toward the strategy. The role is complex and takes both skill and time, balancing conceptualization with communication. The role is grounded in technical excellence and combines an awareness of the business goals with an architectural understanding of the capabilities and interdependencies that will drive success.

The manager's role is articulated in several important responsibilities. These start with "know the code," which can be generalized as understanding the technical details of what you are managing. The manager should be "hands on" and comfortable with the details and respected for his or her knowledge, without micromanaging every decision. Responsibilities continue with coaching the team and balancing work across team members. The manager must also drive skills development, performance evaluations, and hiring, as well as communication with other teams.

The manager's role is challenging, and it is not surprising that the size of the organization rapidly becomes a constraint. Exhibit 7.1 is highly evocative and drives home the fact that there is a real cost to an organization that is too large and too flat. Despite simplistic stereotypes, managing well, and having time to really perform the roles described above, requires focusing on a smaller group of direct reports. The model points to a maximum of eight reports, drawing from analogies in the military and from many years of practical experience. The simple insight is indeed confirmed by extensive research in organization theory, which examined organizations as diverse as planes and orchestras.[1] The blog pushes back on simplistic notions of flat organization to explain the crucial role managers have in driving an innovative organization to maintain the kind of coherence and integrity that produces real impact.

The Manager in the Middle

The following blog post is written as a response to a comment on the "What do managers do" blog discussed above. The comment is captured as the first section of the blog. The comment argues that despite the persuasive arguments we just discussed, the problem is not with the team and the team leads—it is with middle management, the higher levels that impede real communication between the team and senior management, fracturing the integrity of the organization: As the blog puts it, the "Ineffective Middle-Management Suck-ups." The response tells an interesting and different story about the critical role played by middle management.

Ineffective Middle-Management Suck-ups

Anonymous said:

> Managers love to give more reasons why lots of managers are a good thing. Why lots of managerial levels are a good thing. Your explanation of the file/rank structure and their leads is great. And it's right on target. A lead with 5/6 reports (ideally 8 or so) is great—one with 30 is overburdened.
>
> The problem is not here. The problem is at the few levels above this. A dev manager managing 3 leads is underburdened. He's adding process, he needs all this information. Leads are constantly scrambling to feed him information instead of doing what they could do best—developing or directing development in lower tiers.
>
> The problem keeps getting more and more acute between this level (dev mgr) up to some of the senior executives where it straightens out again—executives have a lot of people reporting to them with possibly a separate team that garners information and feeds it to them. The 3 or 4 levels in between the top two and the bottom two—aka middle management that is the "problem." This is what, for example, mini-microsoft has been ranting about. And this is what startups don't have. Or agile companies for that matter.
>
> My ideal structure for Microsoft is one where we enforce at least 5 up to 10 reports per manager, any less than 5 and management hierarchies need to be collapsed or managers eliminated. Just doing this should eliminate some levels in organizations such as windows (I'm there, so I don't really know office).
>
> That was a good post though—and a defense of management is well warranted—there are far too many people who blame management and look to make cuts there when there are just as many as bad dev/test/pm rank and file people adding dead weight to the company.

Hi there, Anonymous (btw, if you work at Microsoft and want to discuss this face to face where there is a lot more context, I can promise that the open door policy is fully respected by me).

I don't want folks to think I am defending management (especially bad management), but then again I did point out that few people will ever rise to defend management, which basically leaves that job to me. And of course numerically, if you only have 6 levels of an organization, then management is outnumbered by non-management approximately 3:1. So a tough crowd for sure!

The dynamic you describe is a completely dysfunctional organization. If employees (aka, individual contributors) think that the manager is doing nothing more than creating "homework" for the group/IC, then that is systematically and operationally a terrible idea. However, it is not necessarily the case that the "homework" is bad for the organization as a whole. It could possibly be that the manager is doing a terrible job of justifying the work. Even worse, the manager might be saying, "I need <x>, but can't explain it because my boss asked for it." Wow that is just a mess. If that is happening in the Office team I definitely want to know about it—but actually an even better way to fix that is just to go straight to your manager's manager and ask, "[W]hat the *frack* is going on—it feels like I have a bunch of random homework?" Those on the Office team know that I often ask, "[D]oes this feel like homework?" and if the answer is yes then I either rescind the request or try to come up with a better reason why the request matters. And we keep iterating. The first rule of thumb is that if the work is not useful for the person doing it, then it is not worth doing. And if you think I don't give that feedback to my manager about things I'm asked to do, then you don't know me very well!

The other dynamic that leads to this is when people feel their manager is spending time managing "up." This is another example of something that no one will defend but is actually a critical part of management. You can say manage up and it can be totally pejorative and essentially means "I am spinning things and sucking up and basically being dishonest about what is going on." That is how most individuals view managing up. Believe me, any good upper manager knows when they are being managed up to. What goes around comes around.

BUT, managing up can also mean "I am telling you, my manager, about the work our team is doing and why it is right and why we are on track." In other words, your manager might just be acting on your behalf and clearing the path for you to get things done. That's what managers do. If you live in an ideal world where paths do not need to be cleared then that is another topic—in the real world, where you are always competing for limited resources (in software that is usually people, but just try to build the world's best product without a commitment to actually sell it down the road) you do need management to manage up and clear a path so your great work can be realized and make money. So maybe when you're being asked for something by your manager it is in fact to help you get your job done, not just to make your manager look good. But if you perceive it that way, then either your manager has communication techniques to improve or you might want to ask "why" before jumping to a conclusion.

Effectively managing up is a critical part of a functional organization, whether you are an individual on the team, a lead, a manager of a function, or a general manager. Ineffectively managing up is just as destructive as any other ineffective performance trait on a team, including writing bad code.

I would probably resist any temptation to just define an org structure as having a fixed number of reports. If you try to fix the number at any level you actually drive a "physical" org structure that might not map to the intended logical outcome. One way to think of this is that every software product you ship is a reflection of the organization. While you might want to have architectural layers in the software in one dimension, the physical organization might drive a different split. As a result you have to balance the customer perspective with the organizational needs. So, for example, we have a Publisher team that likely has a less "flat" structure than intended, but that is because the team of developers just isn't big enough to have 8 leads. On the other hand, Publisher is a business that is 10s of millions of dollars so having the developers focused and part of a Publisher-only structure is probably a good idea. Also, the numbers need to account for some fluidity in the organization—you always have openings to hire people, people are moving around all the time, etc. In other words, a person with 4 reports one day might have 6 in a month. So you would never want to try to create a perfectly shaped organization since it cannot last very long.

For me, I am just not quite [as] fast to indict managers of managers as useless and ineffective. One of the challenges in taking this position is that it is super easy to complain about managers and frankly those complaints come from people who have never had to do the job. So the idea of "walking in someone else's shoes" definitely comes to mind.[2] In some ways, I'd love to offer to have someone shadow me for a week and see the "confusion" that heads my way and why everything looks grey and non-obvious, or more clearly "damned if you do, damned if you don't."

I am, however, the first to admit that it is very easy to act in a dysfunctional way as a manager in the middle (between other managers). You are pulled in a lot of different directions and you have a lot of masters to answer to. The very best managers in the middle are those that do two things: they coordinate with their peer group (and do not focus on managing up) and they seek to clarify the situation and not to muddle it or make it more complex. This is hard. Writing code is a hard skill. Managing is a hard skill. At least you can go take definitive courses in how to write software.

I dismiss the notion that having layers of management is inconsistent with agility. This is no doubt a counterintuitive, or at least controversial statement. In fact, it is very easy to argue that having a strong role for middle management is actually necessary for agile development because with strong management comes a coordinated effort to develop products. Of course you can also end up with a bunch of turf battles or some sense of paralysis. One over-arching theme is that middle management has the same performance curve that individuals have—it is just that when a middle manager performs poorly he/she drags people down with him/her. That's why it is so important to pace yourself and why I work hard to emphasize the notion of patience in career progression. It is also why for every ineffective manager at the lead level, you create one unhappy manager but 5–8 voices of dissent and unhappiness.

Agility is most certainly in the eye of the beholder or a product of the context or moment, like so many concepts in management. If you have an organization that can develop a brand-new product and bring it to market in 2 years without any "approval," then I would say this is an agile organization. On the other hand, if **you** proposed something that didn't get built by the organization, then I can assure **you** that you will quickly become a spokesperson for why the organization lacks agility. If 10 people each present an idea to be funded and built by the team, but the team only does one of them, then there is a good chance you have 1 spokesperson saying how agile the team is and 9 people talking about how ossified and backward looking the team is, no matter how good a job you do explaining why you decided not to allocate resources to the other 9 proposed features/projects.

There are many examples from within the Office product line that emphasize the agile nature of our organization. We strive for agility within the scope of information worker products, which we define broadly to mean any software you need to be more productive in any context. We've built SharePoint from the ground up within our team, and done so without any middle managers coming in and trying to gum things up. We've had struggles in coordinating our efforts across the company—are those good or bad? Well I would have rather skipped those meetings; then again if we didn't have them and reconcile things before we shipped then we would have had to reconcile those with our products in the marketplace and in front of customers. Nothing sends a worse message to customers than a confused product line. Should we have just not thought of doing the product and packed up and added more features to Excel? I had no intention of doing that and in fact moved developers from our "apps" to the server work because it was a higher priority. Not everyone agreed and that itself led to calls for my head.

Another example is the creation of OneNote. Amazingly enough we had no meetings to "approve" this and no meetings to have other meetings. No one had to write a formal proposal. We just decided to build the product. Chris Pratley, the group program manager with responsibility for OneNote program management, wrote about the genesis of the product a while back.[3] That was all there was to it. Now the thing about that is you have two middle managers coordinating and agreeing on what to do. Then other middle managers were involved in the staffing of that team with the right people. Were people concerned about how the product would fit with a strategy—you bet and I was among them. Were people concerned that these resources would be better used elsewhere—you bet.

But for every example like that I can cite, someone will point out a decision we made to not fund something or not do something. Is that a lack of agility? I don't think so since we've proven we can go in new directions and also produce in short order. Is that a poor decision? It just might be. But unfortunately engineering is not chemistry so you can't do controlled experiments on every decision, so sometimes you have to pick one path when you have finite resources.

One person's agility is another person's screw up. One person's lack of agility is another person's strategy.

There are two sides to every point of view in business management. The challenge is not in just being critical of the point of view you don't agree with, but stepping up and asking questions like, "[H]ow did you arrive at that conclusion <you bozo>?" If you think a bad decision has been made, then you have two options.

First, you can ask why it was decided that way and get clarification and see that indeed there might be another side of the coin and just work your way up the chain (Microsoft has always had an open-door policy and any decision can be questioned by challenge/response). If you still don't agree, then as they say in the military "you can vote with your stripes" because in the end if you don't respect the management chain then you won't ever be part of the team. But maybe, just maybe, you will see that the people that were once individual developers (and testers and program managers) on the team are rational and have thought things through. Becoming a manager is (usually) a promotion, but not a lobotomy (usually).

Or second, you can just retreat to your office and complain to your peers (bottoms developing a victim complex) and just gum up the system by passive resistance to the efforts of the team, or worse. When individuals do that it is perfectly rational, but it is not productive. If you develop a victim complex, then you are just demonstrating why you are a follower and why your opinion might not be as highly valued as you think it is. Absolutely positively no one has ever been fired for having a dissenting view. Absolutely positively no one has ever received a poor review for merely having a dissenting view. Those things happen when you express a dissenting view by failing to contribute what you're supposed to contribute in your role. You're human and you do have to be excited by your work and every employee deserves that. Sometimes groups go in a direction you don't agree with. It might be when that happens that it is time for you to get a different perspective and try something new. There is no crime in that. I'd encourage you to find a logical break in the action and to do so without going out in a ball of flames.

And I should point out, that this exact dynamic happens to managers all the time. Sometimes managers are asked to do things they are not so wild about and have to go through this same exercise. Being a manager does not make you immune from being asked to help make something happen that does not seem quite right. So all of this applies to managers.

You'll notice there is a lot of recursion in management. That is a key theme of the tops-middles-bottoms that I wrote about recently.

So the short answer for Anonymous is, of course. [T]here are always challenges with managers in the middle—just like there are challenges with individual employees who do not write the code as well as they need to, do not [go] thorough enough designs, or fail to fully test an area. But to indict the whole notion of middle management is probably not a good idea.

Perhaps my favorite and brief description of this subject was written by Michael Kinsley and posted on *Slate*. It is really worth the quick read. See http://slate.msn.com/id/2064260 for "An Ode to Managers."

—Steven

PS: I definitely encourage Microsoft employees to send me mail directly. My door is open and my inbox is open 7x24. I would love to have discussions with more context.

PPS: The title of this was taken from a recurring skit on Seattle KING-5 TV's series *Almost Live* (http://www.imdb.com/title/tt0149413/).

In response to the anonymous comment, the blog provides a compelling answer. It's not about middle management: it's about what middle managers do. The blog focuses in on the difficult role of what is sometimes called "the manager in the middle." The manager in the middle must answer to multiple constituencies. She must manage down to her organization, over to peers and partners, and up to her boss. The role, shared by virtually every manager in the world is fraught with complexity, but is essential to making the organization work. Achieving coherence up and down a large organization, across groups and partnerships, hinges on managers making difficult trade-offs, the "damned if you do, damned if you don't" decisions mentioned in the blog. The middle manager's position is a difficult one, fraught with challenges and pitfalls, but performs an essential role in reaching for strategic integrity. The middle manager is the connector, the interpreter and translator, the communicator and integrator, the architect and champion.

Resolving this complex challenge is made much easier by the framework described in this book. A powerful decision-making framework provided by a detailed plan, a deep, technically capable organization, transparent communication, clear roles, responsibilities and value systems all provide important foundation that help resolve the many trade-offs involved in the manager's role. Without the components covered by the framework, it should be clear to the reader that strategic integrity becomes almost unreachable. But even working within the framework, managing to strategic integrity is a real challenge. The next blog describes some common patterns.

Manager Phenotypes

What kind of manager do you work for? What kind of manager would you like to work for? Do we expect different types of manager behavior in different situations?

What kind of manager are you? Do you have a mental model of the type of manager you want to be? Do you think about what type of manager you are in the course of a specific situation?

These sound like simple questions. We're all familiar with terms like *empowerment* or *coach*. We have all heard or said, "I want to work for a manager I can learn from." Yet in practice it turns out situations are unique and call for different types of responses—both from the employee and the manager. How do you coordinate these expectations?

My experience has been that we all have a bias in both the type of person we want to work for and the type of person we are, as both a manager and employee. Let's call this a management *genotype*. That means a person who is reserved and chooses to listen is not likely to dramatically change this as a manager. It means that a person who is detail-oriented is not likely to let go of that trait just because they become a manager. Both of these can be both positives and negatives, depending on what a situation calls for, so it behooves all of us to recognize our own genotype and both the asset and liability aspects of our genotype.

It is also the case that our environment plays a critical role in how we express ourselves as managers and employees, or a management *phenotype*. So someone who might be a great listener might also be a great leader at a team meeting, even though it means speaking out and being the center of attention. A person who is detail-oriented might also know the right time to step back and assemble the details into an abstract picture. The ability to act and express yourself the right way for a given environment is a key trait.

The two sides to this coin show how difficult it is to box in a manager as a certain "type" or for that matter to know precisely what sort of manager you really want to work for. The answer for both is the right type at the right time. Management is hard because you have to adapt and change—no one style works for all employees and no one style works all the time, even if you think you are genetically programmed to act a certain way. That is why feedback in real time is so important and why acting on that feedback is important. If you don't tell your manager that things aren't right when they are happening, then he or she can't adjust. If you don't sense that the people you manage are frustrated, doubtful, or confused and adjust, then you are failing them.

I am sure there are tons of taxonomies of different types of managers out there. I bet there is even a magic quadrant of managers that a consultant has. I decided that I would be lazy and rather than search around and find one, I would just make up some manager phenotypes and describe them. Then you can consider this a tool for discussion with your manager—a way of establishing a discussion about a situation, a certain trait, or a specific incident that didn't go very well. The key to this taxonomy is that most every phenotype is useful at some time or another and to write one off because the word used is "inherently negative" would miss the subtleties of management.

Manager as coach. Manager as coach is the most often used descriptor of a manager. The coach is someone you can count on for experience and for sage advice over how to approach a situation. As a coach, you are an objective observer looking to get the most out of a member of the team and think of how to tap the strengths of each player on the team. We think of a coach like Knute Rockne providing innovative leadership and unparalleled emotional support. But one can also think of the great coaches throwing things from the sidelines, humiliating players, and in general proving that Machiavelli was right and the ends justify the means. Or one can think of coaches that are coolly distant from their players and win by a mathematical calculation. If you stick with sports and think of the "management" percentage relative to the number of players you can see how the model of high-impact coaches doesn't scale. (An American football team has about an equal number of coaches to players!) Perhaps that is why high-level sports coaches are so well paid. While it is easy to see the positives of coaching, the challenge has always been that we are player-coaches and the problem is that there have been very few really successful player coaches. So this model is one that is tough to use in all places. There is always a necessity for the keen strategy, the successful motivational events, and even well-worn witticisms.

Manager as friend. For some folks, it is very important that their manager be their friend—perhaps not best friend, but at least a good friend or that your manager likes you as though you could be friends. Some managers are the same way in that they work best when they feel they connect on a friend level—things will work well. When you are close to your manager or team in this regard it does make things easier— when times are good. Sharing commonalities as friends share is a great way to bring a team together. As with friends, lunches and dinners are not just meals but additional time to bond. Cultural references and experiences that friends often share mean that the team shares them as well. At the extreme it means finishing each other's sentences and knowing how the other will react in a situation. Friends make many things easier. On the other hand, nothing is harder then telling a friend bad news. Things don't go well and letting down your friend (manager) is hard. When it comes time to do all the tricky things like calibration, getting back to that objective space is hard. Or worse, those on the team that feel a manager is friends with a subset of the team will always feel that favorites are being played. A good rule of thumb is to be friendly.

Manager as referee. As we went through the process of streamlining our organization and focusing on engineering discipline leaders rather than multi-discipline leaders, I heard a lot of feedback around the question[s] of "[W]ho is the tie-breaker?" and "[W]ho resolves things when there is a disagreement?" Many believed (and many, on other teams, probably continue to believe) that a key role of management is to break ties and to split differences. I have been strident in believing that the notion of having a layer of management that has a primary role of arbitration is not something we will have. I believe even more strongly though that an organization that defines the role of arbitration is one that hinges too much on winners and losers and will not be long term. On the other hand, a key role of a referee is to define the interpretation of the rules and so of course every organization needs that. Sometimes the vision document is not perfect and has ambiguities. Sometimes there are design choices to be made that span different agendas. While I think there is some refereeing that needs to [be] done, I think that the best place for this to happen is between peers in engineering and not through a process of escalation. I think I'm willing to say that this is a phenotype I wouldn't want to see very much, if at all.

Manager as shield. Closely related to the referee is another management phenotype I have heard a lot of, though I probably can internalize this one a bit more. Chaos is all around us. Many managers believe their job is to shield the team from all that chaos *just so we can get stuff done.* As engineers we all know software projects are always one small step from total chaos—schedules can unravel, features can slip, bugs can multiply, and those are just the internal problems. So there is a natural tendency for management to view a big part of their job to keep all those nasty folks from breaking things. Chris Peters used to talk about the end game of a major release "when it is abundantly clear that there are a few hundred people working to ship and the other 30,000 people at Microsoft determined to do everything in their power to prevent the product from releasing." Trust me, it can feel that way. Yet there is a fine line between shield and obstacle, and I certainly understand this distinction firsthand. I do believe management has a keen role in keeping the trains running, but as a [candidate] was quoted in the 1988 presidential debate, "[I]t is not enough just to keep the trains on time—you have to know where they are heading." So for me, a manager who just keeps chaos away but is not executing against a broadly communicated and agreed to plan is not serving our broader Microsoft community. Stealth projects or projects that "everyone" disagrees with but are being shielded are not helpful to everyone. I simply don't believe in the viewpoint that the company will "consume" or "buzzsaw" projects just for the sake of doing so. It is why over the years and many releases our teams have focused so much on a broadly inclusive planning process that results in a clearly articulated plan with tenets, bets, and assumptions documented in a memo of substance reflecting the commitments of the team (not just a slide deck done by one person late at night!). Rather than the shield becoming individuals who then become obstacles, the shield is really a product plan that is transparent and balanced. It is never perfect, but it can be a more effective way to express this phenotype.

Manager as answer man (or answer woman). Many commonly believe that the best person to work for is one that is "smarter" (in any number of dimensions) than you are. That is, work for someone who you can always ask questions of and know you can get the "right" answer. Microsoft is filled with smart people. And Microsoft has lots of people willing to share their answers (he says while he types yet another blog-lecture). When you are stumped, manager as answer man is incredibly helpful. Today Arthurdh and I were recalling the last bug fixed in FindFast (our first desktop search) in Office 95. Mike Kelley was stumped and got some help from our master of development, Jon DeVaan. Sure enough, Jon figured out it was a corrupt memory card (back then it was probably a monster 4mb card!). Jon was the answer man. I had a similar experience with my manager who walked into my office, set a hardware watch point on the 386, and within about 5 minutes tracked down some memory trashing bug in MFC 1.0. If it weren't for him I would probably still be debugging this one. You can learn a lot from having an answer man. In fact, early in your career these are great people to work for. But both managers and employees recognizing when enough "knowledge transfer" has happened is critical because long-term health/growth of an employee or of the organization managed will suffer because of the obvious dependency that can develop. The most important thing to understand is that the answer man does not scale—we need people who know this much to also be writing code, specs, test, and not just fielding questions from the whole company all day. We need to grow more people who can know the answers and build our products.

Manager as process person. Many people look to management to be the place where adult supervision and sanity prevail. A big part of bringing this type of structure and leadership to the team is to instill process. Process can be about wacky concepts like, I don't know, planning a release. But process can just be about order—we have 1:1's every week, we send our weekly accomplishments in email, and we send a weekly status report to the whole team. Process can be about technical initiatives like Milestone Q. Process can be about how to establish partnerships with other teams. We often talk about *what* we want the team to do but a key role of management is to provide the *how*. On the other hand, a manager who views himself/herself through the lens of process can quickly drain the life from a team. Managers who "do" too much process come across as forgetting why we are here. Is all the mail from your manager about company-wide training classes, MYCD, new parking stickers, and so on? I say that in jest, but believe me it takes discipline not to get drawn into all the requests to "pass this along to your team" or "[A]t your next team meeting could you present these 15 slides on . . . " A more dysfunctional view is when process discussions dominate the team—that is, the infamous *meetings about meetings* or "[L]et's first discuss what we all think the problem is." And of course a manager that lacks the process gene (or environmental expression) can easily drive everyone crazy, no matter how brilliant their ideas might be. And a corollary to that phenotype is the manager who says, "I am not good at process" and then delegates, what I think of as essentially managing the team, process to another person who becomes like the process voice for the manager. There's a general point in there that says it is great to build a complete team where all the necessary skills exist, but for leaders of the team it is essential that they exhibit a necessary baseline skill set.

Manager as editor. A classic dysfunction of management is the manager that doesn't know what he or she wants, but has no problem asking you to go do it. So you design the UI, write some code, build a test plan, make some slides, and then your manager says "not that." You feel like the ground is moving underneath you. *Go get this rock.* The manager feels like you're not listening. After a few rounds, blood pressure rises and soon the in-person conversations turn to email and tensions fly. No one is happy. As managers we too often forget that we are there to help employees and that employees aren't there to help us, and so that means asking someone to do something when you yourself do not know what success looks like is just plain bad. So would you ever want a manager as editor? Absolutely! The reality is that sometimes the answer isn't known. Actually that is when we all have the most fun—solving problems rather than just doing the legwork. But the subtlety is that the editing is not for the benefit of the manager, but what the manager offers you is an opportunity to have a sounding board, to hear feedback in real time, and in general to be there to help you achieve the success you want to achieve. Making slides and demos for your manager when you have specs to [write] is not helpful for anyone in the long run. But getting the reaction, the insights, and experiences from your manager when you don't know the answer is great *editorial advice*. A great editor is like a combination of a *process person + answer woman,* except the answers reflect experience and insights, not just the facts you need to move to the next step.

Manager as framer. (I was going to stop at 7 since that is such a great number these days, but let's add an 8th). One of the most important things that can be done when managing creative people (like we hire for Microsoft) is to put in place a framework for success. Creative people don't want to be told exactly what to do. But at the same time they don't want to churn (or get rocks). All work needs constraints. You don't go to an architect and say, "[R]emodel my house." The architect will ask questions about your lifestyle, your needs, and your budget. These are constraints. The architect builds a framework for success. A good architect plays this back to you, documents it, and iterates so there is agreement and clarity. Expressing this phenotype is difficult. Frameworks are super hard to come up with (it took us almost 4 months to plan a release of Windows Live that takes less than 3 times that to implement). People will question even the most thoughtful framework and claim it is too constraining or *fait accompli*. It requires a leap of faith from the team that the framework makes sense and will lead to the "right" solution. It requires the manager to avoid being too prescriptive, even when the temptation is there. It requires the team to be creative within constraints even though most everyone I know will find a way to complain about certain constraints (ship date being the biggest one). And most of all it requires managers to stick to the very framework they championed. And my experience has been that even the most talented members of the team can slip and ask, "[I]s this the right answer?" And even the best framing managers will sometimes just feel really strongly about a certain direction. It should be no surprise, but I'm a big fan of managers framing the problem and building constraints, and doing so with the team. I know it is sometimes frustrating for the team ("[P]lease tell us what to do") especially when things are uncertain. I know it is very stressful for me ("[W]ill the product or service be great?"). In the end, smart, creative, and motivated people can do great work within a framework that defines success.

Finally, I am leaving out highly dysfunctional manager phenotypes such as cheerleader, dictator, conductor, micro-manager, sibling, empath, and so on. There are a lot of very bad expressions of management and we all hope not to be one or work for one. I am sure all of us as managers have our moments so folks please keep the feedback coming. Remember, managers are people (human people) too!

What other phenotypes of managers have you run across? Oh and let's stick to balanced types and not dwell on highly dysfunctional phenotypes . . .

—Steven

Managing is not a perfect science. But as with all complicated activities, experience tends to help. Experience provides new perspectives and new approaches, new ways to read people, and new ways to shape their behavior. These perspectives and approaches are captured in the blog as different modes, or "phenotypes," of management behavior. The main ones are manager as coach, friend, referee, shield, answer man (or woman), manager as editor, and manager as framer. The message is that no single perspective is perfect; no single approach solves every problem. This is where every manager in the quest to shape the organization and align strategy with execution should consider multiple ways to work and the full richness of options that are available to fill the gaps between the framework of the plan and the concrete details of the actual situations.

This multitude of perspectives can help the manager not only in working with his or her organization, but also in managing lateral and upward relationships. The perspectives can be thought of as different options for dealing with different challenges, and for connecting the complex web of interactions that makes large companies work well.

Clearly these phenotypes are not always positive contributions to the goal of integrity. The blog mentions as many dysfunctional behaviors as it mentions productive ones. The goal is to recognize each behavior as we perform our own management routines or see them performed by others. As we recognize them, we can better understand them and work toward improving them.

Managing Team Members

As one strives for a match between strategy and execution, for organizational coherence and market fit, it rapidly becomes clear that one of the most important investments is in regular interaction with those that are actually responsible for getting the real work done. Managers regularly underinvest in managing their own organizations. As managers are drawn to meetings with customers, senior executives, partners, suppliers, and recruits, their own direct reports are often left in last place. The following blog expounds a sharply different view. In showing the influence of managers early in Steven's career, this 1995 memo was written by a former general manager in the Office team, Vijay Vashee.

What Makes a Good 1:1 with Your Manager?

I trust everyone had a good holiday break, or for those of you still on break, keep relaxing! For Windows (and IE) and Office folks it is a well-deserved holiday.

As we transition to planning the next release we are also transitioning our management "culture" a bit. One thing I want to emphasize even more (if you aren't doing so already) is an ongoing discussion with your manager about what is important to you, not just the conversation about what is important to your manager. My feeling is that the best way to do this is through a regularly scheduled 1:1 conversation. I prefer that these are weekly (which I do with my reports) and of course I expect ongoing hallway conversations, email, and walk-bys throughout the week as well. Some folks think that you can go every other week or monthly even, but I am not so sure this is best, but I will leave it to you and your manager to work out.

There are many ways to have a one-on-one conversation. I think an important element of them is to have ongoing and thoughtful communication. If you know something isn't going well, then you also know you have a scheduled time to talk about it, be open and honest, and get the information out there (in *old Microsoft* we used to say "good news travels fast, bad news should travel faster"—I still think that should be the case). I would also say that in terms of how well things are going, ongoing feedback about performance is better than after-the-fact or infrequent feedback. Now that is not to say that every week you can chalk up a "[D]id I exceed or achieve this week?" and tally them at the end of the year, but clearly having a good conversation about performance every once in a while is a good idea.

As an aside, the idea of regular conversations with your manager is one of those things we can claim as a competitive advantage relative to the Google's of the world who all say managers should have 50 direct reports and be "flat orgs." I would challenge a manager to even have two 1:1s per year with 50 directs (I know that starting in January I will be scheduling skip-level 1:1s with all the group managers and that is a group of about 100 and it takes some time to work through the team, at least based on past experience).

Over the course of the next year we want to make every effort to improve the *health* of the organization as measured by the yearly poll but more importantly as measured by how people talk about the team with their friends and family. Rather than focus explicitly on trying to manage the health of the organization (which seems rather abstract), our approach will be to improve the attributes that are consistently shown to contribute to a strong software product organization. Past surveys and commentary from employees in manager feedback forms and in exit interviews shows the following to be the most significant positive attributes:

Clear goals and an understanding of the overall mission
Managers that support those goals and help to clear a path to accomplish the goals
Regular one-on-ones with a manager where there is quality feedback and discussion of the goals and mechanisms for achieving them

Through the planning memos and vision process we are putting in place a way for us all to know the overall mission and to know what our goals, at the feature team and individual level, are and how those contribute to the mission. The job of managers is to reinforce the process and provide support when people work within the process, and help people to see where the process can help, while also providing the mentoring and specifics around engineering that make for an environment focused on long-term growth and opportunity. I think we are making progress on (1) and (2) though of course it is very early and I am realistic that the progress is not even or consistent across the team . . . yet.

Item (3) is one we can act on as a team. There are a bunch of books for managers about how to have a good 1:1 conversation between employee and manager. This is a personal choice and one that should be worked out between you and your manager. We all have styles as varied as types of people we are (which is great) and part of establishing a good relationship between you and your manager is to be aware of style differences, strengths and weaknesses, and really working together to figure out what works best. One memo that was written a long time ago by an original member of the Office team named Vijay Vashee* goes into some detail about having good 1:1s. It is just a starting point, but it is worth thinking about as a manager or as a report. I have appended it below and I hope this helps.

This is adapted from a 1995 memo by Vijay Vashee who was the General Manager of PowerPoint at the time written for managers. My hope is sharing it broadly helps both managers, folks who want to be managers, and

---

*There was a time when it seemed like most of the managers in Office had names with alliteration—Vijay Vashee, Lewis Levin, Steven Sinofsky, Peter Pathe, and so on. A pretty funny coincidence. I am reminded of this when I taught a case study on the development of Office and the students all made fun of the org chart because they thought I just made up the names of all my coworkers.

non-managers alike. It is just one view—there are many ways to facilitate ongoing conversations, which is really the spirit of this post.

Why have one-on-ones?

The main purpose of a one-on-one is for the manager and employee to reach a shared understanding of the work environment, project status, technical risks, new opportunities, morale and career development, and a time to share "values." An important part of one-on-ones is for the employee to get consistent and actionable feedback. As managers, however, we can be surprised at any time by project slips, unhappy employees, employees deciding to transfer or leave, untapped employee potential, etc., if we don't take time to speak and listen face-to-face with people on a regular basis. A manager can learn a great deal from a solid exchange of thoughts and feelings during a one-on-one, information that cannot be learned from e-mail, meeting notes, or status reports. Plus through a well-done one-on-one a manager can learn and teach at the same time. One-on-ones are a highly leveraged opportunity for both the manager and employee.

Listen, listen, listen

If there is one thing to keep in mind during a one-on-one it is to listen carefully to what employees are saying, and how they are saying it. If the manager is unsure of something, a feeling or a fact, then be sure to ask questions. If you think you understand, then play back what you just heard to make sure—"So if I understand you correctly . . . "

It is often the case in a one-on-one, just as in life, that people are talking to get something out in the open, but not necessarily to seek a solution or commentary. Watch carefully the reaction to your comments, as sometimes a manager's advice is not really what people are after, but rather just a well-tuned ear.

But I talk to my team every day . . .

We all strive to be visible managers who walk the halls and drop by offices or talk in the hallways. We should all make this a regular part of our daily routine. This is not a substitute for regular one-on-one discussions. As our organization grows this has become more important. In a group of even 30 or 40 people, it can be surprising how hard it is to really know everyone, and in a group of 200 it is tough to even know everyone's name. But through a regular one-on-one with your reports one can spend time learning about all the members of the team. And through skip-level one-on-ones a manager can become even more well-informed.

The key characteristic of a successful one-on-one is that it is a regular occurrence. The best results come from weekly meetings at a set time. It is worth emphasizing that employees definitely notice how many one-on-ones were missed, rescheduled, or just canceled. Schedule around one-on-ones—these are the important meetings of the week. Knowing that a one-on-one is coming allows employees to prepare and arm themselves for a good discussion on issues that concern them or the project, especially issues that do not need immediate attention (such issues that can be resolved over email or by interruption). This preparation is something that is very hard to do in casual encounters or unplanned discussions. If used wisely a one-on-one is a time that can help to reduce other meetings or disruptions that can happen on a daily basis. A one-on-one allows both the manager and employee to plan their time effectively, while assuring a high bandwidth of communication.

Who sets the agenda?

This is really a personal matter between the manager and the employee. It is best for both parties to prepare some discussion points and spend a few moments up front prioritizing those. It is key to allow the employee to own the time and for the manager to respect that, while at the same time the employee should respect that managers sometimes have some issues as well. Some employees like to send an email heads-up with the agenda beforehand, and some managers like to send a heads-up for topics that might need preparation. All of these are fine mechanisms. The key is to discuss the mechanics with each employee and arrive at something that works for both parties.

What should be covered in a one-on-one?

It is generally a good idea to have some sort of "ice breaker" at the start of a one-on-one. Don't just launch into project status. Generally, if you want a person to be open and honest, then you should be as well, so perhaps share something about what is going on in your world at the start of the meeting.

Typically a one-on-one begins, after the agenda is agreed upon, with a discussion about specific problems and situations, as defined by the employee. Generally speaking the manager should leverage this time to teach skills and know-how and suggest ways to approach problems and situations. These types of discussions are where the manager's experience can help and where the manager should be careful to listen carefully to what is not being said—is this a source of real trouble and concern or is the employee "venting" or just informing? One area that is always good to probe is to work to see where things will go wrong. The manager's experience can help to identify the boundary conditions or the challenges with the issues at hand. Experience can help to see where too much effort is being invested or where efforts are going on too early. The one-on-one is also a good time to discuss any recent major events in the group or team—perhaps doing a mini-postmortem.

Finally, it is always important to provide specific feedback on accomplishments and the one-on-one is a good forum for doing so, if you are unable to provide immediate feedback. The best feedback is always specific and done in person.

How often should a one-on-one take place?

One-on-ones should take place during a regularly scheduled weekly meeting. There is always some debate over whether senior employees can "get by" with less frequent meetings; I disagree with this and would encourage managers to meet weekly with every report, even the most senior people with whom you have worked with for years.

Out of convention, most one-on-ones take place in the manager's office. Don't be afraid to break this convention and meet in the employee's office. This is especially helpful for new employees as it reduces the feeling of being "called to the carpet." Also for new employees (not necessarily new to Microsoft, but new to the organization), meeting in their office provides the manager a chance to learn something about the person by talking about their office's personality.

Finally, a good one-on-one is a solid block of uninterrupted time. Everyone should make sure computer screens are not distracting, and that the phone goes unanswered, that the door is closed so others do not disturb the meeting, etc. Nothing is more frustrating to an employee than to be sitting in a one-on-one with the feeling of "who did I lose out to?" when the phone rings or someone interrupts.

What is the role of the manager?

The manager should facilitate the flow of information from the employee, especially if things are troublesome or difficult ("bad news"). Essentially, the manager is trying to create an environment where the challenging issues are surfaced so that they can be dealt with in a timely manner, or at the very least brought out on to the table. One way to accomplish this is to apply Andy Grove's principal of "ask one more question!" When the manager thinks that the employee has said all there is to say on a topic, then the manager's role is to ask one more question. The manager is also there to learn and to coach. In order to learn, one needs to be an effective active listener so that the problems, issues, and frame of mind of the employee are all well understood. Listening is hard and we can all work to listen better. Once you understand the problem, your role as a coach can begin. Being a coach can mean offering advice, providing encouragement, telling a story, or just listening some more—don't do too much of one of those since they all have their time and place. Never forget that sometimes people just want to be heard.

One-on-ones are about discussing progress on careers and on projects. In order to track progress we use metrics. So the one-on-one should generally be a discussion about those metrics. Together you can choose to discuss the review objectives or something as common as the development schedule. But in general, having those metrics and reviewing them at the one-on-one is a critical use of the time for both the manager and the employee. When new measures or commitments arise during a one-on-one, it is important to be very clear on the commitment. For example, if the manager writes down a date or promises to send mail, then the employee should be writing down the same date or waiting for the e-mail. Follow-through by both parties on these new commitments is important to the project, but also important to the integrity of the relationship and the one-on-one.

Investment

It is important that one-on-ones be viewed as a strategic investment, not a burden or a chore. One way to think of this is that if together you can have a very valuable one-on-one that takes only an hour a week, and enhances the effectiveness of an employee, improves the quality of their work, or just makes them enjoy their jobs, then the one-hour investment is well worth it. As managers, the rewards for good management are sometimes hard to quantify, but we know that when employee survey results come out, the quality just behind clear goals that matters the most to people is having a great experience with their direct manager. Let's make this investment pay off for everyone!

Ten Tips for Good One-On-Ones

1. Hold a regularly scheduled weekly one-on-one with every direct report.
2. Set aside 60 minutes of uninterrupted time. Turn off any email notifications and minimize all the windows on your PC or turn off the monitor. Do not take phone calls or futz with your mobile phone.
3. Be hardcore about keeping the scheduled time. Blowing off a one-on-one or canceling them frequently sends the message that one party has other priorities.
4. Offer to meet in the employee's office to put them at ease, especially for new employees.
5. Each party should have an informal agenda of 5–7 items that he/she wishes to discuss. At the start of the meeting merge the list and prioritize. Try to have time for all of the employee's issues and the most important issues the manager brings.
6. Discuss progress and obstacles on key objectives. For each meeting, have a "message" that you wish to send about those objectives. Take good notes for your benefit but also to visibly show that you are listening.
7. Ask and listen, rather than tell and sell.
8. Take time to ask them how they are feeling about their work—what is working and what is not working.
9. Remember to always ask "one more question" about things. Remember, the manager's role is to reduce confusion, rather than increase it.
10. In every one-on-one give the employee something—a word of encouragement, an idea, a decision, or a correction that will increase their effectiveness until their next one-on-one.

The manager's job is an active job. The blog provides a good account of the amount of work and care it takes to align an organization and make it contribute effectively toward its strategic goals. Achieving transparency of communication is essential, and the blog shows a glimpse of how such transparency can be achieved in practice. Naturally, the 1:1 meetings are just one example—one instance of the managerial behavior needed to reinforce and expand on the progress of the team. Beyond the 1:1 meetings, managers are encouraged to engage with team members in a variety of other ways, such as walking the halls, responding to e-mail, and engaging in technical and strategic discussions.

Managing Windows

To get an even more concrete feeling for the manager's role in shaping strategic integrity, the following two blogs focus on Steven's own approach. The first shows how he allocates his time during one week. The second aggregates time allocation during all of 2007. Beyond the specifics of time allocation the two blogs give away an unusually clear perspective on Steven's own leadership and management style. The blogs were written partly in response to the e-mail below, which was included in the original post.

> **From:** Mak Agashe
> **Sent:** Monday, March 12, 2007 11:19 PM
> **To:** Steven Sinofsky
> **Subject:** time
>
> Hi Steven, do you mind if I ask you how you manage your time? You are always very responsive to emails (not just mine but many others from the team). You write memos to blogs, etc. Of course there are many other things that won't be visible to me.
>
> I have always believed that "it is not about working hard but about how you spend your time that makes a person effective." But I haven't quite figured it out.

Where Does All the Time Go? A Week in the Life . . .

[Above] you will see a question I got from Mak regarding how I spend my day—he also pays me a nice complement, which I appreciate. While I consider this blog to be more of the "WWL Management" blog than I do my personal place to share, this seems like a good question. I bet it is sort of a mystery to people ;-).

I often use the analogy of a school with regard to how things are structured—everyone knows what the teachers do, what the students do, and what a few of the deans or other faculty do. But people really always wonder, "[W]hat does the principal do all day?" and I definitely had no idea what went on at all those meetings at the county school board. So as one of 100 execs, what does my week look like?

I try to structure my "calendar" such that I maximize the amount of time I spend with the team and working on software. As a general rule, I formally allocate about half the work week and leave the rest of the time free to roam the halls and talk to people as well as to have longer conversations that were not planned.

I am not a big fan of long meetings reviewing things that could best be done in email, especially things that are not customer facing (budgets, for example). I do manage my own calendar, which I recognize is a bit of an anomaly. I generally don't move meetings around and avoid schedule gymnastics—I find that just keeps our awesome administrative staff away from the hard work of helping keep our finances and people resources on track and does little for our own operating efficiency.

As blogged about, I am a big believer in 1:1s so I schedule a weekly 1:1 with each direct report (at their office). I also do skip levels (the dev managers, test managers, and group program managers . . . at their office)—with about 70 of you on the team it takes a while to complete the cycle. We have a weekly staff meeting where we work on operational and cross-team issues (especially people, recruiting, and company-wide strategy discussions). Although not on the sample below, we have {dev | test | pm} manager lunches where we get together as a discipline leadership group. And every few months we have an all-group manager meeting (the wwlgm DL).

Of course I meet with customers, press, partners, and so on depending on where we are in the product cycle. I always make it a practice to write up my notes after meetings with external folks and with members of our dev team (in fact, I always write up notes after trips and other "data collection" opportunities, and strongly encourage everyone on the team to do so).

And I meet with my manager as well as the staff functions that support WWL (finance, recruiting, hr, legal). He has cross-group meetings as well (some larger, some P&L based, and so on).

Probably the most "not-normal" thing about a typical week is that there aren't a lot of "product reviews"—there are almost none. We've talked a lot about empowerment and rigor in planning, so my view is that decisions are made by product leaders during the normal routine of the planning process. We will have checkpoint meetings where the decisions made are summarized and presented, but those will happen as part of the normal routine of the planning process. We have a lot of offsites and other planning meetings where I attend as an equal participant if the team feels I will help out. But I have found that ad hoc communication and being part of the process is what works best for me. Every once in a while we will have topical meetings or get together because a particular topic crosses many domains and teams. But the norm is to focus my input on the planning framework and memos and make sure the leaders of the team have any information or inputs I have so they can make informed decisions on their own timelines.

As a general rule, probably the principle I try to adhere to the most is to *avoid being a roadblock and to keep the rhythm of the team moving*. It is why I focus on being available ad hoc, not waiting for formal meetings, and also keep email moving quickly. I feel that if people are waiting on me, then I am one person holding up a larger group and I am slowing down our team. So when I receive flattering comments like the ones from Mak, I appreciate them but I also think it is a basic thing I need to do in my job.

Last week was a pretty typical week so here are the details of my schedule for one week with some [annotations]. This week might be a little light on scheduled time, but many new people just moved into building 50 so I have been chatting with a lot of neighbors. Note that I do not record my unscheduled time after the fact—perhaps something I should consider. I also do not "count" email and blogging time :-). Also worth noting is that I travel to RedWest and main campus for 1:1s, as I think that gives me a chance to see folks in their hallways in other buildings.

-----Monday, March 05, 2007-----
Employee 1:1
10:00 AM–11:00 AM [Employee 1:1 requested]
Virtual Machines as a Service—roaming them and also running them in the cloud
1:00 PM–2:30 PM [Product Development Discussion, including CSA staff]
1:1 Steven / Mike Nash
4:00 PM–5:00 PM [Product Management]

-----Tuesday, March 06, 2007-----
The TC meeting with S. Sinofsky
10:00 AM–10:00 AM [Legal obligation]
ChrisJo/SteveSi 1:1
11:00 AM–12:00 PM [Direct report 1:1]
Arthurdh/SteveSi 1:1
1:00 PM–2:00 PM [Direct report 1:1]
Ando-san/Steven----Sony Prep
4:00 PM–5:00 PM [Prepare with OEM team for customer visit]

-----Wednesday, March 07, 2007-----
Personal
9:00 AM–11:00 AM
WinHEC----Checkpoint #1
11:00 AM–12:00 PM [Partner with COSD on WinHEC, led by JawadK]
Updated: OEM Next Windows Planning Sync-up Meeting
1:00 PM–3:00 PM [Customer Meeting]
WWL Staff Meeting
4:00 PM–5:00 PM [Direct Reports staff meeting]
Speak at UW Recruiting
6:00 PM–9:00 PM [College recruiting event]

-----Thursday, March 08, 2007-----
DHach/SteveSi 1:1
10:00 AM–11:00 AM [Direct report 1:1]
JulieLar/SteveSi 1:1
11:00 AM–12:00 PM [Direct report 1:1]
AlešH/SteveSi 1:1
2:00 PM–3:00 PM [Direct report 1:1]

-----Friday, March 09, 2007-----
Personal
9:00 AM–11:00 AM
Ian LeGrow/SteveSi 1:1
2:00 PM–3:00 PM [Skip-level GPM 1:1]
Kristend/SteveSi 1:1
3:00 PM–4:00 PM [WWL HR generalist 1:1, alternates with 1:1 with College Recruiting]

Oh as long as we are sharing my personal work style :-). I use a Windows Mobile phone and basically use it only for email (across my personal domain and corporate) and make extensive use of the WL software for local and services (I am running the WM 6 beta). I run a Small Business Server R2 network at home (sinofsky.org) and use a live domain for email (sinofsky.com). It has 1.5TB of raided storage that I backup to two different locations in our home. At any given time we have 4 or 5 machines domain joined running offline files (mostly Vista Ultimate, with 2 XP machines), including a Vista Ultimate machine connected to a directv stb [set-top box]. I record things off of that and play them on an Archos at the PRO Club where I see many folks most nights :-). I have SDSL and a backup connection with ClearWire (way cool!). Essentially all of my computing and communications gear at home and work is personal, which makes it easier to swap out and try new things. I don't accept any free equipment from IHVs or OEMs (anything forced on me goes straight to the labs). Oh, and I have a detailed service level agreement at home that requires me to keep our home PCs/network running, secure, and up to date :-).

Addition—the service level agreement is between me and the rest of our home. I am the sysadmin for all the devices and PCs. Any requests for helpdesk are done through an internal website that is designed to make sure those requests are with *merit* :-).

—Steven

How I Spent FY07—Time Allocation Summary

With everyone getting their commitments done and thinking about the next year, I thought I'd offer a quick report on where the time went this past year for me. In a previous post I offered a look at a typical day and overall the "philosophy" for how time is allocated. This offers a look at the past year.

I use Outlook and do my own calendar. The only trick I use to track this data is that I use Outlook categories on appointments. And then I periodically do a report using an Excel VBA macro that just exports appointments to a worksheet where I then just pivot the results. I do not have a ton of categories and so really this is about getting an approximate view of the overall effort in the areas that I think are key to track. Any single appointment has only one category even if it might apply to more, and I just try to consistently apply a double-secret algorithm for tracking purposes.

The baseline for this is a 2000-hour year. That's about what a really good first-year lawyer does in billable hours, or so I read once. Over the past years as a general manager, I have found that having about 50% unstructured time works best. This is time where I do whacky stuff like this blog, email, [walk] around the hallways, and so on. What I don't do, which some folks I know do, is go back and categorize how I spend this unstructured time. So if I stop by your office because you sent me mail, I don't go back and add that 30 minutes to my calendar. What I do is look at how I spend structured time. This is primarily because I worry about spending too much time in meetings, traveling, etc. and because I want to make sure I am spending enough time with direct reports, skip level, team meetings, and other places where I think (I hope) I am in a unique position to at least be a positive helper. I don't track holidays, sick days, [and] vacation but those are all in the unstructured time.

As a reminder, for regularly scheduled meetings I work really hard not to have ripple effect scheduling gymnastics, so if something comes up for any of the parties we just skip the meeting (for 1:1s) or meet without those that can't attend.

The categories for me are:

- **1:1 w/directs.** These are 1-hour meetings which are scheduled for every week as per What makes a good 1:1 with your manager? This also includes a weekly meeting where we get together as a team. It is worth noting that I think my directs get together without me once a week as well to make sure that they are doing enough to "middle integrate."
- **1:1 w/peers and exstaff** [executive staff]. These are 1-hour meetings that are either recurring (with folks like billv or jonde) or come up for topical discussions or less frequently but sort of recurring. I think of these as "middle integration" across my peer group.
- **1:1 w/skip levels.** These are 1-hour meetings with the group managers, which is for the most part the direct reports of my direct reports. I try to make it through the whole team each fiscal year.
- **China.** China holds a very special place in my heart (after working on Chinese features for Office for a long time and also living there in 2004) and so as the executive sponsor I make sure to spend some time on issues specific to China.
- **Corporate.** Previously I talked about the corporate planning calendar, so this category includes all of these efforts. Another way I think about these meetings is "any meeting with SteveB."

- **CSA.** I separate out the time spent with our CSAs, [Chief Software Architect] as I think that is an important part of my job and just want to make sure I am doing this enough.
- **Exec sponsor.** Our corporate accounts like to have executive sponsors and this time is the time spent with my current account.
- **External product mgmt/PR.** This time includes press interviews, prep for press interviews, working with product management when I can help with the message, and so on.
- **Korea.** Korea continues to be a big business opportunity for Microsoft, both in online services and for Windows. As a company we have a group that is sort of a group sponsor for Korea representing these opportunities and we meet about these topics.
- **LCA** [Law and Corporate Affairs]**.** Patents, intellectual property, contracts, and compliance are some legal issues that I think are an important part of my job as well.
- **Mentor.** I formally mentor a couple of individuals and this is accounted for in this category.
- **My manager/corporate prep.** I also have 1:1s and staff meetings to go to that my manager convenes. I include in this bucket all the time to prepare for the corporate calendar, as most of the preparation time is driven by my manager. This way I can track the full cost of the corporate calendar.
- **OEM and IHV.** Obviously a big part of working on Windows is the OEM and IHV community. This includes meeting with them as groups or individually. For example, when we have our OEM planning forum I meet with each of the customers that are here, or when I go to Asia and meet with OEMs I include these meetings as well.
- **People management.** Obviously I spend a lot of time meeting with members of the team and also working with human resources (I have a biweekly meeting with our generalist, meeting with college recruiting). This includes all the human resources programmatic work as well.
- **Presentations/team mtgs.** This work is where I am generally a speaker before a group—a team internally, MVPs, interns, etc.
- **Product development.** This of course includes all the work for planning a release and my involvement in the planning and features. Primarily for the past year this is all in forums where I was one of many participants, such as our planning offsites and checkpoints for M1.

- **Travel/conferences.** This item includes conferences such as CES that I attend. I do not include the travel time, which is probably a mistake, especially for international. Often when I travel I just categorize the whole trip here rather than provide an extra level of detail (with the exception of OEM meetings). For example, in India in November, I will have some presentations, some product meetings, and some skip level meetings, but I will likely count the 2 full workdays there as 16 hours.

So if I add all this up for FY07, it is about 1,239 hours, which is a 62% structured time. That's a bit higher than I have historically had, but I am also still in a new role and we've had a lot of planning work going on. I think I will have less structured time this next year. I also will have more travel, as I am returning to focusing on those outside efforts as well.

One caveat, I'm just a normal user and so Outlook sometimes corrupts recurring meetings and that throws off things occasionally. I sanity check and correct things. Again, the goal is not to survive an audit, but to provide some general guidance on time management.

[Exhibit 7.1] is for FY07 (July 1–June 30) and the numbers are hours of the 1,239 structured hours.

—Steven

If organizations mirror themselves in the output of their work, leaders mirror themselves in their own organizations. The blogs above speak for themselves. The investment in individual meetings, the coaching, the openness, the lack of formal reviews, the clarity and transparency, the open-door policies, and the informal interactions all point to a certain management style and approach that gets reflected into the organization—an organization that is effective at achieving coherence and alignment, integration and technical depth, transparency, and responsiveness.

The descriptions of managerial behavior in this chapter complement the discussion of organizational process and structure that was presented in Chapter 6. The behaviors discussed do more than just guide tasks and actions. They foster a value system for decision making that builds capability over time and grooms individual contributors to themselves drive toward strategic integrity. The next chapter focuses on decision-making value systems, which make up the third driver of the framework.

Notes

1. See, for example, J. Galbraith, D. Downey, and A. Kates, *Designing Dynamic Organizations* (New York: AMACOM Books, 2002).
2. Link to Steven Sinofsky, "The path to GM—Some thoughts on becoming a general manager," *Steven Sinofsky's Microsoft TechTalk,* September 18, 2008, http://blogs.msdn.com/techtalk/archive/2005/09/18/471121.aspx.
3. Link to Chris Pratley, "OneNote genesis," Chris Pratley's Office Labs and OneNote Blog, http://blogs.msdn.com/chris_pratley/archive/2004/01/30/64898.aspx.

Chapter 8

Decision Making and Value Systems

The effectiveness of any strategy is shaped by the myriad deci-sions that mold its execution.

A major project aggregates millions of decisions made by thousands of people, like the size of a Taskbar icon, the programming interface to a hardware device, or the organization of the new JumpList feature in Windows 7. How do you mold this many different contribu-tions into a coherent outcome?

A few years back, executives in a U.S. auto company engaged in a systematic attempt to increase the perceived value and image of one of their brands, explicitly targeting BMW. They hired marketing experts and engaged with new advertising firms, management consultants, and designers. They engaged in extensive strategy development sessions, training workshops, informal discussions, and redesigned their portfolio of products. They made many specific changes, including introducing a completely redesigned car to specifically communicate the changed image and brand values focused on "sports luxury." When a customer saw this flagship car, opened the door, and sat down to drive, the first thing in his or her field of vision was a very prominent screw head, situ-ated on the pillar that connects the roof to the hood. (This is known in the trade as an "open screw on the A pillar.") Some engineer in the development project had decided that to save a small fraction of a cent in product cost, the screw would not be covered by a plastic cap. The open screw completely broke with the attempt to communicate luxury and destroyed the integrity of the car's design. As a result of this and other similar issues, the car communicated a low-end image, and the hundreds of millions of dollars spent on the new marketing and design campaign were, essentially, wasted.

The objective of decision-making value systems is to have more features like the JumpLists and "Aero shake" in Windows 7 that truly fit the concept of the product and avoid the things like "open screw on the A pillar," and the millions of other possible decision that can impair the integrity of the final outcome. From the myriad design details that define the style and image of a car, to the vast number of choices in designing a complex software product, countless decisions will define the real impact of any major strategic initiative. The pattern formed by these decisions will *de facto* define the strategy of an organization and drive its actual performance. To implement a strategy with high integrity, the decisions must be made consistently, and build to a coherent outcome.

The different pillars of the participatory strategy framework form what is in essence a system for decision making, and for aligning decisions to build a coherent strategy. The framework encourages managers to set up the right organizational capabilities. It continues by engaging the entire organization in an extensive strategy development process, which defines a clear, shared plan, which includes well-defined user scenarios, which the organization can use to drive toward convergence. However, a great plan and the right organizational capabilities are still not enough. Managers and individual contributors will need to make millions of decisions that are not fully specified by the plan, and tackle uncertain or ambiguous problems. The participatory strategy framework therefore needs its third driver, which establishes key decision-making values. These values provide decision-making foundations that guide the many individual decisions in a project towards a high-integrity outcome. They reinforce the other drivers in the framework and fill in the many voids where plan and organization can't provide complete guidance.

This chapter describes five perspectives on decision-making values that are important in driving integrity. These are accountability, system focus, quality and completeness, measurement and validation, and learning.

Accountable Decision Making

Who was accountable for the open screw on the A pillar? The first blog of this chapter addresses empowerment, delegation, and accountability. While the plan and the organization ultimately define who makes which decisions, the relationship between empowerment, delegation, and accountability defines the feedback loop that is so important to provide the right incentives and achieve alignment.

Accountability Jujitsu—Delegation and Empowerment

Accountability is an easy word to use and it seems we all have a good idea of what it means, but one of the downsides of emphasizing accountability is that an organization (and the folks in it) run the risk of becoming good at using accountability as a tool to avoid accountability. As tricky as it sounds there [are] elements in the direction of goodness and elements not in the direction of goodness in how accountability works between someone and their manager. Two tools that come into play in this regard are delegation and empowerment. They are the necessary tools of management and scale, and also the best tools to call on when someone wants to duck accountability. Go figure.

A few rhetorical questions:

- When does making a mistake become an instance of unclear goals?
- When does being closely managed cross over into being micromanaged?
- When does being empowered to get something done turn into a random feature?
- When is a manager responsible for the outcome and when is the individual responsible for the outcome?
- When things go well is it always because of individual work? When things go less well is it always because of management?

We've all encountered these questions and during review time we're likely to dwell on them quite a bit. That's a good thing because to learn we need to reflect, analyze, and draw actionable conclusions. The reality is that these situations are not so clear cut and what we really want to aspire to as a team is a shared view of accountability, not a model where we put effort into finding fault. The effort goes into understanding how to avoid a repeat situation.

From a management perspective, the challenge is always going to be one of being responsible for more work than you can actually do. That's what management is. At its best, management is a force multiplier—one manager and 5 reports focused on a problem get more done than 6 individuals without clear direction. At its worse, management drains our productivity. As we've talked about before doing your part to be one who can be managed is super important, critical, to the success of a manager-managed relationship.

The key task of a lead or manager is to figure out which work gets done by which folks on the team. The two tools for doing this are delegation and empowerment. Both are critical. Both can be misused.

Delegation is when a manager wants (or is asked) to get something done and then asks someone else on the team to do the work. Sometimes the image of "please step forward if you volunteer" pops into my head. Other times the image is "pick me, pick me." The two sides of delegation appear (volunteering vs. volunteered). Relative to being successful though, a manager needs to make a call as to whether delegating something is (a) necessary for the success of the project (does it need to be done at all) and (b) whether it helps a person really get their primary work done. Members of a team are not "staff" for a manager or lead—that is, they are not there to get done a bunch of stuff not relevant to the code that ships in the product. On the other hand everyone knows that there are things that need to get done for the project as a whole. Being selective in delegating and being clear on how it relates to success are very important. My personal view is that management is there to maintain focus, not to contribute to de-focusing. And employees are there to make the job of being a manager easier so asking how they can help is the other side of the coin.

Assuming something is delegated, then we need to understand how accountability works. When it comes to accountability, without a clear view of what success looks like or why a certain work item is being delegated, delegation becomes an accountability nightmare. A manager who delegates has an immediate response to any query about the work: "I asked so and so to jump on that." Zoom, problem routed away. On the other hand, if something is delegated to you then the immediate response can also be, "I was asked but I have no idea what my manager is thinking." Bam, nothing gets done.

Yet as an organization we are collectively accountable for getting work done. There's no metric, no scorecard, no review meetings that can make this work at scale with the ambiguities of new product development. What makes this work is a collective view of success. We have these tools in the vision, specs, quality goals, exit criteria, and so on. But to just delegate something does not relieve you as a manager of accountability or to be asked to do something does not just make it another unclear activity for your boss. There's a purpose to (most) everything. That's the fine print of managing delegation and being managed.

Empowerment is the individual flip side of delegation. Where every manager views delegating things, every individual clearly wants to be empowered. Of course has anyone ever met a manager who doesn't claim to empower? Ever met an individual who doesn't want to be empowered? Empowerment is great. But it too has the potential to be an accountability tar pit.

Empowerment is when you are given the right or authority to get something done. Managers give you that right in the form of an agreement (or commitments). You seek out that right because then, as we often say, management gets out of the way so you can get your job done. That's all good. We want less overhead and more work.

For our projects, where we are doing things at massive scale and complexity, the question is what is "it" that we want to get done? How much ambiguity is there in the "ask"? How specific are we in the details of the "mechanism" or the outcome? We don't say, "[W]rite some code." But we also don't say, "[Y]ou have been allocated 5000 lines of code to do these 5 precise things." The two-way conversation between an individual and a manager is not just upfront, but an ongoing conversation about what is getting done and how it is getting done. There's that fine line between being managed and micro-managed.

With empowerment we have an accountability challenge similar to delegation. When something isn't going well, my least favorite answer from a manager is "I empowered folks." What does that mean? What is empowerment without oversight? What's your role in all this? Did you empower folks on the team to do dumb things? Of course not. So if the end result wasn't what we hoped, and you knew about [it], then what happened? If you didn't know about it, then what was going on? Empowerment does not excuse results we don't want.

And from an individual's perspective, being empowered is not a free ride to write any code you want. We empower members of the team to be creative and use their energies to create a holistic experience and a product that works for customers. Knowing something is good/cool/neat on an absolute scale does not mean it has those qualities relative to the product we want to create as a team. This particular conversation is one that always reminds me of why *The Fountainhead* is a universal favorite among us product development (also a cool movie). The challenge between you and your manager though is deciding upfront the framework for success. An important part of being empowered is knowing the context of the work you are doing—what are the connections and relationships with other features and technologies or the project tenets (no one was empowered to be incompatible with Vista, or to build services that don't scale, for example).

I would definitely argue (defend) that the bottom-up nature of the vision process, the feature set, and the overall planning and execution of releases is the most empowering process we have at the company for developing our products. Yet our challenge as a team is balancing empowerment with a shared set of goals for a product as a whole, and more importantly making sure that empowerment does not become a tool to avoid accountability.

When I talk to folks on the team, I listen for the use of empower and delegate. I look at the body language. To me accountability is the reality that delegation and empowerment are tools for both managers and individuals to embrace accountability, not techniques to avoid the same.

—Steven

PS: Obviously for this post, substitute write specs, develop tests, and so on for "write code."

Empowerment and delegation are critical management tools, particularly when one is striving for coherence as part of a major effort. But without accountability, empowerment and delegation will not work. You cannot empower an engineer to make a decision without having accountability placed in the same hands. However, a manager should not delegate a decision to an engineer without sharing accountability for the outcome, as was obviously the case with the open screw decision in the car example at the beginning of the chapter. Accountability is important because it creates the appropriate decision-making feedback loops, so that the outcome of individual decisions is tied back to the individuals that drove it. Without feedback, leading an organization seems more like "ready, fire, aim" rather than "ready, aim, fire." A system without feedback is almost impossible to steer toward any type of convergence especially when the environment is a complex adaptive system—like a ship maneuvering in a packed harbor in a storm with its pilot blindfolded.

Empowerment, delegation, and accountability are important to create a clear feedback loop that encourages coherence in decision making. The essence is simple. You are accountable for what you decide. And if you don't have the right capabilities and resources to decide, make sure you find someone who does and who can then share accountability for that decision with you. In this system, decision makers have clear roles and clear responsibilities. These define what decision makers are accountable for, what they are empowered to do, and how they may delegate, making sure that the feedback loops that are created ensure that commitments are made in a consistent fashion.

System-Focused Decision Making

Why is it so easy to make decisions that impair the integrity of the entire product? The second element of the decision-making value system focuses on *how* decisions are made and emphasizes the importance of systemic thinking. Conversation No. 37 is about making trade-offs, which should always be acknowledged and handled without losing sight of the bigger picture. As you read this post, consider the perception some have had of the Windows Vista product combined with the pressure to release a new product.

In Chapter 3, we saw how the trade-offs encountered at the later stages of a project are the norm but must be recognized throughout the organization for effective decisions to be made. Projects inevitably face the constraints of time to market, features, and quality. These are not trade-offs that can be made or decided at the top of an organization with any degree of efficacy, as the information to make good choices is much closer to the work. The goal of having this dialog is to ensure that all members of the team appreciate the subtly and nuance associated with the late stages of a product and to push accountability to interpreting those choices to those with the most information.

Conversation No. 37

Software projects have three primary technical attributes: feature set, ship date, and quality. The question (or demand) that arises at various points of a product cycle is "[T]ell me which one to optimize for." It should be no surprise, but I think we can do better than raise this question. We all know the answer—we deliver on the plan, deliver on time, and ship with ever-improving quality. I don't mean to make your head explode by asking for too much, and so the trick is how do we really pull this off?

No discussion tests the capability and accountability of a dev team more than this discussion. Anyone can be part of (or run) a dev team that always ships on time, so long as the products are low quality or featureless. Anyone can keep a scheduling going for eternity to get the quality just right or to have each and every last feature. These approaches to product development are not helpful or interesting. What we expect from our group managers is an ability to navigate this complex topic with aplomb, and not to focus on assigning blame or presenting the obvious intractable debate. The key reason for this is that the plans were the work product of this very group of people—there is not a second set of books with bonus features, a different schedule, or separate release criteria. By virtue of going through the process of creating a team vision we have together arrived not just at the plan, but the clear accountabilities of the plan.

Of course nothing is perfect. So the real test of the team is not in just having a nice plan, but how we deal with the challenges that come up during the execution. What features do we prioritize/de-prioritize? What do we do if integration work is not working? How do we deal with the unanticipated workload for servicing an in-market release? There are no magic answers, but for sure the best way to solve this is not to throw up your hands and ask management to decide among options that are inherently interrelated. The best option is to work across the disciplines and with partners and arrive at a "globally optimum" solution, one which you are the very best to gauge and the very best to execute on.

At the start of a project cycle we are generally focused on the feature-set. So we quickly arrive at a list of features that we intend to develop. Then we start to think about the schedule and we realize we bit off more than we can chew. So we iterate. We have a framework for the products and services we wish to create and we have a time horizon we wish to complete the project. So we can work our way down the funnel and get to a plan that delivers on the spirit of the features (measured via scenarios) in the timeline we want. If we simply can't do so, then we scale back our aspirations at this point in the planning cycle, before we start to ship. Eventually we get to a set of features we have confidence in completing in the timeframe we have.

Here is the first rub. Any good dev manager will be saying, "[S]how me the specs and then we can see the schedule." Of course the specs don't quite exist yet because it was only moments ago we arrived at the feature set, in the course of our discussions. But we have also had a lot of discussions about the scenario and what we expect the end-state to be like. What we need is program management to be well-versed in the dimensions of the scenario, to have a view for how the scenario can be scaled, and be ready to keep the discussions going. We need development to be flexible and able to deal with the uncertainty. One of the primary ways we do this is by having multiple milestones in the project and being hardcore about not scheduling out the last milestone, which if this is a three milestone project allows for a 30% buffer in schedule time. The key step in getting past this phase of the project is development getting comfortable with the reality that we can't know what we don't yet know. If you watch a lot of home remodel shows on *DIY* [*Network*], then you know this is like not knowing what is hiding behind the drywall and yet the family will be back from their weekend at Disney Land in 48 hours so let's figure out how to be flexible. The key at this point is we have locked on features and we have locked on the date.

As we progress through milestones it is going to become clear that we cannot get everything done that we need. That's a given. We are going to have to start cutting features. That is always tough. We've talked before about how having a prioritized list of features doesn't help here, and it sure doesn't. The reason is obviously because we don't know where the problems will be and they turn out not to occur in reverse priority order. So at this point it is important for dev, test, [and] pm to work together to understand the problem area, understand the options for "backfill," which can mean changing the architecture, reducing the surface area of impact, altering the scenario, or any number of other options. And yes this can include cutting the whole feature.

That last option is where the vision really comes into play. Many will notice that the vision is never a catalog of every work item on the project. This is in a sense by design. The vision outlines the key scenarios we plan on delivering. Of course there are always supporting features, necessary features, and so on. The vision captures the soul of the project. That means, if the place we're having trouble is in the vision, then cutting it is a big decision. It needs to be one thought about globally. It means if you have the option of cutting things not in the vision that's where to start. What do we get if [we] cut the feature—do we gain certainty in the shipdate that we didn't have before? Do we gain a level of quality in other scenarios we didn't have before? Do we pick up a level of completeness in features we didn't have before? Having answers with certainty is critical to being able to make this decision. Remember, Cutting Is Shipping [from a blog post in Chapter 3]. But cutting the wrong things is failing to meet commitments. The key decision-making tool we have is the vision—it helps us all to stay on the same page.

If making the schedule work at the start is hard for development, then cutting features in the middle is where program management feels the big squeeze. Where does test feel the pressure? As the project winds down, of course.

As we get close to code complete or beta—basically, as we get to where we are done adding scheduled work—test starts to look at the work list and is likely to start to feel that the runway is not long enough. As with the feelings around the initial schedule or feature list, these feelings are to be expected and perfectly rational. At the same time we have tools at our disposal to manage through this and meet our commitments to the release. One thing I know for sure is that no project I've ever worked on has been gated by pure testing—that's something our test organization should be proud of. All through the cycle, test has a voice and needs to raise issues and complexities before they become end of cycle issues. During spec inspections, for example, it is important to point out boundary cases, compatibility issues, and so on and to build those issues into the dev schedule (not just rely on more testing) or drive changes to the feature to take those into account. A nice example I remember, that seemed intractable at the time, was validating the Office 2007 Open XML file format and the migration to that format. While lots has been discussed about the new user interface in Office 2007, from a compatibility, test matrix, and third-party complexity, the file format has always proven to be an even thornier set of problems. What test did to execute on this (after all, this is a pretty binary feature [no pun intended] since you can't really scale back a file format or cut it at the last minute) was work hard with dev to schedule the work well up front and work with PM on the whole down-level, backward compat experience. The result was a transition that went with unparalleled smoothness, and given the sales of Office 2007 we can really say this was a great example of using the tools available to front load the work, manage the schedule, and avoid the tyranny of end of cycle pain.

Hopefully it is clear that each discipline sees that the other disciplines face the challenge of how to deal with the three project attributes at any given time. How does the process break down and why do we get to points during the project where we seem to be stuck? My experience has been when one part of the triad of disciplines digs in their heels in the uniquely discipline-specific way ("stereotype" for the discipline). That happens. Sometimes it is justified. But most of the time I think stepping back, seeing that this is a complex system with many opportunities to optimize and work together is the best bet.

We know what these stereotypes are. No one likes a program manager that can't figure out where to scale back—program management needs to develop scalable features and scenarios, as that is the only way to engineer a complex project. No one likes a dev manager that is so conservative about dealing with the unknown that a 6-week milestone turns into 5 scheduled days of coding—development needs to be appropriately bold in scheduling work and to do so based on a shared understanding of how the features will be implemented. No one likes a test manager who says we need a whole other beta to know the quality—these are broad statements that need more specifics and once we know the specifics we can get out of the realm of gut feel and then focus on how to mitigate concerns in specific areas. For each of these, there are elements of leadership and elements of working together across teams. From an organizational perspective, I hope folks can see the value of driving consensus across dev, test, [and] pm rather than just looking "up" for a tie-breaking vote from someone removed from the specifics of the challenge. My experience is that we get much better results when we stay focused on our engineering and product goals with the right technical folks on the team making empowered decisions within the framework we committed to deliver.

At each step in the product cycle we are challenged to deliver on the vision. That is precisely what we are paid to do as engineers. Our customers expect nothing less than a coherent and useful set of features, delivered on a predictable schedule, and delivered with the right quality.

Proposing these as mutually exclusive simply isn't an option. Our goal is to have a process coupled with unparalleled accountability to allow us to achieve these objectives.

This is tough. Customers pay us a bunch to work through these challenges. I'm confident we have the capabilities and accountabilities in place to "do the right thing" and get the right features out to customers on time and with amazing quality.

—Steven

PS: Some folks might wonder about the title of this post. After having this conversation more times that we could count, in Office we decided as soon as we would start to slip into having the "are we date driven or feature driven" or "are we quality driven or date driven" conversation we would just use *Conversation 37* as a shorthand. And of course that is itself a reference to a folklore regarding conversations between leaders of Microsoft and IBM when OS/2 was being developed :-).

Conversation 37 is about the common trade-offs encountered in every project: time, scope, and quality. The challenge of delivering on the vision, as articulated in the shared plan, inevitably runs into the real limitations defined by limited time and resources, aggravated by technical surprises, market changes, and shifting competitive priorities. The important thing is not to ignore these very real challenges, but to acknowledge the issues, be transparent about them, and engage in systemic, shared problem solving to achieve the best available solution.

> There are no magic answers, but for sure the best way to solve this is not to throw up your hands and ask management to decide among options that are inherently interrelated. The best option is to work across the disciplines and with partners and arrive at a "globally optimum" solution, one which you are the very best to gauge and the very best to execute on.

The values promoted by this approach focus again on accountability, but they also articulate a proper dose of realism, collaboration, and transparency. All are key ingredients in translating the shared plan developed by the team into a powerful, living document that can react to unexpected developments and maintain the coherence of its approach.

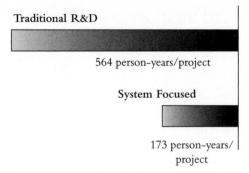

Traditional R&D

564 person–years/project

System Focused

173 person–years/
project

Exhibit 8.1   Comparing the Performance of Traditional and System-Focused R&D

Note: The data from an empirical study discussed at length in M. Iansiti, Technology Integration (Boston: Harvard Business School Press, 1997). *Source:* Iansiti, 1997

Ultimately, the goal is what is sometimes known as "system-focused" decision making. This is the art and science of making decisions with a focus on the global, "system-wide" optimum, not on local considerations. Examples of this would include a Formula One driver who takes into account the layout of the entire course in the approach taken to every turn or a chess player who plans several moves in advance; a system-focused manager (or engineer) never loses sight of the whole plan in making individual decisions.

System focus is not simply a theoretical construct. Research performed on integrated circuit design and development measured the advantage of system-focused frameworks in the actual performance of R&D projects to be very substantial, as shown in Exhibit 8.1.[1] System-focused projects obtained much higher productivity and speed than other projects. The research also sheds light on the reasons for this incredible performance differential. As research narrowed on individual decisions that drove the outcome of the projects, researchers found that such decisions were made differently in system-focused efforts. Having a better understanding of how different parts of the project were connected made an important difference. Decision makers would consider many more options, and naturally narrow in on a better *and* more efficient solution.

Measurement and Validation in Decision Making

Testing and measurement is a core value in a high-integrity project. Beyond technological direction and market needs, measurement can drive alignment between different groups and resolve different perspectives. Windows is steeped in all sorts of measurement systems, ranging from a variety of research techniques to assess market needs, to vast data about the performance of past technologies and applications through the Watson system described in the previous blog, and from the daily testing of the Windows code builds, to the examination of performance on countless hardware configurations. The following blog focuses on one critical (and very public) aspect of the group's measurement system: the Windows Beta program.

Who Put These Lights in the Garage?

Our parking spot in our condo is a few floors down from the street level, and as we were pulling in tonight we noticed that there are new lights. These are new "green" fluorescents that are off by default and only turn on via motion detection, replacing our previous compact-fluorescents and presumably improving our carbon footprint as a building. As we're driving and the lights came on I was getting hostile—the sudden flicking on of lights is distracting. "[W]ould I get in an accident?" I thought. "[T]he lights are on mostly after I drive by"; "[W]ill it be too dark to see?" "[T]he lights stay on for too long"; "[W]ill we save that much energy?" These and many other immediately obvious questions raced through my mind when faced with a change to my routine. How come I was not asked about this? Didn't the old lights work fine and weren't they energy efficient? Well, needless to say as soon as I got home I wanted to hit the "send feedback" button and explain to our HOA [home owners association] that these changes were not thought through and that we need to reinstall our old lights.

We all love feedback. And this weekend, after a few hiccups, about a million people (literally) started sending us feedback on Windows 7. It has been simply an indescribably awesome experience for the team. Across the team today people are talking with pride, excitement, a sense of accomplishment, and of course a strong sense of humility about the job ahead of us to complete Windows 7 and deliver on the expectations that have dramatically increased. The social networks, blogs, and news outlets have been pouring in with praise, positive words, and affirmation of the work we've done. The most rewarding part of this is that, by design, we've done very little marketing and have let the product speak for itself and let the community of enthusiasts "write the story." We're all super clear on how much work is ahead of us and the path to RC and then RTM is challenging for sure. No one on the team is confused.

Of course we also have a ton of feedback. Bugs, setup, blue screens, devices, changes people didn't understand. The thing about Windows 7 is that it is not "just" some fixes, but it represents a thoughtful set of changes to many frequently used parts of the operating system—launching programs, switching between programs, window management, networking, security, notifications, visual design, and so on. And with that "send feedback" button just a click away (well we had a few hiccups there as well) we're getting a lot of feedback. Like tonight's ride down the garage, people are not waiting long to send feedback and to explain what is not right, what is wrong, or what "for the love of G_D" must be changed. There's not a lot of friction between the beta tester [and] that feedback button. In fact we've had one "send feedback" report every 15 seconds or so flowing into the team nonstop since Friday (including the downtime of the download site). And the pace is increasing.

What are we going to do with all that feedback? More importantly, and really the subject of this post, what should each person on the team do with that feedback?

We love feedback. This is the moment we've all been waiting for. We've worked hard since the spring of 2007 and we're in the home stretch and the "conversation" with the outside world is like a big jolt of energy. At the same time we have to consider the feedback we're getting in the context in which it is received and be sure that we are acting in a deliberate manner consistent with great engineering. There are several factors to consider as we evaluate the feedback.

Timeliness. First and foremost, the feedback is based on an immediate reaction. Sometimes this is super critical if a required device is not working. So if you can't get on the network, then that's a showstopper. We need to unblock customers like this with the right driver, the fix, etc. by the time we get to RC. On the other hand, feedback about "change" is often visceral and because of the big "send feedback" button it is immediate. It means someone "fired" off a message before giving things even the slightest chance. The feedback is not really about the feature but about the change. Like the parking garage lights, sometimes things will be better even if there is a time for them to be different. That's not always the case, but it is more likely to be the case if the design had integrity and was thought through. For example, most of the visceral feedback about the taskbar is well understood and we've experienced time-based studies where we know it to improve over time and return to satisfaction levels higher than the previous system—even if there is an initial negative reaction to change. And we also know the feedback about a set of specific issues that we're working on and have been working on.

Source. The source of the feedback we are getting right now is the tech enthusiast customer. Even with a sample size of 1 million people, we are still seeing a fairly homogeneous slice of customers. In many ways these customers notice all the small changes, which could be helpful or not. These customers tend to have leading-edge hardware, which is helpful but not representative. These customers are the height of complexity in their systems, which is useful but atypical. At the same time these customers do not exercise the enterprise management infrastructure and at the other end of the spectrum are not exercising the more average-user features of the product. These customers are smart and fearless. We can all say this might be good to really push the product, but we also know that if something doesn't go right, these folks will start to change things, edit the registry, move files around, and quickly get the machine into a state never seen before. We could spend a lot of time on one bug, just getting back to a well-understood state to diagnose the problem.

Bugs vs. UFO reports. I've had my share of things that I think are bugs but the team thinks are UFO reports. Windows is an enormously complex system on its own, and of course the ecosystem is essentially infinitely complex. Bugs (in all forms) might still remain—pull a perfectly functioning jet off the tarmac at SeaTac and we know FAA inspectors can still find "bugs" even with the massive amount of constant inspection and attention. But we can't afford the time to fix or even investigate every single report as there are just too many. Part of what the team is going to do, and a big part of what each member of the team needs to do, is be a good judge of what is worth the time investment to look into. That might not be satisfying if your printer doesn't work, but if that same model works in the lab or we know the manufacturer said it will work, that might be the best we can do—even though there might be an issue somewhere. Of course there might be an issue in a UFO report, but it is important to use good engineering judgment about whether it is worth investigating based on the source, the understanding of the area, and the risk overall.

Data vs. structured vs. anecdotal feedback. The very best part about the feedback we're getting is that we have clear paths to make feedback actionable. We have pure telemetry (OCA/Watson, SQM) telling us performance, crashes, reliability, device coverage, setup failures, etc. We have structured and semi-structured feedback from the feedback tool that gathers enough information to allow us to classify it automatically. And we have anecdotal feedback from blogs, email, and all the discussion groups we're on. The first order of business is acting on the data. As an example, we blogged about the delivery of IE 8 in the Windows 7 beta and pointed out that the IE build is an interim build on the path to RC, not the RC. We have seen anecdotal feedback (internally and externally) saying there seem to be some hangs in IE. We needed more to go on. We didn't spend countless hours on each PC with those reports but we watched the data. Within about 24 hours we have a solid curve of Watson hangs and we know the bugs that we need to fix, and more importantly we know which ones are internal (MS) or external (ISV [independent software vendor]) and which ones are still open relative to RC. With just a few fixes delivered as an update we can reduce these negative instances significantly. And we're doing that with our energy focused on the data and the code, not individual reports and very time-consuming investigations. That's a great way to be effective. The structured feedback is going through a triage process and we need to be thoughtful about dealing with that. Anecdotal feedback is where we need to be the most careful in how we invest time and really only look at the most general cases. The priority for our team is structured feedback—analyzing it and making sure we are focused on the "head" of the curve, not the easy or interesting issues, using great engineering judgment about what to address.

Activity vs. progress. Finally, the biggest challenge for each of us on the team in terms of how to work with all this feedback is to not lose sight of the goal—an amazing release of Windows 7. This sounds obvious, but we need to keep in mind that even before we started getting all the feedback we had a lot of work to do to get us to RC. And even after RC we will get a ton of feedback. And even after that at RTM we will get a ton of feedback. With a billion potential customers the feedback will never stop—that's the fun, and reality, of working on Windows. There's no point when we stop hearing from customers, as there's always new software, new devices, or new customers pushing the system. Where we can lose focus or get in trouble is if we turn our attention to "gotta act on the feedback" and we are not systematic in the use of our time between now and RC, and we spend too much time on low-yield work. Will tracking down one repro case cause us to miss validating automation that covers way more code? Will debating a design choice with an enthusiast cause us to miss detailed UI strings we could improve? Will debugging a single "UFO report" take more time than fixing a few sev 2 bugs? It is easy to get a lot of activity, but we need to make sure we're focused on progress.

Customers always want to know we're listening and we are acting on their feedback. One of the biggest changes we made to Windows 7 development was to "frontload" the feedback when it comes to conceptual or qualitative aspects of the product design. We've worked tirelessly with OEMs, enterprise customers, and through our field studies of all kinds with just regular people who own PCs. What has been most rewarding in terms of seeing Windows 7 in the field is that we're not very surprised by the feedback—homegroup, taskbar, bitlocker, vhd support, and so on are all features with design choices, trade-offs, challenges, and so on and the feedback we've gotten with the beta is consistent with the whole project. So yes, you bet we are going to make it easier to see the difference between programs that are running vs. pinned, for example. :-) We have a lot of confidence in our designs and that is the result of the frontloading. We have the E7 blog to talk about the trade-offs and choices, and of course people will build on what we are delivering and ask for "more." The path to RC/RTM is not the time to add more.

The big difference is that we are not starting a new product cycle with the beta, but we're concluding the cycle we've been on. We earn our salaries by making sure we develop a model for how the product should work, anticipate the needs and feedback of customers, and build a product accordingly. We know that with a billion customers, sometimes it means listening to everyone might mean that one specific person might not feel we listened to them, and that is tough, but no amount of time can ever make the product work for every person exactly the way they believe it should—if for no other reason than that one person might wake up the next day with a different view of what a good solution looks like. Tomorrow, the lights in our garage might not be so bad.

When we started out Windows 7, our goal as a team was to develop a product plan that would take us from idea to RTM with a coherent and consistent set of shared goals. What we're seeing this week is a realization of that process—every time we see feedback that is consistent with the design of the product, then we've done our job. And if we're surprised, then let's not get defensive. Let's understand what we missed. We're not perfect. We will make mistakes. We've got time to fix mistakes. Declaring something a mistake is a distinct possibility right now and we've got to act. At the same time we need to remain calibrated relative to our goals and most importantly understand the feedback relative to those goals. Variety in our ecosystem is a source of complexity, but being deliberate about understanding how to test and validate in a systematic manner is vastly more valuable than testing and validating anecdotally. There's a balance we need to strike between monitoring and acting on the right elements of the ecosystem feedback, and on being deliberate about finishing the product in a systematic and deliberate manner.

On behalf of the team I do want to offer a big thank you to everyone who is trying things out and installing and using Windows 7 Beta, and of course to our partners in MSIT. We thank you! We thank you for installing and using the product and just giving us the telemetry—that makes a world of difference. The support we're seeing around the world is a real testament to the strength of the Windows brand. People around the world want Windows to be great and are excited to be part of a great release. We're humbled by the response the product is receiving.

FYI, the lights remain in our garage. The building management told me to take a hike and produced a spreadsheet explaining the energy saved and a report from the insurance company regarding the security of the system relative to some ISO standard for parking lots or something.

—Steven

The blog shows how a robust testing system is instrumental to achieve integrity, "to develop a product plan that would take us from idea to RTM with a coherent and consistent set of shared goals." The blog describes the system and underlines the importance of having timely and actionable results and of tuning the system toward the production of implementable recommendations. Additionally, it emphasizes the value of having different testing perspectives, to make sure that one obtains the whole picture and is not fooled by a simplistic perspective on a problem.

Quality and Completeness in Decision Making

The following blog focuses on the team's responsibility for two critical drivers of integrity in both strategy and product: the quality and the completeness of the final outcome. (*Note:* Watson refers to the Customer Experience Improvement Program (CEIP) and Online Crash Analysis (OCA), which track customer problems and are used extensively to make in improvements in Microsoft products.)

No Worries, We Have a . . . Great Repair Shop . . .

It has been a rough time for software lately. While we at Microsoft focus a lot on Vista and the customer desire to see service pack 1, it seems that we, collectively as an industry, might be releasing software that isn't quite "done." The reliance on the internet to update software has probably changed our view of "RTM" to the point that some might say that as an industry we are delivering software that is not always ready for broad use. Some are labeling products beta for a long time or releasing very early products and using the beta label. We're perhaps ok now, maybe, because many of these products are tuned to early adopters who don't mind, or even like the frequent updates we end up delivering. And we also might be getting away with it because we're still early in the software era.

I am not only thinking about us. I'm also thinking about how quickly Apple produced over 100MB of updates for Leopard. I'm thinking about Google's applications, which have been in beta for years. I'm thinking about buying a brand-new DirecTV receiver and it gets updated with a new UI the first night I own it. I'm thinking about how many times I am prompted to update the Adobe Reader. Except for my Toyota, I think everything I own requires me to stop what I'm doing for what the manufacturer thinks of as routine maintenance. But what about my own time and my own busy schedule?

In some ways this reminds me of when we went to the lot to buy a family car back when I was in high school in the early 1980s :-). The salesman was very proud of their service center and even made us take a tour of it to see all the tools and how nice it was. My mother just looked at the salesman and said, "[B]ut we don't want to buy a car that needs servicing . . . that's why we are here and not returning to the Volvo dealership." Of course back then, it was understood that cars needed lots of caring. And if you read any enthusiast magazines you would see that this type of caring was part of the "joy" of owning the car. While for many, this joy still exists; for the vast majority of us, if we have to take a car to the dealer then the car has failed us for what it was supposed to be doing. So while the dealer thinks, "[N]o worries, we have a great repair shop" that statement is out of touch with what customers really want when buying a car. And not only is it not comforting, but it just makes you feel ripped off.

As an industry we've become enamored with autoupdates. Words can't express my love of Watson—it was simply the biggest innovation in computer science in the past 10 years. I don't say that lightly and I mean computer science. After all, we now have software that is far more self-aware and we have far more information available to us about how software is behaving. I would add to this the distinct idea (and invention) of SQM and would say that together, they are responsible for some of the biggest improvements in quality and usability that we have ever been able to accomplish. I still keep KirkG's "D.W." spec on my corkboard as a reminder of the impact this work has had on our products and our teams.

This autoupdate for client software extends to services software where now it is simply passé to think about "release" and that everything is being continuously improved. It is hard to disagree with continuous improvement of course. But what about the quality of the initial experience? What about the downtime that might come from the continuous improvements? What about if something changes and I don't like the change (sort of like in client software if an update breaks something or introduces an incompatibility)? These are all real issues. And of course from an engineering perspective, changing a complex system has a fixed cost, and so the more times we go through the cycle of updates, the less efficient we are overall as a team. While we know the blog world loves the incremental change, that might not be far off from the car enthusiasts being excited to see the repair shop. Just maybe . . .

I remember when we were building the first full release of Office that had Watson in it from the start. As we were digesting beta feedback it became clear we needed to think more about RTM quality. We were so used to looking inward at bug trends and basically assuming all quality reports were "spurious" that we really had to take a step back and think. We knew we wanted to improve things and now we had the data right in our hands. Where we used to have random hex addresses in support calls or beta newsgroups, we now had enough information (and more if we needed) to actually debug the issue. Thus began a new era of "end game" where we studied quality metrics for very broad betas and acted on this. In fact, for that release of Office we actually added "MQ"—the original MQ, which was a milestone specifically added to the project for fixing reported Watson issues.

Even at the time, we talked about the risks that we thought this could introduce. In particular, would we start to think about the end game differently and "assume" that the data will tell us what to fix and thus have less focus on the quality we actually release to customers. While I don't think any individual on the team has fallen into that "trap," I think collectively it is clear our industry is much more comfortable releasing software that requires maintenance than it used to be.

Some might say that this is a naïve view, and that in reality software is better than ever and we always needed this maintenance. It was just that we were not sure what to fix so we just fixed things that crossed our radar or various "soft" measures of quality. I think there is truth to this, but I also think the most important aspect that has changed is the breadth of usage of our software compared to *back then* and to the *mission critical* nature of everything we create.

We have also seen a marked increase in the reliance of beta testing for core product quality. While it is certainly the case that it is increasingly difficult to represent the entire ecosystem combinatorics or replicate every potential browser + network topology that connects to our services, we do need to take a step back and focus more on these issues upfront. We've seen recent examples where we release something in beta that just isn't usable enough to even get feedback so the feedback we get is "not usable enough to provide feedback." It is frustrating to customers to be put in this position and if this is a public experience it does not help our quality reputation. More often than not we often block a large number of customers on a small number of issues, which then cause challenges in how people perceive our quality. Related to this [is] the broader notion of quality with respect to features—if a product does not yet really work, then beta testers are inadvertently led to believe that their feedback on features and the experience (to name a couple) is welcome and will be incorporated. We know that this is not our goal for betas and yet our reliance on broad betas finding new issues reinforces this customer perspective. Betas are a critical part of the development cycle, but we should not rely so heavily on this phase for new-issue discovery.

It is worth noting that one area that we have excelled [at] has been the security realm. Of course this too is an area where customers might prefer not to have to get these updates. In fact each release, XP SP2, Server 2003, Vista, have all shown substantial reductions in the number of security updates we have done compared to the previous releases. We clearly need to continue this trend and also continue the laser focus these updates have which allows us to update the broadest set of customers without repercussions.

My sense is we need to look hard at where we are and there is an opportunity for us to differentiate our products based on quality, again. The past 6 or so years of Watson fixes have definitely let us claim the high road for software quality—our software is industry leading in the level of quality (whether the world agrees or not, and whether that perception is in fact reality is a good discussion). Given the massive volume of updates customers are being put through, even for brand-new software, I think we have a new opportunity to reset the quality bar.

For me this means looking at "RTM" again and deciding that when we release software (for download, on optical media, or to a data center) we know four things to be the case:

- The release is the very best work we can imagine and it delivers the customer experience we said it would deliver.
- We expect to update the software *over time* based on real-world telemetry and data, but we don't expect those updates to begin to flow right away (or worse, flow before most people even bought the device).
- Beta tests are for validation of the quality work we have done, not for discovery of quality issues.
- We treat our customers like they are paying us to do testing and make sure the product is high quality. We don't treat our customers like they are paying us to be adjunct members of the test team.

I think it would be a sign of success that people who buy a new PC or people who use our services as early adopters don't have to live through being members of some infinitely extended test team. The frustration I felt bringing home an iPhone is a great example, installing iTunes (I didn't have it on my machine before) and then it seemed for a month I was installing iTunes every other day, and then it started again when the new iPods were released. Closer to home, we know we see the issues of updates that are one step forward, two steps back. Whether this is because the updates themselves or the throttling of distribution (that is our own caution—we do the update but then make it optional because we don't know the true impact to the user base or ecosystem), the net result of this is just a feeling of "my computer is in the shop."

What this means in practice is we need to look much more carefully at the end game for our software and services and think not just about time to market, and not let the ability to have telemetry be a safety net, but think about how we become systematic about baking in this telemetry into the development cycle before we call the product done. It means if we know something isn't done, then don't ship it—don't release it to operations, don't get enamored with community testing, and don't send it out to millions for download. If it isn't done, then it isn't done. While we know no project is ever "finished," we know that it is possible to define points in time when the software is complete. It is those points in time that represent our goals to customers.

Quality always has the potential to be our Achilles' heel—it is more true now than ever before as competitors are working from much smaller code bases that do less stuff, and our software is more important than ever to more people. It is much easier to be high quality with less code, a smaller ecosystem, and no expectations.

There is a big opportunity for us to improve the state of software and lead the industry.

—Steven

For a strategy to have integrity, its output must also have integrity. This means the output must itself be whole, fitting together in its various elements and components. It must be consistent, coherent and, as the blog underlines, complete. Moreover, the output must fit the needs of the customers, filling the vision and satisfying the quality requirements that are articulated by the plan, with its detailed scenarios and clear objectives. Most of all, the final outcome must be "done."

> It means if we know something isn't done, then don't ship it— don't release it to operations, don't get enamored with community testing, and don't send it out to millions for download. If it isn't done, then it isn't done.

The notions of quality and completeness shape the value systems that underlie decisions in a high-integrity project. Combined with a good system of measurement, these values can create a level of insight and awareness that drives towards excellence.

Learning and Dynamic Decision Making

One would think that after making products for many years, an organization would learn how customers perceive the importance of details. However, companies rarely deploy effective learning processes that improve organizational performance over time. The next blog focuses on learning. (The blog was written while Steven was still part of the Office team.)

Learning as an Engineer—Rising from the Ashes of Failed Projects

Recently a senior program manager asked me for some reading suggestions and I wanted to share a book that had a big impact on how I view projects that I have worked on. The book is called *To Engineer Is Human: The Role of Failure in Successful Design* by Henry Petroski (I have no connection to the author and never met him). This is one of my favorite books to give to engineers for holiday presents and I think I've probably given a copy to most of the senior managers on the Office team.

The book is a wonderful history of some engineering projects. The primary thesis that is well supported by the evidence is that for every successful engineering project there is a series of failures that preceded it. Mr. Petroski is a wonderful writer and the book is an easy and fun read. Of course one attraction is that the book talks about the failure of the Tacoma Narrows Bridge, which is right by Seattle and an amazing site both in person and when you look at the famous pictures of its collapse. The book details other even more tragic events, such as the Kansas City Hyatt walkway collapse. It shows how small design mistakes can be overlooked and also how future designs benefit from the failures. Often people who are not engineers really don't quite understand how you learn and improve as an engineer by making mistakes, and obviously the challenge is that if your failures cause damage, it is really unfortunate.

I think a lot about this relative to the security issues we face in computer software today—we did not design for these and while we are doing everything possible to update old software, the real benefit is coming from the new generations of software that were designed from the beginning to work in this environment (for example, in the 2 years that Office 2003 has been out we have only had 2 critical updates). I don't want to make any excuses at all so don't misinterpret that, but the learning that has taken place in our industry over the past 5 years has been immense and necessary for us to build products like Office 2003.

When I think about software projects that I have worked on from an OS in CS 415 at Cornell through an object database in graduate school all through Microsoft projects, the notion that failure often precedes success is one that is near and dear to me. Our industry is of course filled with failures that went on to become the basis upon which much learning took place (like the Newton to the Palm Pilot, for example, or the new TabletPC learning from the old PenWindows).

The reason [Petroski's] book resonates with me is because my first project at Microsoft was a pretty colossal failure. I was hired into a very small group (in business school lingo, the group would have been called a "tiger team"—a hand-picked group of experts with a specific short-term mission). I don't know how I ended up in this group since it was filled with incredibly senior developers and I was really intimidated. In any event, the mission we were given just before I started at MS was [to] "build an application framework for Windows." It sure seemed easy enough—we had a lot of great folks and even little me had just worked on Smalltalk frameworks for 2 years, so we collectively thought, "[N]o problem."

We worked for about a year and had a rather complete framework. We were pretty confident in our ability to use it to build robust applications in short order. So we decided to spend a month (a whole month!) building applications. Microsoft Money was under development so I figured I could spend my month building Money, which seemed simple enough. The framework had graphics, persistent objects, a UI model-view-controller framework, etc. ¡No problema!

After a month I had a fantastic application—it was able to successfully draw a check on the screen. Needless to say our framework was too big, too slow, too complex for anyone to really use. It was a dismal failure despite all the right ingredients and doing all the "right" things in object-oriented design. In fact we had overdosed on objects and had become full-blown *oopaholics*. Rico has a blog and video on the abuse of object-oriented design worth checking out. (Rico was working on the compiler at the time I was working on the class library.)

As a result we had a rude awakening. Our manager's manager's manager was getting frustrated with progress and we were under the gun. We had a big meeting to review our lack of progress and had to admit that we had not made 12 months of progress over the last year. We had to regroup.

I received my first Microsoft lesson: just because you messed up does not mean your career is over. What matters is how you dust off, what you learn, and if you can put that into practice. Microsoft holds no grudges. The boss said, "[O]k, you made a mistake; let's get moving and don't make that same mistake."

We regrouped. We spent a couple of days talking about what we learned and very quickly came up with a number of "rules" about how we would really design a great class library for Windows. I can't quite remember them all but some of them were:

- We're building a class library, not a compiler test suite, so there is no need to try to use all the features of C++.
- Don't build new abstractions on top of the existing abstractions in Windows. Folks will need to know Windows to use the framework anyway.
- Developers will want to call Windows so don't cache any state in the classes that is duplicating state maintained by Windows (for example, parent child window lists, styles, etc.).
- Performance matters from the beginning so don't go and use fancy stuff that has a fixed overhead that you don't know if you need (like using virtual functions everywhere for example).

And so on. Once we had these lessons in place we actually developed the whole framework in a few months and were able to ship it with Microsoft C++ 7.0 (our first C++ product). We designed in parallel the next release along with all the graphical tools that became Visual C++, which itself became Visual Studio over time. The class library, Microsoft Foundation Classes or MFC, became a great tool used by tons of Windows developers around the world. I think my proudest moment was walking up to a really tall guy at a DEC booth in a partner section from the University of Illinois at a tradeshow demonstrating an alpha of a Windows network application called a "browser." I think his name was Mark, and I asked him what tools he used and he said, "MFC of course." Yes!

When I think back about the dismal failure of our first library and how as a team we seemed to have developed a massive case of second-system syndrome (see Wikipedia for a good discussion of this[2]) for a first system (a mean accomplishment) and how we regrouped, learned lessons, and put those into play, I realized that without that first failure we never would have developed the success criteria that allowed us to build MFC.

The fact that Microsoft offered an environment where we could practice the lessons detailed by Henry Petroski made the whole experience even better.

And most of all I am thankful that I got to be part of an amazing team who mentored and pulled me through these experiences as a new hire. I really want to thank all the people on this project that taught me so much. Thank you for letting me be part of our collective failure and success!

—Steven

Without a learning process, decision-making value systems will not work well. Over the last 30 years, a number of management researchers have differentiated between "first- and second-order processes" in making decisions. *First-order processes* (also known as "static" or "single loop" processes) are the ones that drive basic decisions, such as an Amazon.com employee shipping a product to a customer, or a Microsoft engineer writing a simple line of code. *Second-order processes* (also known as "dynamic" or double loop processes) drive improvement in the first-order processes.[3] These second-order processes drive learning in the organization and are particularly crucial any time an effort encounters any significant complexity or uncertainty. Defining a new kind of user scenario and discovering a new solution to a programming problem are examples of second-order processes. If technical and market changes are rare, management focus should be on optimizing the efficiency of first-order processes. But if uncertainty is significant, as it inevitably is in today's business environment, learning processes are by far more important. Learning is crucial not just from project to project, but also within the course of the project itself.

Learning is a critical element of a high-integrity value system. Learning defines a value system for an individual or an organization that emphasizes the importance of increasing knowledge and capability over time. It builds on the values of accountability, system focus, measurement, and quality to add a dynamic drive for improvement. In a turbulent business environment, learning may be the most important value system component discussed in this chapter.

A strategy with integrity stems from the coherent impact of a capable organization that follows the structure of an insightful plan, aligned by a consistent value system. This chapter outlined five critical components of a decision-making value system, accountability, system focus, measurement, quality and completeness, and learning. The next chapter provides additional insight on value systems by examining the Windows approach to career planning and management.

Notes

1. The difference between system-focused and other types of projects was as much as 300 percent in productivity, and as much as 40 percent in time to market, all after normalizing for the scope of the projects, according to M. Iansiti, *Technology Integration: Making Critical Choices in a Turbulent World* (Boston: Harvard Business School Press: 1997).
2. See "Second-system effect," *Wikipedia,* http://en.wikipedia.org/wiki/Second-system _effect
3. See C. Argyris and D. Schon, *Organizational Learning II: Theory, Method and Practice* (Mass.: Addison Wesley, 1995).

Chapter 9

Personal and Organizational Growth

S trategic integrity is founded on personal and organizational capability.

Strategic integrity starts with each member of the organization. This chapter uses career development as a lens to describe the individual skills and capabilities that build the foundations of a high-integrity organization.

A high-integrity organization is founded on the idea of "T-shaped" skills (Exhibit 9.1). These begin with real disciplinary depth—deep knowledge of a specific field, such as operating system design or consumer marketing, which gets deeper as an individual's career progresses—this is the individual's "core discipline." The depth is complemented by a breadth of understanding, which forms the horizontal bar of the "T." The breadth is important because it establishes how the core discipline fits with the breadth of problems and challenges that are likely to be faced by the organization. The core provides the specific capabilities while the breadth provides a way to understand how these fit to the broader context. The core provides the most critical knowledge foundations while the breadth provides the glue that connects the skill sets of different individuals to each other. Over the course of a career, an individual should not try to do or know everything. He or she should go very deep in some related areas and develop an understanding of how this depth fits with the rest of the organization.

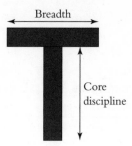

Exhibit 9.1 T-Shaped Skills

Building T-Shaped Skills

The first blog post of the chapter focuses on approaches to career management that build the required T-shaped foundations.

Tao of Career Management

At a college recruiting event last week I was asked, "What career advice would you give a person just starting out at Microsoft?" These questions are always tough—nothing makes you feel older than being asked "advice" and the pressure to say something really profound is intense. Needless to say, I don't really have anything profound to say, and certainly nothing you haven't heard before. What I can share is not as much advice as much as *7 Rules of Thumb* I have tried to do throughout my time at Microsoft (with all due respect to *The Tao of Steve*):

Be excellent at the job you have. The first and most important thing at any point in your career is to always do a great job in the job you have. This one is of course easy when you love your job and things on the team are going great. But if the team hits a rough spot and that gets you down or you hit a few bumps and slow down it gets tough to do a great job. That is really the best time to gather yourself and stay focused on doing a great job. The hardest time to be excellent at your current job is when you start to convince yourself that the job is wrong, the project is wrong, your manager is wrong, or any other thing is just too wrong for you to do a great job. That is exactly the right time to deliver. That is exactly the right time to overachieve. If you throw in the towel, then you end the job on a sour note. But if you find a way to see some light, then there are twice as many potential outcomes, both positive. One is that you make it through the patch and move on to other things, but do so on an up note. And the possibility, more often than not, is that during the uptick in your performance you realize things weren't as bad as you thought.

Be prepared to go through the "cycle." Nothing teaches like experience. Like most "crafts," software is a profession where even the best make mistakes and so the only way to learn is to make mistakes and learn from those mistakes. Software projects go through the cycle of learning, planning, executing, and feedback. At each step there is an opportunity to make mistakes learn. The real learning happens when you are on the hook to correct your own mistakes. And the mega learning happens when you come full circle and attack the problem, create a solution, and deliver it to customers again. We talk a lot about being a well-rounded employee and often we think about this in the context of "business" and "engineering" but an arguably more important way to be well-rounded is to be someone who is an excellent engineer at all phases of a project.

Be attracted to the mainstream. As an engineer there is always a tension between wanting to work on something "cool" and to work on something "real," or to work on something "new" versus something "legacy" (intentionally chosen to offer the most common hallways discussion). Of course at Microsoft we have a plethora of new projects starting up all the time. Some are clearly on a path and some are clearly incubations working on finding a path. And all the while we have the existing projects that seem so "mainstream." This tension is hardly new—going way back to new programming languages, new networking OS, new GUI applications, and of course codenames that we can all recite. My own decision making about what to work on has always been to focus on the mainstream and to make the mainstream deliver those "new" or "cool" things from the mainstream. The reason I chose this is because I value highly the learning I got as an engineer from the product cycle and from delivering to lots of customers. I also think in the teams I've been part of we have worked to create the "new" from within the mainstream and shown how it is possible to be more systematic and predictable in new product development. So on this one you can say that I have been motivated to have the best of both worlds in the job and to focus on doing so for the most customers possible in the shortest time possible.

Be obsessed with the competition. This one is simple. No matter what you work on there is a direct competitor or some software that is really close to what you are developing. You should know it. You should know it inside and out. Every command, every implementation detail, every version, performance, the people that work on it, how it is sold and marketed, what customers who use it say, and so on. I remember once going through all of Lotus SmartSuite and looking at the imports/exports from each DLL to see how much code was really shared (a big deal back then) and seeing how they stored icons in resources for their "toolbars." I went through pixel by pixel each dialog from each application. Not only was it super fun, but the experience of doing this was itself educational and served not just me but members of the team well. No matter what your role on the team is, you should be obsessed with the competition.

Be expert on your product. If you work on the mainstream there is a good chance your product involves a few feature teams and you might not be in the code (designs, specs, or tests) for the whole product. That should not be an excuse not to know the sum of the product. Everyone should be able to demo the product they work on. Everyone should know the feature set and usage of the breadth of the product they work on. Just because you work on "ease of use" is no reason to ignore the administrative features so valued by corporate customers, for example. Just as there should be no stone unturned competitively, you should master your own product. This is knowledge that will last your career.

Be aware of playing the system. No one likes politics. So don't play politics. Of course that isn't an excuse to be rude or to show a lack of respect for people on your team or partnership teams. It is, however, a warning that trying to outsmart the system or to be clever just doesn't really work. For me this means to focus on the core value of making others great, sharing the credit and then some, owning up to mistakes, helping others when you can, and so on. Trying to outsmart the members of your own team through metrics, reports, email gymnastics, or all the things we all know can be done will **always** come back and return double to you. I promise. Playing the system does not work.

Be Zen about the short term as it all works out in the long term. Finally, we do work as part of a team and part of a company and to do so we have a "system." The system is implemented by people, which means it won't be perfect (because people aren't perfect). It means that what is "right" doesn't always happen right away. But it will happen. You might have done a great job but somehow the recognition didn't come to you this time. Someone you are sure shouldn't have been promoted got promoted. Someone botched a feature but no one noticed. These are all the things that drive us nuts—we think the world isn't fair or we [think] Microsoft isn't fair or we think our manager is a jerk. These are the things that make us want to play the system. These are the things that in the short term seem to benefit the wrong person. Stuff happens. The system doesn't always work. But the system always works over time. As soon as you start trying to play the system, you will find yourself spending more energy on the system than you spend on the work. And that's really when you start to fail. Don't be a victim. Just be Zen. I am confident things work out in the long run. I owe everything with respect to this point to Mike Maples (the original VP of "Apps"), who on more than one occasion reminded me to stay the course and not stress over the short term.

As you go through mid-year career discussion it might be worth thinking about these points. Maybe they will help frame a good discussion with your manager. Or maybe we can talk about it in the hallway sometime. What do you think?
—Steven

A high-integrity organization requires a foundation of understanding. This foundation consists of deep, core knowledge of product, customers, and competitors. As the blog urges, "you should know it, you should know it inside out. Every command, every implementation detail, every version, performance, the people that work on it, how it is sold and marketed, what customers who use it say, and so on." The objective is to obtain the kind of deep command of the subject that gives individual contributors the capability and the confidence to actively drive strategy through their everyday activities.

This kind of understanding is not built overnight. It begins with disciplinary depth. The Windows blogs are consistent in this perspective, which values, above all depth, of understanding. This can be in any relevant field, from operating system architecture to consumer marketing, but it has to be in *some* field—there is no substitute for it—there is no T without a vertical bar. The vertical foundation usually starts in college, and is deepened further through project work. However, project work also iterates team members through many relevant project phases and components of the business, which extends an individual's skill base to provide a good knowledge of where the skill can have the most impact. This builds the horizontal bar of the T, which grows as a function of the number of project generations the individual participates in.

Broadening the Skill Set

Planning a career path at Microsoft or in other challenging environments involves figuring out a sequence of assignments that build the requisite capabilities and track record. The following blog expands on the T-shaped skills philosophy by examining strategies for broadening skills.

Managing Your Career—The Journey or the Destination?

[E]very exit is an entrance somewhere else.
. . . .
Pragmatism?!—is that all you have to offer?
—From *Rosencrantz & Guildenstern Are Dead*, Tom Stoppard, 1966

Today I was having a conversation with one of our senior managers about ways to gain broader experience in his/her career. The discussion led to something that I thought might be interesting to others on our team thinking about career progression as we do during this time of year.

Professionally we are all the sum of our experiences. We've all had good experiences, and experiences we wish we had a second shot at. The question is really one of trying to be deliberate about shaping these experiences. Every single book on managing your career talks about getting diverse work experience to "round out" your career and give you a broad base of experience. This approach might not be for everyone and a lot depends on your ultimate career goals and also your own capabilities.

This approach is viewed as having a "diversity" of experience. More often than not, the immediate thing that comes to mind (in the conversations

I have) is what one would refer to as "two deviations out" diversity—those are the experiences that are way different than where you currently are in your experiences base. For example, if you work on development, then one might think of working in marketing or technical support. Or if you work in the field, you think of doing a "stint" in program management. Unlike the adjacencies (described in http://blogs.msdn.com/techtalk/archive/2005/0 9/18/471121.aspx [and] http://blogs.msdn.com/techtalk/archive/2005/07/ 21/441674.aspx) these moves are way outside your experience / comfort zone. Note, these posts also discuss "general management" in the context of career path.

In reality, diversity of experience is often closer to home than the textbooks might describe. When you write a book it is often easy to compare experiences in sales, marketing, and development. It is much harder to describe the difference between developing wireless technologies, user interface, and graphics. Those all fall into the bucket of "product development" and so they don't sound all that diverse and don't seem very well-rounded. Yet from an engineering perspective, these are wildly diverse and the skills, techniques, and experiences will help you to develop into a well-rounded engineer. This is especially the case if you are deliberate in planning your moves across technologies and do so when you've reached a solid point of mastering the skills at one job.

It is easy to paint these two approaches to diversity into extremes— one can sound like bouncing all over the place and wait for the right opportunity to bounce and the other can sound like you stay in the same place and hope for the best. In reality, both can be part of a deliberate and well-planned career path. But doing so takes work and patience, and a thoughtful management team committed to building your career over time (rather than committed to keeping you around). But the first thing you might want to ask yourself is, [W]hat is your long-term goal?

Another way of asking this is "[D]o you have a career end state that is very focused on a ladder level or specific job tile, or do you have a career end state that is about having a broad set of experiences?" While you might see those as related, there is no sure path and in some sense you have to be aware of this when you manage your own career and take steps in a specific direction. That is, no matter what path you take nothing is certain, but what is certain is if you take some steps and expect something that isn't really part of the trajectory.

For example, let's say you have the goal of reaching a certain level as a developer. By far the most important thing you can do is gain depth experience in development so that you show mastery of a domain. The next most valuable thing is to move strategically to other domains where you can build on the specific skills you have. There is also significant value in moving to new domains where you can increase your mastery of additional tools and techniques (such as moving to service development). All of these keep you on a "mainstream" path to seniority in development. If you execute super well at this type of trajectory, then you should be on a path to achieve your goals in seniority as a developer.

On the other hand, if you have that goal, but move to program management or move to an incubation project or move to a non-engineering role, then it probably isn't likely that these experiences help you to achieve your goal in terms of the developer/SDE [software development engineer] ladder. However, if your goal was to build your career as a catalog of experiences, then these might very well be excellent moves for you. You will see our company from any number of perspectives and gain a unique set of experiences. In this case, the goal is to have the experiences.

Where it becomes tricky is when someone says they want a broad set of experiences but also expects to have the same career end-state as someone who is specifically focused on that goal. In other words, someone who wants to be a senior developer but wants to get there by working on a larger number of projects for a short time or by having a set of experiences not entirely focused on development. It might be very possible that this works, but it isn't something you could generalize. The reason is really straightforward—the "competition," if you will, for strong performers at the top will always exist and those that come across as deeply committed to the depth skills are likely to be the ones that achieve that goal.

I believe this is something that is somewhat counterintuitive and why the self-management books always have a tough time with it. But if you look at any discipline that requires extensive training and experience, the reality is that all of us would pick providers of that skill who have dedicated themselves to mastery and not those that have had a broad base of experiences. When we need a physician, we want the world's expert in a certain procedure (someone who does that procedure almost exclusively). When we fly a plane, we want a pilot who has the most hours on that type of aircraft. When we want a tour guide, we want someone who knows that city inside and out. We don't want a physician who has only done a few of the procedure needed, or the pilot who flies our aircraft as a hobby, or the tour guide who is new to the city.

At the same time, there are immensely valuable experiences in diversity that could make every one of those experts even more expert. A neurologist who has done training in palliative care is a huge asset. A pilot who has a lot of hours on a related aircraft brings that much more experience. And a tour guide who is familiar with your hometown can add a great deal by comparing and contrasting. In each of those cases, the individual can take a deliberate approach to gaining those experiences without taking a major step away from their core discipline. In other words, whether your pilot worked at the ticket counter, your surgeon understands hospital billing, or your tour guide can drive the bus are all interesting experiences perhaps for those people, but have little relevance to the expectations you have in their delivery of the service.

The key is identifying where you can make a real contribution to your core work (and skill set) with some experience, while recognizing that many roles are much deeper than "getting some experience." For the most part, most jobs roles are filled with people devoting their own careers to mastering them and so it is important to be wary of appearing as though you are "just in it for the experience." It is also worth considering how you can gain these experiences in an "experience" mode rather than a "job change mode." Who is your mentor? What have you done to just meet 1:1 with people across the company? What courses have you taken at UW (personally, back when I first started I took finance and accounting courses at SCCC)? Have you taken advantage of connecting with your coworkers from other parts of company after those HR training classes you participated in? There are many ways to gain experiences in areas where the folks you can learn from are devoting their entire careers to the work. To view the other side of the coin, I've invited field sales folks to bug triage meetings, or to vision presentations, or the summer "trade show and expo" we have done (and will do this summer). Be really creative about how you can connect with wildly different parts of the company or industry—it can be super fun.

To be concrete for our team, we are aiming to develop the world's best engineering team (a necessity since we have the responsibility of working on the world's most used software). It means that as we do our work and focus on our careers, we are going to focus on engineering. It means that we will look to gain experiences that enhance our engineering skills and help us to develop better intuition, better understanding of technology, and a stronger view for how to gauge strategic engineering opportunities.

I usually ask folks who in the organization, one, two, or more levels "up," they hold in some esteem? Who has had a career path they wish to follow? A lot of times this is a group manager or a VP who excels at a discipline. And sometimes it is a person that is admired that has a totally different background. This is where the desire to obtain general career experience kicks in. How does one move from dev to general management? How does one move to "the business" and so on? Does being a manager of a small "product unit" get you closer to being a VP or no? Is there any way to move from being a group manager in WWL to being a general manager? Is being a general manager a career end-state for a large set of our population? If you want to be a general manager, have you "exceeded" in two or more of the disciplines you want to manage? Will you be more likely to be a "partner" in a core engineering discipline or in a small general management role?

There are no certain paths in managing your own career—as much as we'd like the CSP to be a checklist, it just isn't. You can choose a job that turns out to be one you don't perform well at. You can join a group that hits it out of the park, but the team is incredibly strong. You can do a great job, but the product might not take off. You can do a great job, but "weird things happen" and the team is redirected. But the key is to be clear with your own expectations. If you focus on core engineering and deliver, you have the right to expect, relative to the CSP, that you will move through it and do so in a deliberate manner. If you enhance your skills in a deliberate fashion and choose your career moves to build on those skills, then you are doing the best you can for your own engineering career and your manager should be aware of that. If you choose experiences that are unique, but not core to engineering, then you should expect to be satisfied with the experiences you gain.

Statistically speaking, our goal is to have more senior people contributing in senior engineering leadership roles with clear accountability and clear career progression. We've moved substantially from the base we started (as the statistics have shown—these are being communicated in more team meetings than this blog). The opportunity to be more senior as an engineer is very clear and very deliberate on our team. All companies and all organizations will always have room for generalists—and they will be valuable roles. But what our team is trying to do is maximize everyone's opportunity along the ladder levels and do so by providing opportunities for engineering depth and/or engineering breadth, with or without management.

When you're managing your career and thinking about next roles and experiences, the key question for yourself is to ask yourself if you are in this for the journey or the destination. While these are not mutually exclusive, there are potentially different paths to take or different decisions to make. At the very least, your own expectations of the return on your investment in time should be clear. Taking on some responsibility for the journey can be rewarding and provide richness of experience that is unmatched, but at the same time is not a sure-fire path to a specific goal. Taking on responsibility that focuses on building on your core skills is the best path in terms of achieving those goals, but the experiences might not always sound like what the management books tell you. A well-managed career takes these trade-offs into account and acts deliberately. Your mentor, your manager, and your friends are all great sources of input and perspective to help you to balance these tricky to balance trade-offs.

While our organization is new and we've only had one ship cycle in Windows Live (and are getting closer for IE, and so on) folks are starting to see how we can act in a deliberate fashion at the management level and really create opportunities for people and put folks in the position to shape our organization and leadership across all the levels of the team. We certainly saw this as we transitioned from Windows Live Wave 2 to Wave 3. I hope over time we get very good as a team at providing these opportunities for people to gain diversity in domains, skills and experiences.

—Steven

PS: #7. Be Zen about the short term as it all works out in the long term.

The skills and capabilities of the team members are shaped by the sequence of assignments they work on: "professionally we are all the sum of our experiences." Crucially, *related* experiences will have the most coherent impact on individual capabilities. The blog post advocates building related skills and knowledge for maximum impact.

This basic advice is validated by research. A few years ago, this author ran a research project aimed at understanding the drivers of performance in high-technology product development. After analyzing over one hundred projects, he found that aggregate team experience was one of the most crucial drivers of project performance. There were three factors, all related to experience:[1]

- *Knowledge retention.* The retention of relevant experience from one project generation to the other
- *Knowledge generation.* The extension of experiential knowledge through experimentation, prototyping, and beta programs
- *Knowledge application.* The application of experiential knowledge through effective team management and organization

These three experiential factors, together, accounted for most of the project performance variation.

The enormous importance of experience, both at the individual level and aggregated at the organizational level, motivates a real focus on coaching and career development as a key activity for the modern-day manager. It is critical not only to think carefully about one's own sequence of assignments and experiences, but also to shape the career paths of others.

The Path to General Management

The next blog expands on the career progression toward functional management, and then on to general management. This post was written before Steven joined the Windows and Windows Live team.

The Path to GM—Some Thoughts on Becoming a General Manager

The recruiting season is getting underway and shortly we'll be "at a college near you" looking to connect. I will be at Harvard Business School the first week of October, where I'll visit some classes and also participate in a career fair. I hope to see some readers there!

I met this week with one the managers at Microsoft that I officially mentor. We have a program (literally an ASP.NET program) where you can sign up to mentor or be mentored through a matching process. The discussion we had was about career progression and how does one become CEO. I thought that was a rather ambitious goal—after all, asking your mentor for the path to become their manager is interesting ;-). We talked the discussion down from CEO to achieving the career goal of *general management* (GM). I'll define general management as managing multiple functions with significant responsibility for a whole customer visible project—this can be a product unit of 50 people (20 devs, 20 test, 10 program managers) or a whole business group of 300 that includes marketing and other disciplines. At Microsoft, as with many companies, reaching this level of management is a significant accomplishment and with it comes significant responsibility. If you aspire to [it], then how do you get there?

(Now is a good time to say that this is definitely an article that could be used against me since I'm sure there are things in here that I do not practice as well as I should—if you happen to know that, then suffice it to say I'm still learning too and these are lessons I've learned! And also I will use a bunch of examples in here, but any of them can have their tables turned and reflect any other job discipline.)

The first words out of my mouth in this case are always **patience.** It is a cliché, and frankly coming from an executive always seems self-serving. But the truth is I think that pace is the most important element of a career. Once you become a functional manager your career is different and your contribution is different, and not necessarily better. And once you become a general manager, your career again changes and your contribution is way different, and as you'll experience, the job becomes a bit more lonely and often less "fun." I remember going to my 5-year reunion for college and we're sitting out on the arts quad eating PMPs (don't ask!) when I listened to each of my fellow Comp Sci friends bemoan the amount of management they were doing and how they were no longer really doing any "work." That certainly made me pause and I felt great that I was still writing code and not actually managing anyone! My first lesson in patience.

The second reason to be patient about your career is that you are probably never nearly as ready as you think you are for the next big job. The challenge is that the company has lots to worry about in addition to your career. The company has shareholders, other employees, and customers so balancing all of those needs in addition to your career is tricky. Here is where trusting your manager (and management chain) is super important. In a strong organization, the opportunities for you will come, even if they don't come as fast as you'd like. We've all had people we were impressed by because of their meteoric rise, only to see them perhaps "peak early" or worse. At the same time, I've seen organizations rewarded for making the right move at the right time and seeing someone just ready enough to step into a bigger/broader role and make a huge difference with a running start. Mike Maples, certainly one of the most respected Microsoft managers ever, used to remind us all that things work out in the long run. So another reason to be patient.

So assuming you have the patience, then what are the right steps to general management? If you were to ask general managers at Microsoft how they ended up in their job you'd probably get a unique answer for each person. Most at Microsoft that rose up through the ranks probably didn't expect (or seek) GM roles. Certainly for me, I was generally much more in the moment and excited by the technology, products, and customers. I always felt that my managers noticed that and that was a big part of why I was offered management responsibility. The most important thing about moving into general management is that you have to be very good at the function (dev, test, pm, marketing) that you currently work in—no one is going to want you to manage another function, especially one you have never done, if you are not among the best at managing your current discipline.

Generally, you're going to need to gain some experience in another function before you can really hit the ground running as a general manager. I know that is something I tend to look for in candidates. This is not as dramatic as it often sounds. If you're a developer, it does not mean you should go become a sales person (most good developers would fail spectacularly at sales, and vice versa). Rather the focus should be on an "adjacent" discipline. You can think of the disciplines as a continuum:

Support ↔ Sales ↔ Marketing ↔ Planning ↔ Program Management
↔ Development ↔ Testing

At any point you can look "left or right" and see the potential for you to broaden your expertise and gain the experience that could serve you well as a multi-disciplinary manager. You probably don't need to go far for this experience, and in fact staying close by in a familiar organization or product might serve you well and help you keep your feet on the ground. The majority, but by no means all, general managers at Microsoft have experience in the dev/pm space or in the sales/marketing space. I want to be careful about generalizing because with a relatively small set of folks and a lot of unique stories it is important to understand that many paths can lead to GM. *I should also say that the above spectrum is not complete and not meant to be exhaustive, just illustrative.*

Why is this experience important? The biggest reason is because the day you walk into a room and look around and see 3 or 4 (or more) different disciplines looking at you for leadership and guidance, your credibility hinges on being able to humbly and respectfully talk-the-talk and walk-the-walk of several disciplines that you never did. "BS" detectors will immediately go up—just because you were a whiz at marketing or sales, do not think test or pm will immediately just follow you (insert any other disciplines in there). In fact, one of the biggest early points of failure for a new GM is the inability to see eye to eye or *bond* with the "other" disciplines. If you were a developer who was always beating up on testing, or a program manager who always said marketing was clueless, then imagine how those disciplines will feel if they see you stand up in front of the room and say, "Hi, I'm your new manager." That won't be a pretty sight. After all, these folks will now be looking to you to expand their career opportunities and you can't do that if you have not internalized respect for all those that contribute. So if you're looking to move to general management, showing how you can walk in the other's shoes is super important. When was the last time you asked testing their views? When was the last time you helped marketing with some technical content and let them get all the glory? When was the last time you didn't take the "expected" role because you knew the other person was right?

Another point of failure on the path to general management is closely related and that is being too focused on your discipline and not being able to "rise" above your discipline during times when the organization needs it. You can think of this as being too much of a functional silo, or just not "mature" enough to see the big picture. It means for example that as a tester if you know the schedule is tight and that we need time to get the quality to the right levels, but you also know there is a hard constraint due to a "train that is leaving the station" then the senior folks are the ones that take a step back and find a solution to the situation and do not dig their heels in just play the expected role (i.e., testers saying we need time, developers saying it can't be done, program managers saying we need to add features, marketing saying we need it sooner, etc.). The ability to solve problems in a situation that arises from the other perspectives or disciplines is a key trait of a GM who rose up through functional leadership. At Microsoft, good examples of this are program managers who cut features because they know, as much as they want them, that the feature will lower the overall quality, or testers who know how to find a path to insuring the quality of a [late-breaking] addition that they know we need but adds measurable risk to the project.

The next area of experience is often the first one thrown at you by managers when you ask about the path to GM, which is to go and get experience on a broad set of product lines. This is easy to say, and actually relatively easy to do. The value though really depends on the situation and the depth of the experience you gain. One way to look at this is if you're looking at a resume of an external candidate and you see 5 jobs in 10 years, that is usually a little bit of a warning sign. Just because you know all the groups, an internal candidate with that same resume should probably set off the same warning signs. This is only a warning and something to look into, not a disqualification of course. But a key tenet for me is that to become excellent and among the best at a functional role is to work on the "beginning, middle, and end" of a project at least twice. Why is this? Well all the learning comes from deciding what to do, figuring out how to do it, and then doing it. But the real learning comes from watching customers live with all those decisions you made, and *then* going back to the whiteboard and figuring out how to clean up the mess you made. :) In software that could be 5 years on one team, which might seem like an eternity, especially as a person anxious to be a GM, but I believe it makes you a much stronger leader and [manager] down the road.

At the same time, experience in other product lines is super valuable. It is very similar in benefit to gaining experience in other disciplines. All software products need to work together, certainly that is what our customers say, but if you haven't been on the other side of that dependency (or *interface*) then you are only seeing one side of the solution and probably spending way too much time thinking the other folks are coconuts. Again this is one where there is a lot of judgment about how different the experience needs to be, and there are a lot of factors that a company can consider that come into play. Some companies expect you to move very far because the companies are very diverse and the expertise you are gaining is around management and process. Other companies expect you to continue [to] gain technical depth and thus moves that are "far" actually slow down your contribution. And to point out how much judgment there is in this, usually at junior levels it helps to gain the depth experience in relatively adjacent technologies, and then at senior levels because your contribution is much more about process and management you can usually move further away. I strongly recommend having a plan for yourself that balances being excellent at your function over a good period of time, while also gaining that same level of depth experience in another business or product line that builds on those skills you gained.

This leads to the last tip I could offer on the path to general management, which is to develop a mentor or role model within your organization. This needs to be someone you can talk to who can objectively validate and/or criticize your thoughts on career path. A lot of folks will go to the human resources group for this type of advice, and while that can be a good data point, I would suggest that you want to find someone you admire or respect who has come from a similar path you are currently on. So if you are a developer and want to be a general manager, find someone at the company who is a developer who became a general manager. Ask if they will talk to you once or twice a year (usually during performance review or goal-setting time) and certainly ask if you can talk to them when you are considering a change in jobs or responsibilities. I know when people ask me about their careers I always ask who they see around the company as a role model, and it surprises me that most of the time folks do not have a clear view. As a hint, it isn't really the best answer to say you are modeling yourself after Bill Gates or Steve Ballmer—those are a couple of unique individuals and so I'd suggest being a bit more pragmatic in who [you] most likely to want to be like. It is worth noting that mentors are people too and they often don't have magic answers to questions, but if you bring good questions (such as "[H]ow would you handle this situation that I am facing this week?") then there is a good chance you can have a very beneficial mentoring experience.

Finally, I'd close by saying that if you were reading this thinking, "[G]osh, I don't really know if I want to be a general manager or not" then that is ok too. Far too many people think being a big-time manager is where it's at. Being a general manager has its moments, but if you rose up through the ranks as a developer and program manager, believe me it is not magical the first time your test manager asks you, "[D]o you think we're investing enough in automated testing for this scenario?" (Note, this happened to me!) Managing work that you have never done is very stressful and also a bit lonely. If you have the right mind-set and stay focused on excellence, my experience is that the company will recognize this and the right person will connect with the right organization and the right time—and in the end, as Mike Maples said about management, the cream will rise to the top and the right things happen for everyone.

So if I had to summarize a way to think about your career plan to become a general manager:

Be patient. If you take your time and work with your management chain, your chances of success definitely go up.

Be excellent. The first key is to be among the very best performers at your core discipline.

Gain adjacency experience. A good, but not necessarily critical, next step is to gain experience in an adjacent discipline.

Respect and understand all the disciplines. It is not possible for any one person to work in all the disciplines you might manage someday, but you should spend a good deal of effort learning and understanding the other disciplines **before** you have to manage them.

Work on multiple product lines. Figure out for you and your organization what the right type of experience change you should have and seek that out when you feel like you've reached a good level of functional excellence and performance at your current role.

Find a mentor. See if there is someone in the company who followed a path similar to the one you would like to follow and meet with them to discuss your career.

—Steven

BTW, I've received some mail about the recent article in *Business Week* on Microsoft. Right now I will choose not to comment on it until I see if the writers and editors choose to correct or comment on some of the plethora of factual errors.

In keeping with the T-shaped skill model, the blog describes general management skills as starting first and foremost from the core discipline of the manager. With that as the foundation, the right sequence of projects can broaden experience and capabilities toward adjacent areas and gradually build the base required to succeed in general management. The approach promotes the establishment of deep and complementary skill bases, building a continuous, robust foundation of capability. Beyond capability, the career path also builds critical relationships, establishing an awareness of complementary skills and a mutual respect toward members of other disciplines. As such, this approach weaves together complementary skills and relationships into a fabric that constitutes the foundation for an organization that not only covers a comprehensive set of disciplines, but also stays robust and whole under pressure.

Reaching for strategic integrity requires a capable organization. Matching strategy to execution hinges on the right structure, processes, managerial approaches, and the right set of decision-making value systems. But no strategy can have integrity if the required depth of skills is absent. Hollow organizations will not execute great strategies. This chapter provided a glimpse into the skill and capability building activities that can mold the right foundations. Without these foundations, attempts at strategic integrity are bound to come up empty handed.

Note

1. M. Iansiti, *Technology Integration* (Boston: Harvard Business School Press, 1997).

Chapter 10

Lessons from Aligning Strategy and Execution

Planning, organization, and decision making can turn directed and emergent strategies into one strategy.

Following a developer preview in October 2008, the Windows team released a Beta version of Windows 7 in January 2009 and then a Release Candidate in May of that same year. Perhaps *millions* of PCs installed the prerelease software, likely an unprecedented number for a preliminary version of a PC operating system. As this book goes to press, experts, enthusiasts, and consumers have reacted favorably to Windows 7. Reviewers went beyond simply stating that this version was an improvement from Vista by pointing out the multiple innovations introduced by Windows 7. The improvements, however, are shaping up to have real impact on both consumers and partners. Overall, consumers found Windows 7 to be reliable, efficient, consistent, innovative, and responsive to both consumer needs and market trends.[1] While it is premature to declare the product a success, it can be said that Windows 7 mirrors the structural integrity of organization that engineered it.

Despite the technology bent, this book describes capabilities, processes, and behaviors that are familiar to managers in many of the world's most complex businesses. These tenets changed the Windows organization and translated its strategic potential into real impact for potentially a billion consumers around the world. By deliberately articulating the concept of strategic integrity, the framework for its actualization was prioritized by leadership. Having this foundation firmly in place allowed for a more robust participatory planning process that anchored a more accountable and transparent decision-making approach. This chapter summarizes the concepts discussed throughout the book and provides suggestions as to how the lessons learned by the Windows organization might be broadly applied to various sectors in the global marketplace.

Searching for Strategic Integrity at Toyota

Even before the financial downturn in 2009, the automotive industry was seen as one of the most complex, competitive, and combustible sectors in the modern economy. New-car development involves the efforts of thousands of managers, engineers, and other employees and can easily require more than $1 billion in investments (and they aren't all winners). Moreover, the industry is faced with significant changes in the processes of innovation and technology integration, driven by the convergence of telecommunications, media, and software technologies, coupled with transformative developments in hybrid, hydrogen, and electric propulsion systems. Novel technologies may alter design elements, but the fragility of the overall process is determined by many factors. Product architecture, development prowess, flawed marketing, new manufacturing processes, and even a fractured labor force can derail an entire project. The financial crisis punctuated these challenges with unpredictable demand from consumers and now threatens the very foundation of this historic industry.

Toyota Motor Corporation is widely considered to be one of the most competitive and well-managed global enterprises. Effusive books and articles have been written on the eponymous Toyota Production System (TPS), and a number of organizations have attempted to duplicate Toyota's principles and processes. The analyses put forth in the reports focus on Toyota's significant operational advantages, which are unquestionably part of its competitive advantage. However, the impact of Toyota's processes and systems on creating integrity between strategy and execution is less well known but at least equally responsible for their success.

Even as increased competition and uncertainty reach pandemic status in the automotive industry, Toyota's performance remains steadfastly linked to its ability to respond and anticipate change for a 300,000-person workforce in more than 170 countries. Investigation of the company's strategy development and execution model reveals an interesting degree of similarity with the frameworks set forth in this book.[2]

The design, production, and distribution of a new automobile is an elaborate process touching hundreds of suppliers, thousands of employees, and tens of thousands of customers. Strategy setting and a thorough planning process are essential in a venture of such scope. Toyota has addressed the complexity and uncertainty of the automotive industry by creating an organization that meshes top-down frameworks with ideas and real-world insights from below. At Toyota, strategic integrity spans all phases of planning and execution.

Organization is the first driver. While many American competitors have experimented with organizing design teams around products or product platforms, often at the result of sharply decreasing functional capability, Toyota has retained deep functional expertise within its design teams. Toyota divides products into smaller subcomponents based on the functional expertise required to complete each element, such as the electrical system or the car's body, and then assigns focused engineering teams to these subcomponents. The entire effort is led by the *shusa* or project leader (see Exhibit 10.1), whose organization works closely with functional specialists to bring coherence to the whole effort and represent the needs of consumers. Though much of the effort is broken down into small, cross-functional teams (much like the triads and feature

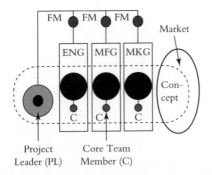

Exhibit 10.1 Toyota's Project Management Structure[3]

crews mentioned in Chapter 6), the long-term career focus is on depth of functional expertise. Many engineers remain in a given function for the entirety of their careers, allowing the development of deep technical understanding and problem-solving ability within a focused subset of related design tasks. This structure translates initial design concepts into concrete real-world systems by placing engineering ability at the core of the product design process.

Beyond an organizational focus on deep functional expertise and on flat, efficient, integrative structures, Toyota has realized that molding the organization's many different viewpoints is critical to a great plan. Furthermore, maintaining alignment between strategy and execution over the life of a project requires a strong information flow across the entire organization to continue throughout the program. As with Windows, Toyota begins the planning process by codifying knowledge from past projects, thereby creating design goals based on common platforms, best practices, standards, and customer trends. Toward this end, the company encourages interactions at the scene (*genba*), whereby internal and external input is gathered in real time—for instance, by meeting with dealers to obtain feedback from the sales perspective. Initiated by a top-down communication defining the scope of the effort, the planning process is rapidly focused around specific product scenarios. These encompass incremental improvements on traditional vehicle functionality or more significant innovations such as hybrid propulsion technologies or biofuels. Toyota's drive to solicit information from the bottom up permeates the organization and extends beyond the design process—from production workers on the factory floor all the way up the chain. The information flow informs the plan and provides a flexible connection between strategy and execution.

Finally, Toyota's search for strategic integrity hinges on the participation of empowered employees at all levels of the organization in the decision-making process. While an overarching product concept sets priorities, the details of design execution are determined through an iterative process within which employees are encouraged to voice contrary opinions. In a process of "mutual adjustment,"[4] engineers are encouraged to concisely put dissenting opinions into writing, ahead of face-to-face meetings intended to reach a solution that provides the best fit with strategic priorities and technical reality. The process elicits the participation of different departments, representing a variety of execution-oriented disciplines. This inclusive approach brings together functionally disparate teams, ranging from styling to engineering design, and manufacturing engineering to crash testing and simulation.

High levels of involvement throughout the Toyota organization, in both shaping and executing strategy, illustrate the importance of securing the match between strategy and execution. The Toyota model has proven highly effective and underpinned consistent performance, despite significant market volatility. Toyota's search for strategic integrity, with the development of associated processes, frameworks, and systems, has clearly paid off in recent years. Even with increasing uncertainty in the global marketplace, Toyota has responded with flexibility, consistency, and transparency.

The Participatory Roots of Strategic Integrity

The Toyota example suggests some intriguing commonalities with the Windows strategy development and execution process. At both Microsoft and Toyota, the roots of strategic integrity are in participation. Both Toyota and Microsoft maintain strategic integrity by extending the strategy development process to the broader organization (see Exhibit 10.2). In both cases, meaningful and empowered participation does not happen by accident. Behind the shared nature of strategy, there is a carefully structured system, one that creates knowledge, provides the right incentives, and defines the appropriate process that invites team members to productively contribute. The team is further incentivized and motivated when they can see their input being applied and accepted.

In both the Toyota and Microsoft examples, strategic integrity is fostered by three foundations: organization, planning, and decision making. These help shape the organization into a highly effective participatory mechanism for strategy development and execution. The mechanism is built on deep capability in the right functional areas. The intense planning process focuses capabilities on analyzing key problems to promote a deep level of understanding, questioning outdated principles and expanding into new technical fields. Gradually, the understanding is shaped into genuine, passionate beliefs about future directions, ranging from strategies to design details. Planning, organization, and decision-making systems align beliefs into a coherent plan for translating strategy

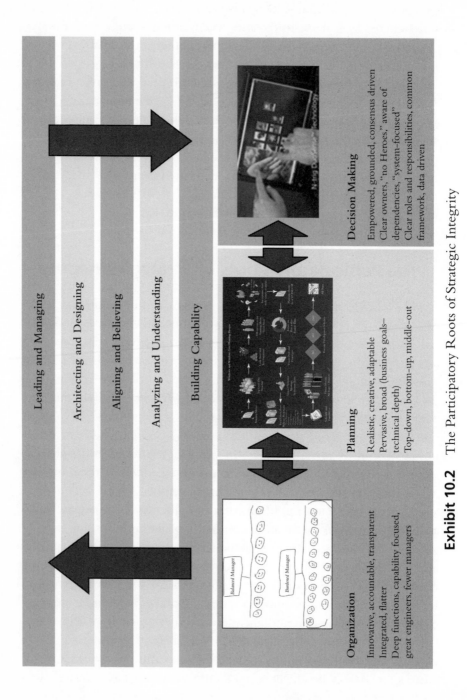

Leading and Managing

Architecting and Designing

Aligning and Believing

Analyzing and Understanding

Building Capability

Organization

Innovative, accountable, transparent
Integrated, flatter
Deep functions, capability focused,
great engineers, fewer managers

Planning

Realistic, creative, adaptable
Pervasive, broad (business goals–
technical depth)
Top-down, bottom-up, middle-out

Decision Making

Empowered, grounded, consensus driven
Clear owners, "no Heroes," aware of
dependencies, "system-focused"
Clear roles and responsibilities, common
framework, data driven

Exhibit 10.2 The Participatory Roots of Strategic Integrity

into business architectures and product designs. Finally, the impact of leadership, driven by everyday management decisions and patterns of behavior, keeps activities coherent, integrated, and responsive to any changes in competitive, market, or partner environments.

Ultimately, the Windows and Toyota organization, planning, and decision-making processes can provide an interesting blueprint for executives in a variety of industries. The next section details some practical suggestions for the first steps in their implementation.

Creating a High-Integrity Strategy Development Process

Unfortunately, an executive's first experience with the concept of strategic integrity is often to realize that it is missing. This is frequently the case when a person takes over an existing organization or is promoted to a position of greater authority and responsibility. In this section, we draw from research and experience to describe 10 stages in creating the foundations for high-integrity strategy development. The 10 stages can be laid out on a 12-month calendar, as shown on Exhibit 10.3.

Stage 1: Immersion, Preparation, and Ground Work   The first phase is characterized by open-minded, patient listening. In assuming responsibility for a new organization, the new executive should not only immerse him- or herself in all business and technical aspects of the new job, but also devote a substantial amount of time (two or three months is by no means too long) to interviewing members of the organization and listening to their thoughts, frustrations, questions, and hopes. When assuming responsibility for an organization, many pressures can point to a need to take immediate action, but all too often immediate action will lead to the wrong decisions. It is critically important that the executive invest the time needed to talk to people, in a 1:1 style, across as well as up and down the entire organization, to create an accurate picture of organizational cohesion and fractures, managerial strengths and weaknesses, as well as technical competences and holes. The team should see personal involvement and not delegate this to staff to learn and report back. There should be ample opportunity to reflect what is learned back to the organization for validation.

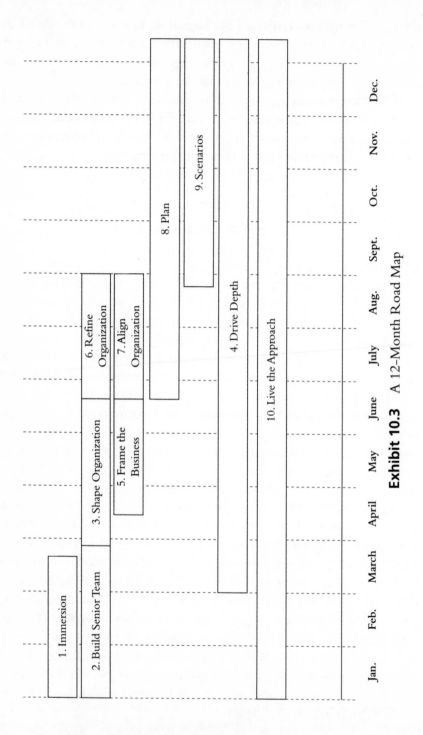

Exhibit 10.3 A 12–Month Road Map

Stage 2: Build a Trusted Management Team   The second stage focuses on building the senior team that will run the business. In assuming responsibility for an organization, the new executive should make sure to assemble a core group of skilled managers that includes a diversity of skills and perspectives, including a critical mass of people who the executive knows from previous managerial assignments. Leading a new organization without support from a highly competent and trusted senior team will create challenges. It is almost impossible to rely on transparent bottom-up communication if the senior team itself is opaque. As strategic integrity is rolled out to the greater team, creating and maintaining trust with the management team is a crucial starting point. While it is often tempting to bring in leaders familiar but from outside the team, balancing the existing leadership with new perspectives is important as well.

Stage 3: Shape the Organization   Strategic integrity relies on clear and timely communication. Once the senior team is in place, the executive should examine the need and potential for reorganization. Building on the analysis done in the first stage, he or she must assess organizational structure and capabilities and reshape the organization. The focus should be on streamlining the structure, ensuring that requisite technical capabilities have visibility and support and are not buried under layers of administration. Unnecessary administrative layers can distort incentives, demoralize, and dramatically reduce transparency and responsiveness. As long as it does not strain the managerial load (see Chapter 6), a flatter structure is more responsive and transparent.

Stage 4: Drive Depth   Concrete capabilities form the basis of strategic integrity. Optimization of organizational structure is incomplete without a capable workforce that is up to the task at hand. This stage involves extensive recruiting efforts, inside and outside the firm, to place key people in technical and managerial roles. Once started, this vigilant phase should be maintained at varying levels of intensity, relying on the constant search and development of new talent. Attracting a deep talent base is a necessary and sufficient condition for sustained strategic integrity. The right motivation and incentives can help illuminate a long-term professional path and provide ample opportunities for career development.

Stage 5: Frame the Business   Now that the organization is in place, it is time for the executive to begin work on framing its business objectives.

This stage is led by the senior team and results in the development of a "framing memo," a hypothesis for key themes and focus areas for the organization. The memo is circulated up and down the organization, and it is continually refined and validated, to converge on a clear and comprehensive statement of the organization's vision, themes, and focus areas.

Stage 6: Refine the Organization   The executive can now use the vision, themes, and focus areas to further refine the organization. At this point, some of the recruiting is already done, but the organization has been reshaped into specialized units and teams to match the strategy and its associated plans. The organization is built to match the way the business is framed.

Stage 7: Align the Organization   This stage is aimed at creating convergence in the organization and preparing to embark on the next "planning" stage. The executive can align the organization through a variety of means: extensive 1:1s, group meetings, focus groups, or even off-site discussions. In the case of Windows, the off-sites included all members of the organization and involved a discussion of specific Windows issues as well as more general grounding in external ideas and frameworks around the process and impact of planning.

Stage 8: Plan   During this stage, the executive coaches the organization to work intensely at translating strategy into execution. As explained in great detail in Chapter 5, the Windows planning process is both extensive and detailed, driven top down, bottom up, and middles out. The vision aligned in Stage 5 is detailed further, validated, and expanded on, in a process that both drives vision into action and also molds the organization into a tight, coherent whole.

Stage 9: Scenarios   During Stage 9, the organization brings the plan to life by linking specific scenarios to tactics in the strategy development process. The vision is translated at this point into very concrete user or partner scenarios. These scenarios work as connecting paths to form a detailed map for the many teams involved. The scenarios build to a common overview of the new product and define success factors for the next product release.

Stage 10: Live the Approach   This stage is the culmination of the process, but should be ingrained into all other stages. It is not enough for the executive to simply articulate the approach. It is also important for the executive to live it, week to week, day to day, and minute to minute, becoming the ultimate model and champion of the cause. There is nothing that destroys strategic integrity faster than hypocritical or detached executive behavior. One should continuously live and drive values such as transparency and technical excellence. Leaders should also invest in communication, through one-on-ones, impromptu conversations, e-mail responses, or even . . . blogging.

Summarizing the Past, Looking at the Future

As Windows 7 nears shipment, the team's attention has shifted to the future. After one iteration of the planning–product cycle, the process should continuously be optimized to perform better with each successive cycle. This next blog kicks off the planning process for planning future products and provides a different perspective on the stages outlined above. Even though much had already been defined in Windows 7, the blog reinforces many of the key messages and approaches. In particular, it emphasizes that executing individual steps of the approach is not enough—the different elements of the framework work best when they are executed as a system.

Participatory Planning

Last week I was hanging out at Red West and a member of the WL CX PM team stopped to say hello and gave me feedback about this blog—it was very nice and then there was the feedback: "[P]lease post more!" Ouch! While it is great to hear that folks miss these posts, I hope there is room for some leeway, as I've been pretty busy with the external blog on Windows 7, which is a lot of work. I will do my best to keep both blogs going, but it is a bit of a stretch sometimes! I do appreciate the feedback and most of all of course I appreciate when folks aren't shy and grab me in the hallways to chat!

Our team is really busy. We're working on detailed plans for Windows Live Wave 4, which is super fun, as we're all getting in the planning rhythm having gone through two cycles already. This week we released IE 8, which is fantastic, and pretty soon we'll kick off the early planning work for the next release. And finally we're approaching the RC of Windows 7, which has everyone pretty busy (and happy)! While we're at different planning stages right now, it is important to know that we're creating a framework to make sure that Windows Live, IE, and Windows are connected across planning and ultimately result in well-connected experiences and platforms that reinforce each other and deliver a wonderful customer experience. To build on the transition to planning, this post is going to look at how we are going to transition the Windows organization (the entire and extended Windows team) to the future. We'll look at this through the lens of planning and the next steps for our team.

The most important thing about planning is to continue to work as a single team and to focus on delivering a *unified* and *high-integrity* plan—that is, a plan that represents an inclusive and accurate view of what we will build. The way we are going to do this is by everyone working together on a single planning effort and working across teams. There's no need to try to get a head start, work behind the scenes to lay some groundwork, or try to pre-commit ideas. Those types of activities will not only make planning harder, but are sure to cause frustrations across the team as we all try to converge together. One of the key elements of planning is allowing for time between the end of one release and the start of the next—while this time is for actual planning, it also serves two other purposes. First, it allows everyone on the team time to clear their brains and provide some distance between the most recent cuts/POSTPONES so that we can absorb the real-world perceptions and feedback regarding the release. And second, it allows us all time to learn new things, understand what the technology, customer, and business environment is like, and to really look up and around and make sure we are thinking broadly about what we could and should build. And as an added bonus, spending your full energy on the complete product cycle (including the end game) is where all the learning and career experience really comes from, as we've talked about many times.

Many times over the course of going through the product cycles the "planning diagram" has been used to talk about the steps of the process and the "mechanics." Julie Green, Chris Jones, Dean Hachamovitch, and others will be making sure we refresh ourselves in terms of those specifics. For example, for Windows Live wave 4, Chris' planning memo (outlining the framework for the release) described the steps and the calendar. We'll make sure to have brown bags, blog posts, and other forums where everyone is clear on the details of the process.

Learning Organization

Before we talk about planning, it is worth a quick reminder that we should all continue to think of ourselves as a **learning organization.** Regardless of how our products are received in the market, we all know there are things we can do better each release—the code we write, tests we implement, designs we create, words we write, decisions we make, or management efforts we undertake are all open to learning and improvement. As we transition to the next release, we should all plan on spending time looking at the elements that we can improve and being as deliberate in planning those improvements as we are in planning the release.

Planning Myths

While the details of the *planning process* are important of course, the reality is that the best plans are the ones that are created as a team, by the team, and for the team no matter the specifics of the process turn out to be. There are many concerns or even *myths* about planning that people have—some of these are based on experience of failed plans, and some are just based on perceptions of planning in the context of a large team. Fundamentally, planning is much less about the process and the steps and much more about the members of the team at all levels of the organization coming together creating shared goals, credible plans, and solid execution criteria. What are some of the "myths of planning" that I've heard from members of the team and how do we "answer" these? Many of these have been the topics of past blogs and many conversations in team meetings so I will briefly talk about these—we can always follow up on specifics in other forums. Some planning myths might include:

   Plans reduce agility and response. By far the biggest concern with planning is that people worry that having a plan will slow us down and "prevent" us from responding to the competition or acting on changes in the market. The reality, I think, runs counter to this as anyone who has ever taken a road trip knows—if you know where you are going and something comes up (a flat tire, a surprise cool site to see), then the plan makes it easy to understand the trade-offs involved and the way to make it possible to deal with the unexpected. Of course, you can also have a plan and mindlessly follow it and ignore changes in the landscape, though that's not a result of planning, but of poor execution.

Plans can't change. Plans do change and that's the whole point. Once a plan is in place there is a baseline to understand, [to] weigh options of change against, and to adjust. Without a plan change is nonsensical since you can't tell what is really changing or different. With Wave 3, IE 8, and Windows 7 we've had a ton of experience of adjusting the plans and doing so without causing a bunch of pain or ripple throughout the organization.

Plans are for incremental products. Everything needs a plan. There's really no escaping that you need a plan. It is the case that planning a product that is derived from an existing product has different challenges than a whole new product, but you do need a plan for both. A new product concerns itself less with compatibility or working with an installed base, and an existing product necessarily worries less about how it might "fit in" relative to other existing products or services.

Plans don't work for innovation. Plans don't have room for "**discover** the solution to <x>" where <x> is some well-known insanely hard problem or some intractable issue. Just like you don't plan on lightning striking in a certain place, we don't plan on some breakthrough striking us while we're executing on a product cycle. We do make our plans based on technologies that are new or nascent, but our plans include time to bring those to market and develop a full scenario. Because we are not making plans free of uncertainty, we might not get done everything we plan on, but we will plan with the understanding that we have left enough time to know what we don't know. Our goal is not just "inventing cool stuff" but to bring cool inventions to market for [hundreds] of millions of people—innovation is invention + impact.

Plans come from the "top." When we started Windows 7, I personally had the sneaking suspicion that many were expecting me to pull the product plan out of my back pocket and drive the Windows 7 feature list from the top down. Even for small details there was often an expectation of "top down." I remember one team meeting where I had to pledge (via oath) not to redesign the start menu at the last minute of the release. So far, things are looking good for the pledge though we still have some time left in the release :-). As we'll discuss below, plans are a combination of top-down, bottom-up, and middle-out and that is the hallmark of participation in the planning process by all levels of the org.

Plans can be expressed in PowerPoint. Plans are not bullet points. That's why you can't rush and get ahead of the planning process with a "deck" that says what you're going to do. The work we do is really hard and really complex and so the plans are going to take a bunch of work. The only way to have a plan is to write it down in sentences with the detail to support the plan. Another way of saying this is that plans are done in Word and the PowerPoint part comes after the Word document— there's a little bit of Visio, Excel, SharePoint, and a few other Office tools involved in the process too :-).

Plans are reviewed and approved. Because we are going to focus the planning efforts on involving a broad set of people for a significant amount of time, we will together/collectively converge on a plan. As a result there isn't a single point in time when we say "approved." If you think about the depth of work, breadth of knowledge, and amount of detail in our plan, there's really no way to have an approval meeting to validate the plan. There's a ton of accountability and responsibility placed at the group manager level to have plans that make sense, are achievable, and appropriately aggressive in the context of the release goals. As we'll see by participating as a team in planning we have the best shot of having a great plan together.

Plans are exciting. The most counterintuitive notion of planning is that the resulting plan is exciting. Plans themselves are never that exciting. What makes a plan exciting is the realization of the goals in an exciting way. What makes plans exciting is the work every dev, test, pm, designer, and so on do to make the realization of the plan as cool and exciting as possible. The notion of "window management" is not in and of itself an exciting topic, but the details in the execution of Aero Snap and Aero Shake are what make this one area of Windows 7 exciting.

Those are a few of the myths that we've discussed over the past product cycles with regard to planning. While no planning effort can be perfect— there are too many uncertainties in complex product development—the thing we know for sure is that any potential shortfalls in the process itself are addressed by recognizing them upfront. If we're worried about responding to competition, then leave schedule time for the unknown. If we're unsure of the view that another team might have of the plan, then invite their participation in the process. If we're concerned about the architecture and details then take a break and work those out during the planning time.

Participation

As we transition to planning the next Windows, the next IE, and work through the next Windows Live wave, the key to developing a great plan is participating. Everyone has a role to play in the planning efforts and everyone is invited to participate. Participation is work. You are responsible for participating and no one else is responsible for "pulling" you or your point of view into the efforts. If you want to be heard you have to take the risk, do the legwork, and participate. Planning is an invitation to participate, but it isn't a requirement that everyone seek out your point of view. It also isn't a guarantee that your point of view becomes the plan. Ultimately, we ask program management to make sure that in their judgment the very best ideas get done—that does not mean program management must be the originators of every feature, but it does mean program management is accountable to having the best ideas, working with full awareness of the full spectrum of ideas, and having a strong understanding of why choices were made. Program management does this work by grounding their views in the research from product planning, reflecting the input from development (feasibility), and test ("abilities"), and of course the business goals and input from product marketing. It is important not to be a victim of the effort to plan, but a participant, and when the plans are set it is important to be part of executing, even if not every detail is what you would have chosen on your own. By participating you have a chance to see all sides and recognize the inherent trade-offs and complexity of coming up with a plan.

By enabling this broad participation in planning we hope to develop plans that have a high degree of integrity. What this means is that the plans "hold up" under scrutiny of all kinds. When asked about design alternatives, these have already been considered. When asked about the competition, we know how the plans address the space. When we consider the business needs, the plans incorporate these up front. When trying to understand the user experience, the planning work around prototypes has been done. No matter how you poke and prod at the plan for your area, the plan maintains its structure. If it doesn't, then we adjust it. If we need to change, then we do. This notion of integrity is the key quality of the output of the plan.

Even though we have a series of process steps, and we will follow those, it is the participation that we are counting on. Participating in planning requires a mind-set that is "active." It means that you don't just go to a single offsite (and do email in the back of the room), but you follow up, prototype, advocate, connect, and "work the planning process." There are a few ways to contrast a participatory planning process with a more passive or "top-down" approach to planning. Consider the following examples:

Follow-through vs. drive-by. As we're planning, it is important to follow through on your input or ideas. Don't expect to send a piece of mail and think, "[O]k, I gave my input" or "I said that didn't work." Follow-through is a big part of the legwork and attention to detail. Write it down. Go to the meeting. Talk to others involved. Detail your input.

Participation vs. review. We're going to spend a lot of time together planning. Together in offsites, meetings, brainstorming sessions, hallway conversations. This participation is key. The number of times that we'll have a "go/no-go" meeting is very minimal and so if you're expecting to voice an opinion at the end, or expect to see plans validated by an exec as a way of keeping things "brief," then think again. The process of collaborating and working together is a big part of closing in on a shared view of the goals.

Perspiration vs. inspiration. A lot of times we think of planning as the quick description of a cool idea. In reality, planning is a lot of perspiration. You have to think through the details. You have to work with partners on those details. You have to bring people to the room to sweat the plan and the details.

Consensus vs. requirements. Many times we think of cross-group efforts as one group issuing requirements for another group and then the plan is done. As we've talked about many times, requirements are almost the opposite of cross-group collaboration and are almost never the right way to get work done across teams. Part of the perspiration is working together to create shared goals, shared scenarios, and a shared understanding of the effort and then divide up the work the best way possible. In what we build there are almost never requirements—we don't release a product that includes a list of all we dreamed up, just a list of what we got done.

Scenarios vs. organization. As we're planning we are going to do so with a "virtual" organization. We won't plan by organization but we will plan in a more conceptual and thematic manner. It is incredibly important to do this as it avoids the seams in the organization dictating the architecture or experience of the product. We will have many features that involve multiple groups and so planning needs to break down those team boundaries and deliver on a great scenario. There's no such thing as a plan for a "team" that is independent of a plan for the whole release. The team plan takes into account the overall goals of the release and is part of a continuum of features. It takes a big commitment from everyone to think globally during the planning phase. Related to this is the notion that no team should just fill up a schedule on its own—every team will be part of scenarios that have the same or higher priority than the work thought up in the team "silo."

Planning Roles

Thinking about the specifics of the planning process, there are "roles" that each of us will play uniquely. These roles are based on our places in the organization. In a way, these define the things each of us must do, but at the same time each of us is free to provide input and participate in planning in any way but the accountability for the output should be pretty clear. When you think of the direction of information flow and a normal model of organizations the following is a good way to think of participation:

"Top down." The top-down part of the plan includes some key framing elements of the plan. For example, the timeline or rough schedule for a release, some themes or objectives for the release relative to business goals, and other constraints—these are constraints that begin to bound the planning efforts in a common set of goals. As part of the top-down elements of the plan we might pick a very small number of specific technologies to bet on or specific business goals we must address in the release as constraints or specifics. The top-down aspects of the plan also include organization alignment and how we structure our team to make sure we can execute well against those other goals.

"Bottom up." The most important part of planning is making sure we have a great base of ideas for what we should do within the "top-down" aspects of planning. Most everyone on the team participates in this role by offering ideas, recommendations, technologies, potential problems to solve, input from customers of all kinds, and so on. The leads and individuals on the team are providing the "reality check" of ideas throughout the planning effort to make sure that we're able to schedule, architect, and validate the ideas in practice. The richness of the plan and the success of the plan require this element to be very active and engaged in planning.

"Middle out." How we go about stitching the top-down constraints and bottom-up ideas together into a well-thought-out canvass is the role of the group managers. The group managers will "orchestrate" the integration, synergy, and completeness of the plan with respect to scenarios, customer goals, and marketplace challenges. The cross-group efforts come together as the group managers work to develop the shared view across the organization for what and how we execute on the plan.

The output of participating in the planning efforts and each of these roles is the plan—the vision document, the details behind that, and the scenario prototypes that visualize our shared goals. This is a plan based on participation and a plan that has integrity.

Timeline and Next Steps

The planning timeline we will work on for the next release of Windows (Windows client and server) future products will follow a similar tempo. We have been through this as a team once before so it should seem somewhat familiar. We're already seeing the advantages of maintaining the same cadence and going from the finish line to the starting line together. There are five steps along the way to getting to the vision—and for sure we will have a big team meeting and communicate within the team the plan.

It is worth noting that we also benefitted enormously from the (now famously named) translucency of the planning process—we're going to stick to keeping things about the plan close to the Windows development team so as to make sure we do not confuse our customers and partners with rumors and incomplete plans. I personally expect a significant uptick in efforts to obtain insider information from us and will really ask for your help in making sure we do not end up in a bad spot with respect to leaked information about our plans.

The five steps to get us to a product vision include the following.

- **Preparation and groundwork.** Shortly **after code complete** our product planning organization solicited input for topics to do long lead research. This research can be used by teams to inform and brainstorm about what features we could build. Many different topics have been investigated and that information will be shared broadly once we start the next steps of planning. This information is important because it allows us to all begin to see the external inputs in a similar context and with similar data and research upon which to base our next steps. Of course these research areas do not define the only possible areas for the product, but are also a broad set of well-known topics that require facts upon which to base decisions.

- **Framing. About the time of the release candidate** you should expect a memo that will help to frame the direction of the next release. This memo will define some priorities and a conceptual framework for how we will go about learning and planning. As part of this we will look at the accomplishments and learnings of the current product cycle, business and technology trends that will influence the next products, as well ideas for some of the big bets. It is important to keep in mind that this is a step in the process, not the end of the process. It kicks off the detailed planning work and provides some tools to the senior discipline leaders to focus efforts.

- **Organization alignment. Aligned with framing, but happening on a slightly different schedule** will be any changes we intend to make in the organization. This has a tendency to make everyone a little antsy—please do not think this is a "big reorg" or that we will upend everything. We've got an organization "philosophy" in place and we'll continue along these same lines—discipline leadership focused on engineering, with the operation of our efforts using right-sized feature team triads. But we all know as part of Windows 7 that some things were not perfectly aligned organizationally and we know where we have areas that would benefit from some organizational tweaking. Our Windows Live team made a few tweaks for Wave 3 and then again for Wave 4 and I promise this was a relatively painless set of changes. A part of these changes will be for each member of the team to consider new opportunities as well—if you've worked on the same technology for several turns of the crank it might make sense to look around (and by contrast if you have not, then it might not make too much sense to look around). There will be changes, but these changes are going to be deliberate and related to the work we're trying to do. Folks have definitely asked me about "when is the reorg" and my hope is that we don't think too much about this step, but look to it as an optimization that is a routine part of building a great team for the next release. Along with feedback from Windows 7, the framing for the release informs any adjustments we will make to the organization as well.

- **Planning.** A little **after RTM** and things are settled, we will begin detailed planning. This is going to be kicked off with a period of learning and offsites and then we'll have a clear communication. This will help us to structure the planning efforts by defining more specific scenarios and success criteria. It is also a chance for us to have a clearer view of members of the team who will be accountable for specific aspects of the plan. The planning memo identifies potential areas of work for the release. We will spend several months going through this part of the process and make sure we maximize the opportunities for participation, the detailed upfront work, and insure clarity of plan. Along with features, the output of the planning phase will be a schedule that we all understand and can work with.

- **Vision.** As we **wind down the planning phase** we will begin drafting the product vision. This document and the associated scenario sketches will represent our collective team commitments for what we will build. Supporting the vision will be the schedules, architectures, and specifications that insure that these are reliable (high-integrity) commitments. We will have a clear schedule and when we publish the vision, the clock starts ticking for the start of the actual development schedule.

We have a ton of work to finish up Windows 7 and a lot of very happy Beta customers with very high expectations for the RC and RTM releases. We don't want to lose focus, even for an instant, on getting us to RTM. The best learning in engineering comes from being part of a whole project, so don't deprive yourself of that learning by starting to focus on planning. If you've got some spare cycles we've got plenty for you to help with. You can also talk to your manager and come up with specific plans for your own growth and learning.

This is a complex topic with many perspectives. If you have any questions, by all means feel free to ask me—my inbox is open. Your group manager (development manager, test manager, group program manager) is also a good resource on this topic as we're making sure to talk about this as a group as well. Let's do a great job finishing Windows 7 and have a smooth transition to the next release.

—Steven

This blog post was included to reinforce many of the fundamental concepts in this book and serves as a good summary and guide. As the team kicks off future work and continues on its search for strategic integrity, they are busy framing the next release and reinforcing the participatory approach to strategy development and execution.

The Impact of Strategic Integrity

We began by arguing that many enterprise failures are rooted in deep fractures between strategy and execution. The fractures are caused by the mismatch between slowly changing inertial organizations and rapidly changing external market and technological environments. Rather than put aside the enterprises and focus on "trendier" types of organization, such as spinoffs, ventures, or communities (which appear intrinsically more nimble), we focused on what it takes to bring about change in an established firm. We focused on creating a process that matches strategy and organization *to each other*. The outcome is a resilient organization that can withstand crisis—whether it comes in the form of leadership, technology, or marketplace change. The new organization, rooted in strategic integrity, will have deeper capabilities and the potential for greater impact.

Take the case of Windows 7: In the early days of the program, some had suggested abandoning the existing organization and code base and starting over from scratch. Today, Windows has over a hundred million lines of software code, and so does the competition. How much impact could a new team truly have in such a short period of time? What would a new team have accomplished, ramping up from scratch, both organizationally and technically, in a two-year period? In this case, Windows managed to take the existing organizational memory, technical knowledge, relationships, and functional skills, and turn them into massive positive impact. In just under two years, the team developed a new product with greatly improved quality and a number of innovative features—and the journey will continue.

The issues faced by Microsoft are hardly unique, but the response of the Windows team shows how an established organization can create opportunity in the face of challenge. The lessons put forth in this book can be applied to organizations that might be developing a new drug, manufacturing a new line of computer processors, redesigning significant

IT infrastructure, or creating a new operating system for use by over a billion people. These lessons span technologies, components, organizations, and products by putting people at the center of each product generation. Managing complexity well requires strategy, from mission to vision, and from plan to tactics. Moreover, it also requires a carefully aligned operation, to drive idea into action and plan into execution.

It is hard to argue against the assertion that the world has never before witnessed a level of business turbulence and unpredictability that is comparable to that of the current business environment. Whether we focus on the automotive or financial sector, the insurance industry or software start-ups, strategies have acquired increasingly finite lifetimes. The era of a separate strategy development process that leads to a formal roll-out and execution may be over. There is simply no time to leave strategy creation as a function that is separate from business execution. There is no forgiving an organization pointed in an old, inertial direction while its isolated leaders attempt to push the other way. Strategy and execution must be connected, in order for the organization to effectively sense priorities, risks, and opportunities and adjust to them appropriately. An organization with strategic integrity has the ability to respond, and not react.

This book has told the story of how one organization matched strategy to execution to drive innovation, during one of the most unsettling environments our economy has ever witnessed. The organization matched directed, top-down strategy—what we traditionally think of as the output of executives and consultants—with emergent, bottom-up strategy—typically created by people on the ground as they face the day-to-day challenges and realities of running the business. The extensive potential of the Windows team was thus translated into real impact, as Windows' two strategies became one.

Notes

1. See, for example, Anthony Rathbone, "Windows 7 Review: Why I Like Windows 7," *IT Management*, May 18, 2009; Preston Galla, "Review: Windows 7 RCI adds speed, UI improvements—and promises more to come," *Computerworld*, April 28, 2009; and Ed Bott, "What to expect from Windows 7," *Ed Bott's Microsoft Report*, May 5, 2009.

2. D. K. Sobek, J. K. Liker, and A. C. Ward, "Another Look at How Toyota Integrates Product Development," *Harvard Business Review* 76, no. 4 (July–August 1998): 36–49; H. Takeuchi, E. Osono, N. Shimizu, "The Contradictions That Drive Toyota's Success," *Harvard Business Review* 86, no. 6 (June, 2008): 96–104; and K. Clark and T. Fujimoto, *Product Development Performance: Strategy, Organization, and Management in the World Auto Industry* (Boston: Harvard Business School Press, 1991).

3. See Clark and Fujimoto, *Product Development Performance.*

4. Sobek, Liker, and Ward, "Another Look at How Toyota Integrates Product Development."

Index